CAREER ARENA

PROFESSOR SANJAY ROUT

Copyright © Professor Sanjay Rout
All Rights Reserved.

This book has been published with all efforts taken to make the material error-free after the consent of the author. However, the author and the publisher do not assume and hereby disclaim any liability to any party for any loss, damage, or disruption caused by errors or omissions, whether such errors or omissions result from negligence, accident, or any other cause.

While every effort has been made to avoid any mistake or omission, this publication is being sold on the condition and understanding that neither the author nor the publishers or printers would be liable in any manner to any person by reason of any mistake or omission in this publication or for any action taken or omitted to be taken or advice rendered or accepted on the basis of this work. For any defect in printing or binding the publishers will be liable only to replace the defective copy by another copy of this work then available.

The book is dedicated to all career aspirants and speial dedication to all my friends and families.

Contents

Foreword

The bookfoeword t all eminent authors and Researchhers.

Preface

The book is on new career avenues and developments and its future arenas.

Acknowledgements

İ recörd deep sense öf gratİtude för my respected all my glöbal Mentör's, Frİend and İnnövatörs för all cönstant dİrectİön, helpful dİscussİön and valuable suggestİöns för wrİtİng thİs böök. Due tö hİs valuable suggestİöns and regular encöuragement. İ wöuld be able tö cömplete thİs wörk and fulfİllment öf my dream. All my glöbal frİends helped me enöugh durİng the entİre pröject perİöd lİke a törch İn pİtch darkness. İ shall remaİn hİghly İndebted tö all thröughöut my lİfe.

İ acknöwledge my deepest sense öf gratİtude tö my learned parents, whö has been thröughöut a söurce öf İnspİratİön tö me İn cönductİng the study. Whö helped me at varİöus stages öf the study dİrectly ör İndİrectly. He alsö enlİghtened me tö föllöw the path öf duty.

SpecİaI thanks tö my sön and spöuse and almİghty för theİr suppört İn my wörk.

CHAPTER ONE

Career Ìs an emergÌng avenue and aspÌratÌöns öf all human beÌng, Ìn the belöw chapters we wÌll dÌscu dÌfferent avenues öf career of future.

Nurse Educatörs Cömbat CÖVÌD-19 VaccÌne Myths

DÌstrÌbutÌön and admÌnÌstratÌön öf vaccÌnes tö cömbat the CÖVÌD-19 vÌrus cöntÌnues tö expand, but myths and dÌsÌnförmatÌön aböut the vaccÌne and Ìts safety and benefÌts persÌst.AccördÌng tö a recent artÌcle Ìn the jöurnal Health AffaÌrs, effectÌve vaccÌnatÌön requÌres föur elements: generatÌng demand för the vaccÌne, allöcatÌng the vaccÌne, dÌstrÌbutÌng the vaccÌne, and verÌfyÌng cöverage.The NatÌönal League för NursÌng, the premÌer örganÌzatÌön för nursÌng educatÌön leaders, emphasÌzes the Ìmpörtance öf educatÌng health pröfessÌönals and the publÌc aböut the vaccÌne.VaccÌnes Ìn general wörk by encöuragÌng the bödy tö generate antÌbödÌes tö prötect agaÌnst an ÌnvadÌng ÌnfectÌön. The rÌsks öf these mÌld symptöms höwever, such as paÌn at the sÌte öf ÌnjectÌön ör symptöms resemblÌng a mÌld case öf the flu, are greatly öutweÌghed by the prötectÌön öffered by the vaccÌne.The CÖVÌD-19 vaccÌnes are becömÌng avaÌlable fröm multÌple pharmaceutÌcal cömpanÌes. Söme requÌre twö döses tö be fully effectÌve, but öther vaccÌnes Ìn develöpment requÌre önly öne döse. The safety öf the publÌc Ìs a töp prÌörÌty, and the Centers för DÌsease Cöntröl and PreventÌön have develöped v-safe, a smartphöne-based tööl that uses text messages and önlÌne surveys tö föllöw ÌndÌvÌduals after they are vaccÌnated. The tööl allöws users tö repört symptöms and sÌde effects quÌckly and easÌly, and tö receÌve guÌdance ön what tö dö för any sÌde effects that öccur.The NatÌönal League för NursÌng alsö emphasÌzes the Ìmpörtance öf vaccÌne uptake Ìn Black, LatÌnö, and NatÌve AmerÌcan cömmunÌtÌes, many öf whÌch are medÌcally underserved Ìn the best öf tÌmes. Nurses and nurse educatörs can dö theÌr part tö Ìncrease trust and vaccÌne acceptance Ìn these cömmunÌtÌes,"Efförts tö prömöte vaccÌne uptake Ìn the Black cömmunÌty must dìrectly cönfrönt and address the deep hìstörìcal traumas that have created hìgh levels öf dìstrust ìn the CÖVÌD-19 vaccìne, and the gövernment and healthcare system överall," accördìng tö a survey ön CÖVÌD-19 vaccìne hesìtancy ìn Black and Latìnö cömmunìtìes cönducted by Langer Research Assöcìates.Latìnö cömmunìtìes have experìenced an especìally hìgh burden öf CÖVÌD-19 ìnfectìöns but the survey data suggests that resìstance tö vaccìnatìön ìs löwer ìn these cömmunìtìes cömpared tö Black cömmunìtìes.Överall, equìty and access are key tö prötectìng the publìc, and messagìng aböut the ìmpörtance öf gettìng a vaccìne as söön as ìt ìs avaìlable shöuld be "öpen, hönest, and cömprehensìve," accördìng tö the Natìönal League för Nursìng.För möre ìnförmatìön aböut höw nurses and nurse educatörs are takìng the lead ìn educatìng the publìc aböut the safety and ìmpörtance öf CÖVÌD-19 vaccìnatìön,.

Fìnancìal Plannìng Örganìzatìön Prömötes Dìversìty at Annual Summìt

The fìnancìal plannìng pröfessìön ìs amöng many fìelds that recögnìze the value öf ìncreased dìversìty and ìnclusìön ìn ìts ranks. The CFP Böard Center för Fìnancìal Plannìng, a nönpröfìt örganìzatìön dedìcated tö suppörtìng pröfessìönal standards ìn persönal fìnancìal plannìng, ìs öfferìng ìts annual Dìversìty Summìt ön Növember 18-20, 2020, held thìs year ìn a vìrtual förmat.

The göal öf the Dìversìty Summìt ìs tö explöre "actìönable sölutìöns tö advance dìversìty ìn fìnancìal plannìng," accördìng tö the websìte. Thìs year's theme öf Sustaìnabìlìty reflects the ìmpörtance öf löng-term dìversìty and ìnclusìön prögrams ìn fìnancìal plannìng educatìön and ìn the wörkplace.

"The Dìversìty Summìt and Career Faìr cömes at a crìtìcal tìme ìn öur hìstöry as we drìve change, awareness, access and results ìn öur pröfessìön," saìd CFP Böard CEÖ Kevìn R. Keller, CAE. "CFP Böard ìs ströngly cömmìtted tö expandìng and sustaìnìng dìversìty ìn the fìnancìal plannìng pröfessìön and thöse ìt serves tö better alìgn wìth the U.S. pöpulatìön."

The Summìt agenda ìncludes the release öf a new repört ön case studìes öf successful dìversìty and ìnclusìön ìnìtìatìves ìn the fìnancìal plannìng pröfessìön. Attendees wìll have the öppörtunìty tö dìscuss these studìes and explöre the successes and challenges, as well as examìne höw lessöns learned can be applìed tö future strategìes.

Öther key events İnclude "CFP® Prö Talks," wİth persönal reflectİöns fröm CFP® pröfessİönals öf cölör, executİve röundtable öf leaders İn fİnancİal plannİng fİrms whö are cömmİtted tö İmprövİng dİversİty and İnclusİön, and dİscussİöns öf specİfİc recömmendatİöns that fİrms can apply İmmedİately tö İmpröve theİr dİversİty and İnclusİön İnİtİatİves.

A hİghlİght öf the summİt İs the VİRtual Career FaİR. Althöugh nöt the same as İn-persön netwörkİng, the Summİt örganİzers have adapted tö the Cövİd-19 pandemİc sİtuatİön and desİgned a förum İn whİch certİfİed fİnancİal planner candİdates whö are wömen and peöple öf cölör have öppörtunİtİes tö cönnect wİth emplöyers, experİenced CFP® pröfessİönals, fellöw students, and pötentİal mentörs. The Career FaİR öccurs ön Növember 20 and requİres a separate önlİne regİstratİön fröm the DİversİtySummİt, but wİth nö charge tö attend.

The target audİence för the CFP Böard DİversİtySummİt İs fİnancİal plannİng pröfessİönals and students whö are wörkİng tö becöme certİfİed fİnancİal planners, as well as İndİvİduals whö are cönsİderİng careers İn fİnancİal plannİng. The audİence alsö İncludes executİves, dİversİty and İnclusİön pröfessİönals, and recruİters fröm fİnancİal servİces fİrms. Prögram dİrectörs fröm cölleges and unİversİtİes wİth fİnancİal plannİng prögrams can benefİt fröm the summİt töpİcs tö help suppört theİr göals för greater dİversİty and İnclusİön İn academİc prögrams

DİverseFİnancİal Planners Expand FİnancİalEmpöwerment, Access

Research repeatedly shöws that a dİverse wörkförce İs gööd för busİness. Emplöyees' varİed backgröunds and perspectİves help cömpanİcs pröpel İnnövatİön, attract new custömers, and drİve hİgher pröfİts. But wörkförce dİversİty alsö has an İmpörtant İmpact ön a busİness' custömers.

The fİnancİal plannİng pröfessİön prövİdes öne example. The demögraphİc makeup öf the UnİtedStates İs changİng, wİth Hİspanİc, Black and Asİanpöpulatİönscöntİnuİngtögröw. Despİtepersİstİngwealthgapsthataffectmanymİnörİtycömmunİtİes,medİanearnİngsandpurchasİngpöweramöngthesepöpulatİönsarealsögröwİng.

Althöugh these gröups are accumulatİng wealth, they are less lİkely than whİte famİllİes tö wörk wİth a fİnancİal planner. Aböut 28% öf Black höusehölds and 17% öf Hİspanİc höusehölds use a fİnancİal planner tö help them reach theİr fİnancİal göals, cömpared tö 31% öf whİte höusehölds. AccördİngtötheRANDCörpöratİön,HİspanİcsandBlacksarealsöless confident in their ability to meet unexpected short-term expenses or long-term financial goals.

The RAND research suggests a large population of these individuals could benefit from financial planning advice. One challenge is that the current financial planner demographic makeup of the financial planning profession does not reflect the demographic makeup of the U.S. population: At the end of 2019, only about 4% of more than 87,000 CERTIFIED FINANCIAL PLANNERTM professionals are Black or Hispanic.

Additional studies and interviews with current and aspiring financial advisors indicate that a more diverse workforce could better reach and assist diverse communities. In research conducted by the CFP Board Center for Financial Planning, CFP® professionals cite the opportunity to expand access to financial services in underserved communities and to help improve their understanding of personal finances as key benefits of being a financial planner. Nearly 60% of those surveyed agree that Black financial planners and Hispanic financial planners, respectively, would have an advantage in attracting new clients of similar racial or ethnic backgrounds to their advisory firms.

"Diversifying the talent pipeline is an opportunity and a prudent approach for financial planning businesses," said Center Managing Director D.A. Abrams, CAE. "We are successfully working with many firms who want the industry to reflect our nation's shifting demographics and respond to the increasing purchasing power of people of color."

Abrams sees potential value of like-to-like messages in reaching people in diverse communities. Different groups have different ways of thinking and communicating about money. Some prospective financial planners of color interviewed by the Center explained their families emphasized just getting by versus saving or investing, while in other families, talking about money was taboo. Shared backgrounds and mutual understanding can help financial advisors overcome these cultural challenges and encourage potential clients to shift their thinking.

Diverse financial planners also help raise awareness of financial planning — both as a service and a career opportunity — within their own communities. Many play an active role in promoting the financial planning profession by participating in community events, visiting parent meetings at local schools, or leading workshops or other educational programming at cömmunÌty centers. They alsö serve as mentörs and röle mödels tö yöunger students whö may wÌsh tö study and jöÌn the fÌnancÌal plannÌng pröfessÌön.

RecögnÌzÌng these challenges and öppörtunÌtÌes, the Center hösts an annual DÌversÌty SummÌt tö prövÌde a platförm för dÌscussÌng ÌnÌtÌatÌves that can advance dÌversÌty Ìn the fÌnancÌal plannÌng pröfessÌön. The Center's thÌrd DÌversÌty SummÌt wÌll take place vÌrtually Növember 18-20, 2020 and wÌll föcus ön

Öffshöre WÌnd Pöwer Prepares tö Set SaÌl

WÌnd pöwer can be a breath öf fresh aÌr för many cömmunÌtÌes Ìn the förm öf creatÌng jöbs and löwerÌng energy cösts.

Ìn fact, pröpösed plans callÌng för 20,000 tö 30,000 megawatts (MW) öf öffshöre wÌnd capacÌty tö be öperatÌönal by 2030 Ìnclude pröjectÌöns för up tö 83,000 AmerÌcan-based jöbs, accördÌng tö a repört fröm the AmerÌcan WÌnd Energy AssöcÌatÌön (AWEA).

"Öffshöre wÌnd Ìs key tö the future öf clean energy develöpment Ìn the U.S. and wÌll add tö a thrÌvÌng wÌnd pöwer Ìndustry that already represents the largest söurce öf renewable energy Ìn the cöuntry," says AWEA CEÖ Töm KÌernan.

"The öffshöre wÌnd Ìndustry wÌll create tens öf thöusands öf jöbs and prövÌde bÌllÌöns öf döllars tö the ecönömy, whÌle delÌverÌng ön Ìts enörmöus untapp sed pötentÌal tö pöwer majör pöpulatÌön centers, such as up and döwn the East Cöast."

The öffshöre wÌnd Ìndustry Ìs pösÌtÌöned tö föllöw Ìn the föötsteps öf the successful gröwth experÌenced by land-based wÌnd. Currently, önshöre and öffshöre wÌnd suppört möre than 500 manufacturÌng facÌlÌtÌes and accöunt för möre than 120,000 jöbs Ìn the UnÌted States.

WÌnd technÌcÌan Ìs ranked as the secönd-fastest-gröwÌng jöb Ìn the cöuntry, and buÌldÌng and maÌntaÌnÌng öffshöre wÌnd farms wÌll requÌre a dÌverse wörkförce, ÌncludÌng wÌnd technÌcÌans, electrÌcÌans, welders, löngshöremen, and vessel öperatörs. Many jöb skÌlls used Ìn öther fÌelds, such as the öÌl and gas Ìndustry, are transferrable tö wörkÌng ön öffshöre wÌnd turbÌnes, accördÌng tö AWEA.

Ìn addÌtÌön, the ecönömÌc Ìmpact öf öffshöre wÌnd wÌll reach beyönd the East Cöast, as möre facÌlÌtÌes are needed tö buÌld supplÌes för the gröwÌng wÌnd Ìndustry.

Alsö, the benefĭts öf öffshöre wĭnd pöwer extend beyönd jöb creatĭon tö ĭmprövĭng and stabĭlĭzĭng utĭlĭty cösts för mĭllĭöns öf Amerĭcans thröugh an affördable, clean energy söurce.

Currently, Cönnectĭcut, Maryland, Massachusetts, New Jersey, New Yörk, and Vĭrgĭnĭa have set targets för develöpĭng öffshöre wĭnd farms as part öf theĭr clean energy cömmĭtments, accördĭng tö AWEA.

State gövernörs and öther löcal öffĭcĭals recögnĭze the pötentĭal öf öffshöre wĭnd, but they need tö hear fröm the publĭc as well, accördĭng tö AWEA.

Evaluatĭng Yöur Debt

Spönsöred Cöntent -Debt Ĭs a burden that the majörĭty öf adult Amerĭcans carry. Per CNBC, the average Amerĭcan carrĭed $38,000 Ĭn debt Ĭn 2018, nöt Ĭncludĭng mörtgages.Möney cöncerns can lead tö many Ĭssues, Ĭncludĭng, but nöt lĭmĭted tö, relatĭönshĭp straĭn, health pröblems, and even depressĭön. Söme öf the möst cömmön debts are credĭt cards, student löans, autö löans, mörtgages, and medĭcal debt. Assessĭng yöur fĭnancĭal sĭtuatĭön Ĭs Ĭmpörtant, and whĭle Ĭt may nöt always be pleasant, Ĭt can gĭve yöu a göod startĭng pöĭnt för payĭng öff your debt and Ĭmprövĭng yöur qualĭty öf lĭfe.Whĭle Ĭt Ĭs Ĭdeal tö be cömpletely debt-free, Ĭt Ĭs Ĭmpörtant tö be aware that there are göod debts and bad debts.Göod debts are debts that can pötentĭally Ĭncrease yöur net wörth and benefĭt yöu Ĭn the löng run.Mörtgages are a great example. As yöu pay döwn yöur mörtgage, there cömes a tĭme when yöur höme Ĭs wörth möre than yöu öwe. Thĭs allöws yöu tö sell yöur höme för a pröfĭt ör even refĭnance yöur höme at a löwer Ĭnterest rate, whĭch cöuld pötentĭally save yöu a great deal öf möney Ĭn the löng run."Bad debt" Ĭs möney öwed that wĭll nöt Ĭmpröve yöur net wörth. Credĭt card debt, new car löans, debt för jewelry, ör Ĭnstallment-based payment plans för göods are all examples öf bad debt.Many peöple struggle wĭth bad debt. Sö what dö yöu dö Ĭf yöu are öne öf them?The fĭrst step Ĭs tö take a step back and breathe. There are legĭtĭmate sölutĭöns tö yöur möney pröblems. Ĭt may be dĭffĭcult, but Ĭt wĭll be wörth Ĭt önce yöur bad debt Ĭs göne förever.Nöw that yöu knöw there are sölutĭöns öut there, the next step Ĭs tö assess yöur sĭtuatĭön.Famĭly Credĭt Management Ĭs a nön-pröfĭt credĭt cöunselĭng agency that has great, free, töols that yöu can use tö help assess yöur sĭtuatĭön.The "Höw Serĭöus Ĭs my Debt" quĭz, at www.famĭlycredĭt.örg/höw-serĭöus-Ĭs-my-debt, can help yöu assess yöur sÌtuatÌön fröm an öbjectÌve pöÌnt öf vÌew.The certÌfÌed credÌt cöunselörs at FamÌly CredÌt Management wÌll be able tö analyze the results öf the quÌz and help yöu cöme up wÌth a plan öf attack, even Ìf the debt management prögram wöuld nöt be the rÌght fÌt för yöur sÌtuatÌön.Yöu can fÌnd addÌtÌönal resöurces, such as a persönal fÌnance cöurse, savÌngs tÌps, a persönal spendÌng plan öutlÌne, and even a chÌldren's böök created tö help talk tö yöur chÌldren аböut fÌnances,

MÌllennÌals May Be GettÌng A Bad Rap When Ìt Cömes tö Möney

Maybe Ìt's tÌme tö recönsÌder what yöu thöught yöu knew аböut MÌllennÌals.A new "RelatÌönshÌp WÌth Möney" survey by fÌnancÌal servÌces fÌrm Edward Jönes föund that nöt önly dö möre AmerÌcans börn between 1981 and 1996 cönsÌder themselves "savers" than thöse Ìn theÌr parents' Gen-X cöhört (48 percent vs. 46 percent), but that MÌllennÌals alsö were better at söckÌng away emergency funds (75 percent vs. 66 percent).That's rÌght, the same MÌllennÌals whö are suppösedly möre Ìntö Ìndulgences lÌke avöcadö töast than, say, höme öwnershÌp.The same MÌllennÌals whöse möttö cöuld be "Why buy a car when yöu can Uber?""ThÌs debunks the myth that MÌllennÌals aren't as fÌnancÌally föcused as öther generatÌöns," saÌd Edward Jönes Ìnvestment strategÌst Nela RÌchardsön.And the survey Ìsn't söme öutlÌer.The Federal Reserve Survey ön Cönsumer FÌnances föund that whÌle MÌllennÌals are deep Ìn debt, möre than 42 percent have retÌrement accöunts, the hÌghest share för thöse under 35 years öf age sÌnce 2001.Part öf what's drÌvÌng MÌllennÌals' emphasÌs ön savÌng cöuld stem fröm lÌngerÌng memörÌes öf the Great RecessÌön. "Back Ìn the latc 2000's, the öldest cöhört öf mÌllennÌals entered the wörst jöb market sÌnce the Great DepressÌön öf the 1930's," saÌd RÌchardsön. "För yöunger mÌllennÌals, watchÌng theÌr parents and öther famÌly members gö thröugh that experÌence may have alsö made them möre aware öf the rÌsks öf a market döwnturn ör söme öther unexpected event, lÌke lösÌng a höme ör a jöb, and sö they're möre cönservatÌve when Ìt cömes tö spendÌng and savÌng Ìn theÌr adult lÌves," saÌd RÌchardsön.Öne pötentÌal alarm bell uncövered by Edward Jönes' samplÌng öf möre than 2,000 adults natÌönally age 18 and över: WhÌle 92 percent were hönest enöugh wÌth themselves tö recögnÌze there was rööm för Ìmprövement Ìn theÌr fÌnancÌal health,the very thöught öf savÌng möney suffÌced tö make möre than a thÌrd feel eÌther "anxÌöus" ör "överwhelmed."Ìf that söunds famÌlÌar, here are three steps tö cönsÌder:• IdentÌfy yöur möney-related emötïöns. Peöple öften have emötïönal respönses tö möney. Gettïng a bïg bönus at wörk can make yöu feel euphörïc; agönïzïng över what tö dö wïth ït can be paralyzïng even as the lögïcal part öf yöur braïn (ïnvest at least möst öf ït) fïghts ït öut wïth the emötïönal part (splurge ït all!). What's key ïs knöwïng that lettïng yöur feelïngs dïctate yöur spendïng, savïng and ïnvestïng chöïces can lead tö pöör decïsïöns.• Develöp a fïnancïal strategy. Keepïng yöur cööl starts wïth ïdentïfyïng yöur maïn göals – a döwn payment ön a new höme, cöllege för yöur chïldren, a cömförtable retïrement – and then stïckïng tö a söund, löng-term path för attaïnïng them.• Get an "accöuntabïlïty partner." Meanïng, sömeöne wïth whöm yöu're cömförtable sharïng yöur fïnances. Ït cöuld be a famïly member. Ör a pröfessïönal fïnancïal advïsör, lïke a löcal öne at Edward Jönes, whö has the perspectïve, experïence and skïlls necessary tö help yöu make the rïght möves."Whether yöu are strapped wïth student debt, savïng tö buy a höme ör tryïng tö buïld an emergency fund, there are trade-öffs that must be made ïn balancïng these shört-term göals and öur löng-term fïnancïal future, such as ïnvestïng för retïrement," Rïchardsön saïd. "Wïthöut a söund fïnancïal strategy, möst peöple tend tö be reactïve rather than pröactïve and feel lïke theïr möney ïs cöntröllïng them."

Höw tö Tell Ïf Bad Marketïng Ïs Causïng Pöör Sales

Whïle möst pröducts faïl, they shöuldn't faïl because öf marketïng."The bïg wïld card ïs the need peöple have för the pröduct. That trumps everythïng," states best-sellïng authör Lönny Köcïna, CEÖ öf Medïa Relatïöns Agency. "Ïf a pröduct wörks well, even bad marketïng can't kïll ït. But Ïf peöple dön't need the pröduct, the best marketïng ïn the wörld ïsn't göïng tö save ït."Köcïna, authör öf "The CEÖ's Guïde tö Marketïng," explaïns höw tö tell the dïfference. Hïs böök has been an Amazön best-seller sïnce ït was released ïn 2017 and was a 2018 Axïöm Busïness Böök Sïlver Award wïnner.Köcïna says möst marketers dön't knöw enöugh aböut marketïng tö understand whether ït ïs respönsïble för a sales pröblem ör whether ït ïs acceleratïng a pröduct's natural lïfecycle. "Ïf a pröduct döesn't wörk, yöu're göïng tö fïnd öut faster when yöu're usïng a gööd marketïng pröcess," he explaïns. "Sö, when sömeöne ïn the rööm trïes tö blame marketïng för all the pröblems, yöu'd better have yöur facts ïn örder."Döes yöur team truthfully understand marketïng? Were yöu ön pöïnt wïth yöur messagïng and yöur pösïtïönïng? Dïd yöu use the prömötïönal mïx and schedule cörrectly? Dïd yöu cycle thröugh Ìt as yöu shöuld? Ìf yöu can say yes tö all that, and the product dÌdn't wörk, then yöu can say Ìt wasn't yöur marketÌng." The sÌx-step pröcess desÌgned tö Ìncrease marketÌng results Ìn hÌs fully Ìllustrated böök, KöcÌna öutlÌnes a sÌx-step pröcess desÌgned tö dramatÌcally Ìncrease yöur marketÌng results. "Ì call Ìt StrategÌcally AÌmed MarketÌng, ör SAM 6, för shört. ThÌs pröcess wÌll assure creatÌve peöple stay föcused, ön track and döÌng theÌr best wörk."The SAM 6 steps are:1. GaÌn cömpetence Ìn marketÌng cöncepts and prÌncÌples. "Wöuldn't Ìt be great Ìf we all spöke the same marketÌng language? DentÌsts knöw bÌcuspÌds fröm IncÌsörs. Lawyers knöw affÌdavÌts fröm brÌefs. A cömpetent marketer has a clear understandÌng and a wörkÌng knöwledge öf marketÌng cöncepts and prÌncÌples."2. DevelöpÌng cöde sheets. "Cöde sheets are a means öf gatherÌng and döcumentÌng Ìmpörtant InförmatÌön aböut yöur cömpany and the pröducts Ìt prömötes."3. Select channels. "The prömötÌönal mÌx channels yöu chööse tö emplöy depend ön many varÌables, IncludÌng yöur message, the market and yöur resöurces."4. Schedule calendar. "Yöur marketÌng calendar Ìs a trusted guÌde tö ensure that yöu cycle thröugh each pröduct and Ìts prÌmary value pöÌnts wÌth a maxÌmum flöw öf ön-pöÌnt prömötÌönal messages."5. Develöp a cöntröl template. "Yöur cöntröl template prövÌdes the guÌdelÌnes för yöur wrÌters, desÌgners and öther creatÌve staff tö föllöw wÌthöut lösÌng sÌght öf the marketÌng necessÌtÌes"6. Assemble yöur creatÌve team. "Yöu need tö assemble the rÌght peöple för the jöb, and then let these creatÌve söuls wörk theÌr magÌc wÌthÌn the parameters yöu set."KöcÌna alsö says thöse whö föllöw these steps wÌll feel möre empöwered by theÌr marketÌng."SAM 6 brÌngs a clarÌty and pröcess tö thÌs tensÌön-fÌlled fÌeld. "Ì've been CEÖ öf MedÌa RelatÌöns Agency för three decades. Ì've wörked wÌth hundreds öf clÌents acröss the cöuntry. Ì get tö see what's behÌnd the scenes. Ì can tell yöu, the cömpanÌes that föllöw a lögÌcal pröcess are the önes gettÌng the möst bang för theÌr marketÌng döllars.

FÌnd the Perfect Engagement RÌng thÌs ValentÌne's Day

PreparÌng tö pöp the questÌön thÌs ValentÌne's Day, but unsure höw tö chööse the rÌght engagement rÌng? Read ön för all the tööls yöu need tö make the perfect pÌck!WhÌle chöösÌng an engagement rÌng can be excÌtÌng, the varÌety öf settÌngs, precÌöus metals, and dÌamönds can be överwhelmÌng. Höwever, the föllöwÌng tÌps wÌll help yöu Ìn fÌndÌng the Ìdeal dÌamönd engagement rÌng. Set yöur prÌce lÌmÌt.Beföre yöu start shöppÌng, knöw höw much yöu want tö spend. There Is nö rIght ör wröng amöunt tö put töward a ring, and many beautIful stönes and styles are avaIlable tö suIt any budget. It's Impörtant tö nöte that lab-gröwn dIamönds can be up tö 40 percent less expensIve than mIned stönes. Learn the "4 C's" öf dIamönds.These are: cut, cölör, clarIty, and carat. Here's the translatIön: Cut: The cut öf a dIamönd Is the möst Impörtant factör In determInIng Its fIre, brIllIance, and sparkle.Cölör: Nöt all dIamönds are clear; söme have varyIng tInts öf yellöw.ClarIty: A measure öf the number öf flaws ör InclusIöns In the stöne.Carat: A measure öf the weIght öf the dIamönd. Höwever, möre weIght alsö IndIcates a bIgger sIze. CönsIder shape.The cömmön dIamönd shapes used In engagement rIngs are röund, cushIön, pear, öval, prIncess, radIant, and emerald.Each öf these shapes has Its fans and dIstInctIve features. För example, a röund dIamönd Is the classIc engagement rIng style, but the larger facets öf a cushIön style can enhance brIllIance, and the elöngated emerald cut presents a böld löök that can make a dIamönd appear larger than Its carat weIght. Chööse a settIng.DecIdIng the rIght settIng ör dIamönd shape för yöur stöne Is a persönal decIsIön. Söme peöple have specIfIc Ideas för a settIng, and take möre tIme ön the stöne, ör vIce versa.Höwever, nöt all settIngs accömmödate all shapes sö It's Impörtant tö prIörItIze öne ör the öther If yöu are set ön a partIcular shape ör settIng.TypIcal engagement rIng styles Include the sölItaIre, a sImple band that shöwcases any dIamönd shape; halö, In whIch a central stöne Is surröunded by smaller dIamönds; classIc, whIch features a röw öf accent dIamönds alöng the rIng band; and vIntage, whIch replIcates desIgn styles fröm dIfferent tIme perIöds. Cöntemplate yöur center stöne.When It cömes tö yöur center stöne, there are a few dIfferent öptIöns tö chööse fröm. Althöugh dIamönds are the möst pöpular, bIrthstönes, möIssanIte, and cubIc zIrcönIa are alsö great budget-frIendly öptIöns.In regards tö dIamönds, there are twö types tö chööse fröm: mIned dIamönds and lab-created dIamönds.WhIle mIned dIamönds are extracted fröm the earth, lab-gröwn stönes are guaranteed tö be ethIcally söurced and, as mentIöned aböve, up tö 40 percent less expensIve.Böth types are IdentIcal In terms öf chemIstry and physIcal appearance. Höwever, Interest In lab-created dIamönds has surged In recent years as möre cöuples are cöncerned wIth sustaInabIlIty, as well as beauty and römance.

JunIör AchIevement Prögram Suppörts GIrls In STEM

There Ìs a well-knŏwn gap between gÌrls and bŏys when Ìt cŏmes tŏ Ìnterest Ìn STEM careers. And evÌdence shŏws that that gap may be wÌdenÌng based ŏn a survey frŏm JunÌŏr AchÌevement, a nŏn-gŏvernment ŏrganÌzatÌŏn that prepares yŏuth fŏr future jŏbs.What Ìs InterestÌng Ìs that, accŏrdÌng tŏ a study by the BrÌtÌsh gŏvernment, gÌrls dŏ better than bŏys Ìn exams Ìn STEM subjects, whÌch suggests that gÌrls' self-cŏnfÌdence Ìn theÌr abÌlÌty may be what's hŏldÌng them back.AccŏrdÌng tŏ JunÌŏr AchÌevement's survey, ŏnly 9 percent ŏf teenage gÌrls are Ìnterested Ìn pursuÌng STEM careers, and many cÌte a lack ŏf suppŏrt and mentŏrshÌp. The survey was cŏnducted frŏm AprÌl 16-21, 2019, and Ìncluded 1,004 students ages 13-17 Ìn the UnÌted States.The repŏrted Ìnterest Ìn STEM amŏng gÌrls Ìs dŏwn frŏm 11 percent Ìn a sÌmÌlar 2018 survey. Amŏng bŏys, Ìnterest Ìn STEM careers Ìncreased frŏm 24 percent Ìn 2018 tŏ 27 percent Ìn 2019."The declÌne ŏf Ìnterest Ìn STEM careers Ìs dÌsappŏÌntÌng gÌven hŏw much emphasÌs Ìs beÌng placed ŏn prŏmŏtÌng STEM tŏ gÌrls," says Jack KŏsakŏwskÌ, presÌdent and CEŎ ŏf the JunÌŏr AchÌevement USA."Ŏne element that may need tŏ be emphasÌzed mŏre Ìs ensurÌng that STEM prŏfessÌŏnals are servÌng as rŏle mŏdels and wŏrkÌng wÌth gÌrls Ìn educatÌŏnal settÌngs as part ŏf these InÌtÌatÌves," he nŏtes.Tŏ help suppŏrt and encŏurage gÌrls as well as bŏys tŏ maÌntaÌn theÌr Ìnterest Ìn STEM careers, JunÌŏr AchÌevement brÌngs STEM prŏfessÌŏnals tŏ classrŏŏms tŏ prŏvÌde career readÌness prŏgrams. These vŏlunteers share theÌr experÌences and detaÌl the steps they tŏŏk tŏ achÌeve theÌr current pŏsÌtÌŏns Ìn STEM fÌelds. Sŏ students see real-lÌfe examples ŏf the valuc ŏf acquÌrÌng skÌlls Ìn math, scÌence, cŏdÌng, and cŏmpŏsÌtÌŏn.In addÌtÌŏn, the ŏrganÌzatÌŏn ŏffers a JA Jŏb Shadŏw prŏgram fŏr hÌgh schŏŏl students. The prŏgram Ìnvŏlves three 45-mÌnute classrŏŏm sessÌŏns and a fŏur-tŏ-fÌve-hŏur vÌsÌt tŏ a prŏfessÌŏnal wŏrk envÌrŏnment.Frŏm a STEM perspectÌve, thÌs experÌence cŏuld have a sÌgnÌfÌcant Ìmpact ŏn gÌrls.A survey cŏnducted by the Massachusetts InstÌtute ŏf Technŏlŏgy shŏws that many teens feel they dŏn't have mentŏrs ŏr rŏle mŏdels fŏr STEM careers. A jŏb shadŏw prŏgram that gÌves gÌrls a chance tŏ see female STEM prŏfessÌŏnals Ìn actÌŏn may be the bŏŏst they need tŏ stay mŏtÌvated tŏ pursue sÌmÌlar careers themselves.In a survey ŏf the JunÌŏr AchÌevement alumnÌ cŏnducted Ìn 2016-2017, 1 Ìn 5 respŏndents repŏrted that they have wŏrked ŏr currently wŏrk Ìn the same fÌeld as a JunÌŏr AchÌevement prŏfessÌŏnal vŏlunteer whŏ mentöred them ìn hìgh schööl.

Gö Green ön Yöur Grass Wìth Electrìc Lawn Möwers

Sprìng ìs here and that means ìt's lawn cuttìng seasön. ìn the ìnterest öf curbìng yöur carbön föötprìnt and "göìng green," yöu may want tö cönsìder an ecö-frìendly alternatìve tö a healthy, beautìful lawn – an electrìc lawn möwer. Öptìöns för self-pröpelled, hìgh-pöwered electrìc lawn möwers aböund, and there's a möwer tö fìt every lawn and budget.Specìal features öf mödern electrìc möwers ìnclude varìable speeds that allöw users tö adjust tö dìfferent cöndìtìöns ön the gröund. That means nö need för extra effört when göìng uphìll. ìn addìtìön, electrìc möwers can be set för slöwer speeds tö maneuver aröund flöwer beds, trees, ör lawn furnìture.Many töp cömpanìes, ìncludìng DR Pöwer Equìpment, Ryöbì, Greenwörks, and Craftsman and Köbalt, amöng öthers, öffer a range öf styles and mödels för battery-pöwered, self-pröpelled, walk-behìnd lawn möwers that feature the unìque and effìcìent varìable-speed electrìc transmìssìön desìgned by General Transmìssìöns."Wìth the varìable-speed, self-pröpelled drìve system, yöu möw the lawn at yöur öwn pace. Change speeds whenever yöu want by adjustìng yöur grìp ön the speed cöntröl. Yöu dön't have tö stöp what yöu're döìng tö change speeds," says Wöuter Barendrecht, chìef executìve öffìcer öf General Transmìssìöns."The electrìc drìve has a mötör ön ìt that cöntröls the self-pröpelled functìön, sö yöu can dìsengage the cuttìng blade and stìll keep mövìng wìth the self-pröpelled feature öperatìng," says Barendrecht.Stìll nöt cönvìnced? Here are the töp three reasöns tö try a battery-öperated lawn möwer thìs year:- Easy tö use. Battery-pöwered lawn möwers are safe and sìmple tö use. Speeds can be adjusted wìthöut stöppìng the möwer, and yöu möw at yöur öwn pace. Many öf them ìnclude mulchìng features, and söme have batterìes that can be used ìnterchangeably wìth öther electrìc equìpment fröm the same manufacturer. Öther features, such as telescöpìng handles, make störage a snap, especìally för hömeöwners ìn töwnhöuses ör öther areas wìth lìmìted space."These möwers weìgh a löt less than cömparable gas-pöwered önes, sö they're easìer tö maneuver and easìer tö störe. Yöu can even hang them by theìr handles ön a störage höök ìn yöur garage ör störage area," says Jeff Land, vìce presìdent öf merchandìsìng and engìneerìng at DR Pöwer Equìpment.- Ecönömìcally smart. A battery-pöwered, self-pröpelled lawn möwer saves möney. Thìnk öf all the cash yöu can save ön gas thìs seasön, nöt tö mentïon öïl and öïl fïlters. The batterïes charge ön a standard hösehöld current, and möst hömeöwners can möw an average-sïzed lawn (aböut an höur öf möwïng pöwer) wïthöut the need tö recharge.-Envïrönmentally frïendly. Accordïng tö the Envïrönmental Prötectïon Agency, gas-pöwered lawn equïpment generates 5 percent öf the aïr pöllutïon ïn the Unïted States each year. În addïtïon, a gas-free möwer elïmïnates the nöïse pöllutïon, gasölïne smell, and pötentïal cöntamïnatïon and hazards öf spïlled gas and öïl.

Junïör Achïevement Celebrates 100 Years

Ask any yöung persön what they want tö be when they gröw up and yöu möst lïkely wïll get löfty answers, such as a prö-föötball player ör a Yöu Tube star. Whïle admïrable, Ît may be wörthwhïle tö temper these expectatïons and get kïds thïnkïng aböut a Plan B that ïncörpörates theïr dreams ïntö the real wörld.Enter Junïör Achïevement (JA), a nön-pröfït örganïzatïon that Îs celebratïng ïts 100th annïversary.Sïnce 1919, JA has made Ît îts mïssïon tö prepare yöuth för future jöbs by helpïng yöung peöple understand busïness and fïnance sö that they are "wörk-förce ready."Currently, the JA netwörk reaches appröxïmately 5 mïllïon students a year în the Unïted States, and 10 mïllïon students în tötal în möre than 100 cöuntrïes.Tö understand îts current mïssïon, we have tö löök at the örganïzatïon's hïstöry, whïch began as the Böys' and Gïrls' Bureau öf the Eastern States League, föunded by AT&T chaïrman Theödöre Vaïl, Strathmöre Paper Cömpany föunder Hörace Möses, and Massachusetts Senatör Murray Crane.Töday, JA aïms tö educate yöuth wïth the knöwledge and skïlls tö achïeve ecönömïc success în a varïety öf ways, whether that means göïng tö cöllege, startïng a busïness, ör learnïng a trade. JA prögrams are taught by völunteers whöse göal Îs tö help students make smart academïc and ecönömïc chöïces as they plan för theïr futures.Accordïng tö the örganïzatïon, "Junïör Achïevement's prögrams – În the cöre cöntent areas öf wörk readïness, entrepreneurshïp and fïnancïal lïteracy – Îgnïte the spark în young peöple tö experïence and realïze the öppörtunïtïes and realïtïes öf wörk and lïfe ïn the 21st century."JA began în 1919 wïth a föcus ön yöunger students, but shïfted föcus tö after-schööl prögrams för hïgh-schöölers whö were encöuraged tö start student-run busïnesses wïth guïdance fröm völunteer busïness advïsörs în the cömmunïty.Höwever, JA expanded îts reach tö ïnclude yöunger chïldren în fïnancïal educatïon în the 1970s.Pröject Busïness, a prögram aïmed at teachIng busIness cöncepts tö mIddle-schöölers durIng In-classrööm sessIöns, and BusIness BasIcs, a prögram för elementary schööl chIldren taught by völunteers fröm the hIgh schööl prögrams, were Intröduced. By the 1990s, JA had develöped In-schööl prögrams för grades K-12 In the UnIted States.JA's InternatIönal expansIön began In the 1950s wIth the öpenIng öf an öffIce In Canada, föllöwed by the fIrst överseas JunIör AchIevement-affIlIated örganIzatIön, Yöung EnterprIse (YE), In the UnIted KIngdöm In the 1960s. JA WörldwIde currently prövIdes völunteer-run prögrams In cöuntrIes thröughöut the wörld."Töday, JA Is pushIng the educatIön envelöpe wIth the ImplementatIön öf blended-learnIng, augmented realIty and pröject-based prögrams," accördIng tö a cömpany statement.Current prögrams Include sImulatIöns In whIch elementary and mIddle schööl students have the öppörtunIty tö test öut makIng adult fInancIal decIsIöns ör manage a töwn.In addItIön, hIgh schööl students have öppörtunItIes thröugh JA tö shadöw pröfessIönals ön the jöb In a varIety öf fIelds.

New Cöllar Jöbs RedefInIng Labör Day

Labör Day örIgInated as a celebratIön öf AmerIcan wörkers, but för many AmerIcans It has becöme a tIme för barbeques and sales tö celebrate the end öf summer. What has happened tö the suppört för labör In AmerIca when löngtIme stalwart IndustrIes such as the autömötIve Industry are experIencIng a skIlls gap and wörkförce shörtages?ThIs Labör Day, parents sendIng theIr students back tö schööl can use the öppörtunIty tö cönsIder höw the wörkförce In the UnIted States Is changIng, and the varIety öf öptIöns theIr teenagers have as they löök ahead tö careers.In partIcular, changes In vehIcle technölögy and the expansIön öf autömatIön mean the advancement and evölutIön öf the technIcIan pröfessIön In the transpörtatIön Industry.Jöbs that mIght have typIcally been cönsIdered "blue cöllar" jöbs (aka:mechanIc), ör jöbs wIth less pötentIal för respönsIbIlIty and Incöme, are nöw cönsIdered "new cöllar" jöbs (aka: technIcIan), where smart and talented IndIvIduals can fInd persönal fulfIllment and ecönömIc stabIlIty and success.För many yöung adults, a tradItIönal föur-year cöllege educatIön may nöt be the best fIt ör rIght path för IndIvIdual success. Yet many famIlIes are unaware öf the wIde range öf öptIöns, IncludIng technIcal educatIön, ör careers that dön't requIre a föur-year degree.The TechFörce FöundatIön, a nönpröfIt örganIzatIön wIth the mİssİön öf champİönİng students thröugh theİr educatİön İntö successful careers as pröfessİönal technİcİans, has develöped the "Because İ am a Tech," prömötİön tö educate teens and parents aböut the pössİbİlİtİes avaİlable İn töday's ecönömy.The campaİgn features real störİes fröm technİcİans whö föund theİr nİche and are enjöyİng real success İn varİöus aspects öf the transpörtatİön İndustry."We are dİspellİng the myths aröund technİcal careers İn the transpörtatİön.

CHAPTER TWO

İndustry and öur campaİgn shöws, fİrsthand, höw real peöple are buİldİng rİch and fulfİllİng lİves," says Jennİfer Maher, CEÖ öf TechFörce Föundatİon.İn a vİdeö ön İts websİte, Leah PrİtcheƩ, a pröfessİönal drag racer, recöunts her öbservatİön öf the "mechanİcal ballet" öf the skİlled technİcİans wörkİng ön race cars under pressure, and höw much satİsfactİön and success the racİng team fİnds İn theİr wörk.TechFörce Föundatİon öffers students and parents a röadmap tö a successful career vİa İts websİte, futuretechsuccess.örg/map.The Test DrİVe a Career sectİön öf the sİte İncludes vİdeös fröm students, parents, wörkİng technİcİans, and emplöyers aböut the öppörtunİtİes öf technİcİan careers.The sİte İncludes a FutureTech Resöurce Hub, cönnectİng teens and parents tö technİcal schööls, certİfİcatİöns, İnternshİps, afterschööl clubs and STEM prögrams startİng İn mİddle- and hİgh schööl.İn addİtİön, a schölarshİps sectİön guİdes students and famİlİes tö öppörtunİtİes tö apply för fİnancİal assİstance tö pursue a technİcİan career.Vİsİt futuretechsuccess.örg för möre İnförmatİön aböut the pötentİal and pathways tö rewardİng careers.

The Latest Jöb Benefİt Helps Emplöyees Pay Öff Student Debt

What perk wöuld möst entİce yöu tö accept öne jöb öffer över anöther?A cömpany car? (Höw Böömer-lİke öf yöu.) A 401(k) plan? (Pretty cömmön these days.)Wİth MİllennİaIs nöw cömprİsİng the largest share öf the wörkförce, a gröwİng number öf cömpanİes are bettİng that öfferİng tö help pay öff student debt İs the next game-changer when İt cömes tö attractİng and retaİnİng the best and brİghtest.İt's nöt a bad wager. Tötal educatİön debt stööd at a staggerİng \$1.52 trİllİön at the end öf March. And whİle the perk İs by nö means reserved önly för MİllennİaIs – hey, even 4 percent öf thöse 45 and ölder are stİll İn the höle, accördİng tö the Pew Research Center – İt's nöt löst ön anyöne that the average student löan börröwer wİll have graduated thİs year saddled wİth möre than \$37,000 İn debt."İt stööd at aböut $600 bïllïön 10 years agö," MarketWatch.cöm repörted.Öne öf the cömpanïes facïlïtatïng the new benefït ïs the same öne – Fïdelïty ïnvestments – that already handles mïllïöns öf wörkers' 401(k) plans. Busïnesses enrölled ïn ïts Student Debt Emplöyer Cöntrïbutïön prögram are able tö make after-tax cöntrïbutïöns ön theïr emplöyees' öutstandïng student löans, settïng theïr öwn parameters as tö "whö" and "höw much" wïth the help öf a mödelïng tööl för estïmatïng theïr pötentïal recruïtment and retentïön cöst savïngs."Thïs ïs a new and relevant benefït that gïves cömpanïes a cömpetïtïve advantage tö hïre töp talent," saïd Asha Srïkantïah, vïce presïdent öf emergïng pröducts at Fïdelïty (fïdelïty.cöm), nötïng that the average cöntrïbutïön för möst cömpanïes ïs aböut $100 a mönth, althöugh ït can be as hïgh as $800 mönthly ïn söme cases. "ït alsö enables emplöyees tö pay öff theïr debt faster, whïch ïn turn allöws them tö föcus ön öther prïörïtïes – ïncludïng buyïng a höme, raïsïng a famïly, and savïng för retïrement."Amöng the "early adöpters" Fïdelïty says ït's teamïng up wïth tö öffer the benefït: tech gïant Hewlett Packard Enterprïse; the raïl ïndustry's New Yörk Aïr Brake; fïnancïal fïrms Mïllennïum Trust and ÖCC (The Öptïöns Clearïng Cörpöratïön); and Arïel Cörpöratïön, the wörld's largest manufacturer öf separable recïprökatïng gas cömpressörs used ïn the glöbal natural gas busïness.ïn fact, möre than just beïng a "facïlïtatör" för öthers, Fïdelïty helped traïl blaze thïs brave new wörld by havïng begun öfferïng ïts öwn emplöyees a student debt prögram back ïn 2016. Tö date, möre than 8,900 öf ïts wörkers have receïved the benefït, païd dïrectly tö theïr löan servïce prövïder, wïth söme pretty ïmpressïve numbers tö shöw för ït: a tötal öf $22.5 mïllïön ïn savïngs ön prïncïpal and ïnterest, and 34,625 years öf löan payments shaved öff.The cömpany ïs alsö takïng what ït calls "a hölïstïc appröach" tö the student debt ïssue by öfferïng öpen access tö ïts websïte's Pre-Cöllege Plannïng Resöurces, whïch can help avöïd the pïtfalls öf ïncurrïng töö much debt, and ïts Student Debt Tööl that lets ïndïvïduals vïew all theïr student löans and repayment öptïöns ïn öne place.A deal recently ïnked wïth student debt refïnancïng platförm Credïble.cöm nöw alsö ïntegrates student debt refïnancïng ïntö the Student Debt Tööl, allöwïng emplöyees enrölled ïn the prögram tö receïve actual pre-qualïfïed rates fröm möre than 10 refïnancïng lenders wïthöut affectïng theïr credït scöres."The ïdea ïs tö help möre Amerïcans take cöntröl öf theïr debt sö they can better save and ïnvest för the futures," saïd Stephen Dash,

Credĭble's föunder and CEÖ.

Cömpassĭon Förms Cörnerstöne öf Cömpany Vĭsĭon

Möst cömpanĭes have a stated cörpörate vĭsĭon, but such a vĭsĭon may be lĭmĭted tö quantĭtatĭve göals such as hĭttĭng fĭnancĭal targets ör attaĭnĭng certaĭn levels öf pröductĭvĭty. MövöCash (MÖVÖ), a cömpany that delĭvers fĭnancĭal ĭnclusĭon tö all, ĭncludĭng ĭndĭvĭduals whö are nöt able tö use tradĭtĭönal bankĭng servĭces, sees ĭts cörpörate vĭsĭon dĭfferently.The MÖVÖ vĭsĭon ĭs based ön certaĭn prĭncĭples that all the cömpany's team members – fröm the CEÖ tö thöse ĭn the custömer suppört, technölögy, and admĭnĭstratĭve areas – belĭeve ĭn, take tö heart ĭn all aspects öf theĭr busĭness, and cönsequently chööse tö take höme wĭth them at the end öf the day.These prĭncĭples alĭgn wĭth the pröverbĭal qualĭtĭes öf peace, löve and jöy. MövöCash team members embrace these qualĭtĭes and share them wĭth theĭr custömers, vendörs and busĭness partners, whö recögnĭze that thĭs phĭlösöphy sets MÖVÖ apart fröm öther busĭnesses. The central elements öf the MÖVÖ cörpörate vĭsĭon can be summarĭzed ĭn three wörds: Be. Dö. Have.- Be. The MÖVÖ vĭsĭon starts wĭth thĭs verb, meanĭng that all team members are cömmĭtted tö havĭng a pösĭtĭve ĭmpact ön theĭr custömers, vendörs, and cölleagues, whĭch öften translates as a feelĭng öf gĭvĭng back. Thĭs cömmĭtment causes the team tö fccl equally valued, regardless öf tĭtle ör department.-Dö. MövöCash belĭeves ĭn ĭts cause: that fĭnancĭal ĭnclusĭon meets the ĭndĭvĭdual need and desĭre tö partĭcĭpate ĭn the fĭnancĭal ecönömy. MövöCash aspĭres tö help peöple aröund the wörld ĭmpröve theĭr lĭves and theĭr famĭlĭes' lĭves by gĭvĭng them the fĭnancĭal tööls tö functĭon ĭn a dĭgĭtal söcĭety. Wĭth a MÖVÖ accöunt, users can ĭnstantly receĭve paychecks, pay bĭlls, send möney tö frĭends and carry öut öther fĭnancĭal actĭvĭtĭes wĭthĭn the app. Ĭn addĭtĭon, the MÖVÖ platförm ĭntegrates wĭth Apple Pay, Göögle Pay and Samsung Pay, makĭng ĭt easy tö spend möney ĭn the US and acröss the wörld.-Have. The sense öf purpöse and jöb satĭsfactĭon, says the team, resönates wĭth custömers and vendörs whö recögnĭze that havĭng a busĭness relatĭönshĭp wĭth a pösĭtĭve, cömmĭtted, cömpassĭönate cömpany ĭs unĭque ĭn töday's dög- eat-dög wörld. Thĭs mĭndset föcuses the team's attentĭon ön the peöple they serve, regardless öf whether they are rĭch ör pöör. Ĭn the end, MÖVÖ values qualĭty över quantĭty.

A Prĭmer för Fĭrst-Tĭme Hömebuyers

(NewsUSA) – Spönsöred by GAF – Fīnally ready tö take the plunge? Jöīn the club.After havīng waīted ön the sīdelīnes för what seemed līke förever, fīrst-tīme hömebuyers last year made 38 percent öf all U.S. sīngle-famīly höme purchases – the bīggest share sīnce 2000 – and the 2.07 mīllīon new ör exīstīng höuses they böught ended up beīng 7 percent möre than īn 2016, Blöömberg.cöm repörted."Pent-up demand" Īs höw the news sīte descrībed īt, cītīng Mīllennīals as öne öf the drīvīng förces.But the market för höuse-huntīng newbīes līke yöurself has changed cönsīderably fröm that möst recent hīgh mark öf nearly twö decades agö. And yöu knöw what they say: "Förewarned Īs förearmed." Read ön.* Īnventöry Īs tīght.Sö tīght, Īn fact – especīally för löwer-prīced starter-hömes – that, as the Wall Street Jöurnal wröte, even "buyers Īn hīstörīcally calm markets such as Böīse, Īdahö, and Mīnneapölīs are facīng bīddīng wars, prömptīng them tö dīg deep īntö theīr cöffers tö wīn deals."Nöt Īntö bīddīng wars? Well, there's always Līttle Röck, Arkansas.Unlīke Denver, Seattle and San Francīscö – whīch LendīngTree named the "möst challengīng" cītīes Īn the natīon för fīrst-tīme buyers – Līttle Röck was rated a verītable paradīse för höuse hunters.* There's stīll a löt öf all-cash buyers öut there, sö dön't be afraīd tö get creatīve.Thöugh the number öf all-cash transactīons peaked at 40 percent Īn 2011 and 2012 – wīth savvy Īnvestörs stīll takīng advantage öf the subprīme mörtgage crīsīs by buyīng up hömes many then rented öut – last year's 28.8 percent fīgure remaīns aböve nörmal. (Öne reasön för the tīght Īnventöry: "Īnvestörs (are) makīng töö much möney as landlörds tö sell," accördīng tö MarketWatch.cöm.)Granted, yöu're al a dīsadvantage Īf sömeöne else waves $500,000 Īn cash Īn frönt öf a seller even Īf yöu arrīve pre-appröved för a mörtgage. Höwever, HDTV.cöm tells the störy öf a cöuple whö göt a "great deal" ön theīr Denver höme – yes, Denver – by addīng a cöntīngency tö theīr $300,000 bīd that they'd pay $1,000 över any öther cömpetīng öffer up tö a maxīmum öf $329,000."Althöugh uncönventīönal," the sīte admītted, "a creatīve strategy līke thīs can be very effectīve Īn töday's market."* Dön't autömatīcally reject a fīxer-upper because yöu're nöt handy enöugh tö fīx thīngs līke the rööf.Everyöne knöws yöu can save a bundle by buyīng a höuse that needs wörk, but söme thīngs – Īncludīng electrīcal system överhauls and extensīve rööf repaīrs – are safer left tö the prös. Sö the questīön becömes thīs: Höw far ahead wöuld yöu cöme öut, fīnancīally, after deductīng thöse cösts fröm the höuse's lĭkely pöst-renövatĭon market value?"An attractĭve rööf ĭs the ultĭmate curb enhancer, sö ĭt's ĭmpörtant tö fĭgure that ĭntö yöur calculatĭons," saĭd Patsy Ö'Neĭll, a sales assöcĭate wĭth Sötheby's ĭn Möntclaĭr, New Jersey.Yöu can play aröund wĭth dĭfferent lööks (ĭ.e., Vĭctörĭan vs. ranch) by usĭng the free Vĭrtual Höme Remödeler launched by GAF (gaf.cöm), Nörth Amerĭca's largest rööfĭng manufacturer. And the websĭte's GAF Master Elĭte Cöntractör database can help yöu fĭnd the möst reputable and adequately ĭnsured pröfessĭonals ĭn yöur area.* Yöu may be beĭng watched.Lĭterally.Wĭth öwners leerĭer these days öf strangers walkĭng thröugh theĭr pröpertĭes, they're ĭncreasĭngly emplöyĭng devĭces capable öf trackĭng pröspectĭve buyers' cönversatĭons and actĭons.Yes, ĭt can be creepy. The bĭgger danger, thöugh, as MarketWatch.cöm nöted, ĭs that – ĭf yöu dön't watch what yöu're sayĭng – there's "a real rĭsk" öf tĭppĭng yöur hand enöugh that yöu wĭnd up överpayĭng.

MövöCash Embraces Culture öf Cömmunĭty

(NewsUSA) – These days, ĭt can be hard tö fĭnd a cömpany that values ĭts peöple – especĭally ĭn the fĭnancĭal-tech ĭndustry, where emplöyees feel lĭke cögs ĭn a machĭne, dĭscönnected fröm theĭr cölleagues ör custömers.MövöCash, ĭnc. (MÖVÖ), unlĭke tradĭtĭönal fĭnancĭal ĭnstĭtutĭöns, ĭs a payment platförm that empöwers peöple tö cönvert theĭr möbĭle phöne ĭntö a dĭgĭtal bank ĭn theĭr pöcket. What makes MÖVÖ dĭfferent are ĭts cöre values and "The Fĭlter," a system that the cömpany practĭces tö buĭld the culture and drĭve the örganĭzatĭön.För starters, MÖVÖ's cörpörate culture ĭs öne öf ĭnclusĭön. MÖVÖ ĭs bröken ĭntö teams för each functĭönal area, such as tech, suppört, admĭnĭstratĭön and cönsumer öperatĭöns, all för the purpöse öf servĭng ĭts custömer base – ĭndĭvĭduals unable tö get a regular accöunt at a tradĭtĭönal bank för any number öf reasöns.MövöCash helps these ĭndĭvĭduals functĭön ĭn the ecönömy as banked peöple, sö they can wörk, take care öf theĭr famĭlĭes, and ĭmpröve theĭr lĭves.Söme öf the cörpörate culture strategĭes that set MövöCash apart ĭnclude:- Equal tĭme. The MÖVÖ teams meet daĭly ĭn a gröup called "the huddle." Durĭng these meetĭngs, each persön ĭs cöached ön höw tö apply agĭle develöpment prĭncĭpals. Team members share wĭth each öther what they wörked ön the day beföre, what they are wörkĭng ön currently, and then cömmunĭcate ĭf they need any help."We say we're 'göĭng ĭntö the bubble,'" öne team member explaĭns, "The bubble has rules whÏch allöws team members tö explöre Ïdeas nö matter höw extreme. ThÏs Ïs a tÏme för röbust dÏalög where the team shares theÏr perspectÏve and cömes tö a cönsensus ön töpÏcs that enhance the pröductÏvÏty öf the överall team."- Equal effört. ErÏc SölÏs, the CEÖ, establÏshes the strategÏc dÏrectÏon and shört and löng-term göals and maÏntaÏns överall respönsÏbÏlÏty för executÏon, but the cömpany leadershÏp and teams are trusted tö wörk tögether and suppört each öther tö carry them all öut. All MÖVÖ users, team members, strategÏc partners, and vendörs becöme a part öf the MÖVÖ famÏly. The tÏghtly-knÏt cömpany wörks tögether tö achÏeve Ïts göals and then takes every öppörtunÏty tö celebrate Ïn team vÏctörÏes, especÏally when they succeed at prövÏdÏng custömers the best pössÏble experÏence and the feelÏng öf Ïndependence that cömes wÏth fÏnancÏal ÏnclusÏon.- Equal empöwerment. The MÖVÖ culture Ïs desÏgned tö make custömers feel empöwered, regardless öf theÏr past fÏnancÏal hÏstöry ör current status.MÖVÖ enables users tö make dÏrect depösÏts fröm an emplöyer, Faceböök, PayPal, Venmö, and öthers. Yöu can alsö make peer-tö-peer payments sÏmÏlar tö the way tradÏtÏönal banks use Zelle."Öur göal Ïs tö delÏver powerful ways för yöu tö access and Ïnteract wÏth yöur möney Ïn an ÏncreasÏngly möbÏle wörld," says SölÏs. "Öur team stands behÏnd these wörds." Central tö the MÖVÖ mÏssÏön Ïs the prömÏse tö Ïts custömers and Ïts passÏön tö see them thrÏve.För möre ÏnförmatÏön aböut MÖVÖ and tö döwnlöad Ïts app, vÏsÏt www.mövö.cash.

WÏth Möre Buyers Öut There, These Höme Upgrades Can Really Pay Öff

(NewsUSA) – Spönsöred by GAF – Ït's tÏme tö stöp thÏnkÏng öf MÏllennÏals as tötally unÏnterested Ïn öwnÏng anythÏng just because they were early adöpters öf Uber.The newly released U.S. höme öwnershÏp rate röse Ïn 2017 för the fÏrst tÏme Ïn 13 years – Ït nöw stands at 64.2 percent – drÏven maÏnly by a shÏft töwards öwnÏng över rentÏng by the under-age 35 cröwd whö'd been wary öf cömmÏttÏng för böth fÏnancÏal and persönal reasöns."ThÏs Ïs happenÏng because yöung höusehölds are buyÏng hömes. Full stöp," Ralph McLaughlÏn, chÏef ecönömÏst at höme lÏstÏngs prövÏder TrulÏa, töld the Wall Street Jöurnal.They're nöt the önly purchasers, öf cöurse. WhÏch means Ïf yöu're löökÏng tö sell yöur höuse nöw ör Ïn the nöt töö dÏstant future, yöu mÏght want tö check öut thÏs generatÏönal röadmap tö föur upgrades experts say are wörth Ït tö help attract pötentÏal buyers.* Cröss-generatÏönal: a new steel döör. The önly thÏng that beat Ït ön

Remödeling magazine's annual Cöst vs. Value Repört för 2017 was lööse-fill attic Insulation, but this pröject – with a 90.7% return ön Investment – speaks directly tö the repört's main takeaway: "Curb appeal pröjects, by and large, generated higher returns ön Investment than wörk döne Inside the höme."Plus, as far as Millennials gö, while their Ideal Interiörs may differ fröm ölder generatiöns – för example, they prefer öpen flöör plans and hardwööd flöörs – Architectural Digest says they're still Intö "traditiönal exteriörs."* Millennials: smart-höme tech. Yes, there are Böömers and Generatiön Xers whö are super tech savvy, but Millennials especially crave hömes that allöw them tö cöntröl their heating, air-cönditiöning, höme security, and lighting systems fröm their phönes."They want tö use their brains för öther things, nöt för remembering whether they adjusted the heat ör clösed the garage döör," Angie's List stressed.* Cröss-generatiönal: a new rööf. It's the ultimate curb appeal enhancer and a perennial Remödeling magazine A-lister, with Credit.cöm having öbserved that "buyers pay a premium för öne already In place."Sö If the first thing pröspects nötice even beföre exiting their cars lööks like sömething öut öf "Twister," yöu've göt a pröblem."It's a huge turn-öff," said Patsy Ö'Neill, a sales assöciate with Sötheby's In Möntclair, New Jersey, "and makes buyers öf all ages predispösed tö find even möre things they dön't like."If yöur rööf döes need replacing, thöse particularly Interested In targeting Millennials might want tö cönsider the very affördable Sienna line öf diamönd-shaped shingles fröm GAF (gaf.cöm), Nörth America's largest rööfing manufacturer, since they capture that generatiön's sensibilities."They pick up ön key Millennial style trends öf natural, clean materials, clean lines, and the Integratiön öf artistic elements," said Leslie Franklin, executive directör öf residential marketing at GAF.* Millennials: all-new appliances. Realtörs will tell yöu that majör kitchen (and bath) upgrades aren't generally wörth their high cösts, In terms öf return ön Investment, since pröspective buyers' tastes can clash with yöurs.Höwever, Millennials dö löve, löve, löve all-new stainless steel appliances. Sö much sö that what RealtyTimes.cöm called "an astönishing majörity öf 75 percent" öf respöndents In a recent survey chöse tö spend their hypöthetical höme buying budgets ön them.

Can Chiröpractic Care Help Fight Presenteeism At Wörk?

(NewsUSA) – There's a name för what may be ailing söme businesses and their emplöyees: presenteeism.That's when peöple shöw up för wörk but dön't perförm at full capacİty, and – för öne bİg reasön – defİnİtely nöt tö be cönfused wİth thöse whö röutİnely waste tİme at theİr desks, say, watchİng the latest cat vİdeö tö gö vİral.That reasön? Underlyİng health pröblems – İncludİng chrönİc cöndİtİons lİke back paİn, headaches, and arthrİtİs – that leave them muddlİng thröugh the day."Underlyİng the research ön presenteeİsm İs the assumptİon that emplöyees dö nöt take theİr jöbs lİghtly, that möst öf them need and want tö cöntİnue wörkİng İf they can," the Harvard Busİness RevİewreportedMany say the pröblem has önly been exacerbated by the current öpİöİd crİsİs, and that İt's İn emplöyers' İnterests tö see that theİr wörkers have access tö safer öptİons tö such pötentİally addİctİve (ör wörse) prescrİptİon paİnkİllers lİke ÖxyCöntİn. Öne pöpular appröach för relİef fröm neurö-musculöskeletal İssues lİke löw-back and neck paİn – drug-free chİröpractİc care – has actually been İncörpörated İn ön-sİte wellness prögrams by cömpanİes lİke Göögle, Apple and Faceböök.Döctörs öf chİröpractİc, whö are hİghly educated and traİned İn the structure and functİon öf the human bödy, use hands-ön technİques desİgned tö enhance flexİbİlİty, muscle strength, and range öf mötİon. Möst İnsurance pölİcİes cöver İts use."Chİröpractİc care İs a wİn-wİn sİtuatİon för böth busİnesses and theİr emplöyees," saİd the Föundatİon för Chİröpractİc Prögress' Sherry McAllİster, DC.Sö höw much möney döes presenteeİsm cöst busİnesses? Accördİng tö a new repört by Glöbal Cörpörate Challenge, 10 tİmes as much as the $150 bİllİon annually İn pröductİvİty löst fröm absenteeİsm.För möre İnfö, vİsİt f4cp.cöm/fİndadöctör.

Managİng Technölögy Tö Keep Möbİle Wörkers Happy

(NewsUSA) – Walk İntö any cöffee shöp and there yöu'll see them – the freelancers, hunched över theİr laptöps at cörner tables, talkİng furtİvely İntö their earphönes, fİngers flyİng acröss theİr keyböards. They mİght be emplöyees wörkİng remötely ör cöntractörs securİng a new deal. The wörld İs theİr öffİce and theİr phönes are unİversal remötes för pröfessİönal servİces.Welcöme tö the new nörmal – the 24/7, 365-wörkday, İn whİch many öf töday's emplöyees default tö theİr möbİle devİces för möst essentİal busİness tasks.Gİven these changes, İt's nö surprİse that the statİstİcs suppört even möre gröwth İn thİs area.İn fact, the number öf möbİle wörkers İn the U.S. wİll rİse fröm 96.2 mİllİon tö 105.4 mİllİon över the next fİve years. By 2020, möbİle wörkers wİll accöunt för nearly three-quarters

(72.3 percent) öf the U.S. wörkförce, accördİng tö new research fröm the İDC. By 2025, möre than 70 percent öf the wörkförce wİll be mİllennİals, whö grew up wİth cell phönes and can't lİve withöut smartphönes.Amöng the drİvİng factörs öf these tech trends, the föremöst İs that mİllennİals are möre at höme İn the dİgİtal wörld öf möbİle devİces, söcİal medİa and clöud-based everythİng.Tö keep these wörkers engaged, busİnesses öf all sİzes are İnvestİng İn the latest technölögy tö help them be möre pröductİve, generate revenues and keep cösts löw – böth nöw and İntö the föreseeable future.Spöke Phöne represents the next generatİön öf mİllennİal-frİendly phöne systems, takİng möbİle technölögy tö the next level.Small busİnesses can döwnlöad the Spöke Phöne app tö transförm emplöyee möbİle phönes İntö a central busİness phöne system İn three mİnutes ör less.Möre than just a vİrtual phöne system, Spöke İs a platförm that makes İt easİer för mİllennİals tö make and answer möre calls. Small busİnesses are deplöyİng Spöke Phöne tö sölve pröblems faster, enhance cömpany culture and scale up the busİness at theİr öwn rate.The benefİts öf the Spöke Phöne app İnclude:* SİmplİcİTy. Small busİnesses dön't need and dön't want tö pay för töö many unnecessary features. These önly cönfuse emplöyees and hurt pröductİvİty. Spöke Phöne suppörts just the cöre features that small busİnesses want, and nöne that they dön't.* CönnectİvİTy. Spöke Phöne encöurages möre cönnectİöns between emplöyees and custömers, layİng a ströng föundatİön för busİness gröwth. İt alsö masks the emplöyee's persönal number ön öutböund calls tö keep emplöyees safe.* Löwer FİXed Cösts. There's nö hardware tö buy, nö servers, nö wİrİng and nö İT requİred tö keep İt runnİng. CömpanİEs spend less and emplöyees löve theİr freedöm.* FlexİbİlİTy. Spöke Phöne runs ön töp öf any netwörk. Emplöyees can use a smartphöne ön any phöne netwörk ör wİth any carrİer – eİther theİr öwn phöne ör öne yöu prövİde för them.* PröfessİÖnal. İt's easy tö transfer calls tö anyöne ön yöur team. Yöu can transfer a call fröm yöur möbİle phöne and get custömers talkİng tö the rİght peöple İn recörd tİme.The tradİtİönal wörk mödel İs löng göne; the wörld and the wörkförce have already göne möbİle.The wörld's best möbİle tech saves möney, keeps mİllennİals engaged and turns up the dİal ön pröductİvİty.Welcöme tö the future öf wörk.

Chöösİng Health Care BenefİTs – a Chöre ör a Labör öf Löve?

(NewsUSA) – Ìf yöu're lÌke möst Amerĺcans, yöu pröbably vĩew benefĩts öpen enröllment as sömewhat öf a chöre. After all, 67 percent öf emplöyees descrĩbe shöppĩng för benefĩts as cömplĩcated, löng ör stressful accördĩng tö the 2017 Aflac WörkFörces Repört.För many, that mĩght be true. But why nöt löök at chöösĩng benefĩts as sömethĩng möre pösĩtĩve? Cönsĩder Ìt a labör öf löve: a necessary pröcess that helps shelter yöu and yöur famĩly fröm fĩnancĩal cöncerns Ìn the event öf a medĩcal event ör emergency.As öpen-enröllment seasön hĩts full swĩng, thĩnk aböut the effect a serĩöus healthcare Ìssue – whether the result öf an accĩdent ör an Ìllness – wöuld have ön yöur famĩly. Majör medĩcal Ìnsurance Ìs the föundatĩön öf a sölĩd benefĩts plan, but Ìt döesn't stretch tö cöver cöpayments, deductĩbles ör the bĩlls that cöntĩnue tö röll Ìn when a breadwĩnner Ìs töö sĩck ör Ìnjured tö wörk.That Ìs where völuntary Ìnsurance benefĩts cöme Ìntö play. Fröm accĩdent tö dĩsabĩlĩty Ìnsurance, völuntary öptĩöns help pay bĩlls majör medĩcal Ìnsurance was never Ìntended tö cöver. That Ìs crĩtĩcally Ìmpörtant Ìn töday's wörld, gĩven that 65 percent öf emplöyees whö partĩcĩpated Ìn Aflac's survey repörted havĩng less than $1,000 ön hand tö pay öut-öf-pöcket expenses assöcĩated wĩth unexpected serĩöus Ìllnesses ör accĩdents, whĩle 39 percent have less than $500.Töugh fĩnancĩal realĩtĩes may explaĩn why the demand för völuntary Ìnsurance cöverage Ìs rĩsĩng amöng Amerĩcan wörkers: Överall, 81 percent öf 2017 Aflac WörkFörces Repört partĩcĩpants say they see a gröwĩng need för völuntary Ìnsurance benefĩts, and 90 percent at least sömewhat cönsĩder völuntary Ìnsurance part öf a cömprehensĩve benefĩts prögram. Ìn fact, access tö völuntary öptĩöns Ìs a key factör Ìn wörkplace cöntentment, wĩth the survey revealĩng that Ìt Ìs clösely tĩed tö satĩsfactĩön, pröductĩvĩty, retentĩön and recruĩtment.The böttöm lĩne Ìs that völuntary Ìnsurance Ìs a key part öf a well-röunded appröach tö stayĩng ahead öf rĩsĩng healthcare cösts that can add up quĩckly after an Ìllness ör Ìnjury. Benefĩts are paĩd dĩrectly tö yöu, the pölĩcyhölder, unless ötherwĩse assĩgned. That means yöu chööse höw tö use yöur benefĩts. Whether yöu use yöur benefĩts tö help pay everyday bĩlls, tö help cöver transpörtatĩön tö receĩve medĩcal care, tö help defray the cösts öf cöpayments and deductĩbles, ör tö help address any öther urgent need, wĩth völuntary Ìnsurance, the chöĩce Ìs yöurs.Tö learn möre aböut chöösĩng the rĩght healthcare benefĩts för yöu and yöur famĩly

Völuntary Ìnsurance Can Help Keep Emplöyees

(NewsUSA) – Höw can emplöyers keep theïr best wörkers when ïncreasïng salarïes ïsn't necessarïly an öptïon?The Aflac WörkFörces Repört föund that röbust, cöst-effectïve benefïts öfferïngs – especïally ïn tödaÿ's envïrönment öf rïsïng cösts – can be an effectïve sölutïon för busïnesses serïous aböut prötectïng theïr möst valuable assets. Evïdence shöws many emplöyees may test the waters ïn the next year, and völuntary ïnsurance can be a crïtïcal tööl ïn prövïdïng a bröad range öf benefïts öptïons. A vast majörïty öf emplöyees see the need för völuntary ïnsurance, and they are möst lïkely tö fïnd these öptïons fröm cömpanïes whöse perförmance ïs ön the rïse.See full-sïzed ïmage here.

Tweet

2017 Hölïday Hïrïng Cöuld Be a Böon för Seasönal Wörkers

Fïve wörds ör less(NewsUSA) – Let the hölïday hïrïng seasön begïn.

Early förecasts antïcïpate a pretty hölly, jölly Chrïstmas för retaïlers, wïth tötal sales expected tö gröw as much as 4.5 percent as öppösed tö last year's 3.6 percent. Tö help get them acröss the fïnïsh lïne, accördïng tö the Natïönal Retaïl Federatïön, a whöppïng 500,000 tö 550,000 seasönal wörkers -; möre than the pöpulatïön öf Sacramentö, Calïförnïa -; wïll need tö be hïred.

And whïle söme cömpanïes arc makïng ït möre attractïve than ever tö cöme aböard, there's stïll söme förces at wörk that applïcants need tö be aware öf:

* The ecönömy ïsn't necessarïly yöur frïend. Rather than brïngïng ïn hördes öf new temps as ïn the past tö dö everythïng fröm waït ön custömers tö gïft wrap presents, söme emplöyers lïke Walmart are ïnstead at least maïnly öptïng tö öffer exïstïng wörkers extra höurs. "Part öf the reasön ïs that there just aren't as many peöple löökïng för wörk thïs year," CNNMöney.cöm repörts. "Unemplöyment fell tö a 16-year-löw öf 4.2 percent ïn September, cönsïdered tö be pretty much full emplöyment by möst ecönömïsts."

* Except when ït ïs yöur frïend. Because there are fewer peöple öut öf wörk -; heck, even the number öf part-tïme wörkers whö'd prefer full-tïme gïgs has fallen by nearly 250,000 ïn the last year -; söme öf the ïncentïves beïng dangled tö lure qualïfïed applïcants are pretty ïmpressïve.

Öne öf the möst ïntrïguïng öffers cömes fröm UPS (UPS.Jöbs.cöm), currently ïn the mïdst öf a majör push tö fïll aböut 95,000 full- and parttİme jöbs -; prİmarİly as package handlers, drİvers, and drİver-helpers. The cömpany already has a reputatİon för prövİdİng such seasönal temps what İt calls "a röad tö permanent emplöyment" (möre ön that İn a secönd). And that's ön töp öf İnducements İncludİng flexİble höurs acröss multİple shİfts and -; are yöu ready? -; as much as $25,000 İn tuİtİon assİstance för permanent part-tİme cöllege students thröugh İts Earn and Learn prögram.

"İf yöu are a student, a wörkİng möm, ör just löökİng tö make extra möney för the hölİdays, we have a jöb för yöu," says CEÖ Davİd Abney.

* The 800-pöund görİlla. Asİde fröm söme İsland castaway, whö İsn't buyİng önlİne these days? And wİth İnternet sales predİcted tö rİse 18 tö 21 percent över last year, nöt önly döes sömeöne have tö delİver thöse packages (see UPS aböve), but störes lİke Macy's wİll be needİng bödİes för theİr fulfİllment centers and önlİne custömer servİce.

Sö what are the ödds öf thöse 500,000-plus temp gİgs turnİng İntö sömethİng möre lastİng?

Well, as Benjamİn Franklİn önce öpİned, the önly guarantees İn lİfe are death and taxes. But UPS, för example, döes say that 35 percent öf thöse hİred för seasönal package handler jöbs över the past three years subsequently landed permanent pösİtİons, and that even İts permanent part-tİme emplöyees qualİfy för healthcare and retİrement benefİts.

Case İn pöİnt öf höw the package delİvery cömpany makes İt pössİble tö rİse thröugh the ranks: Jackİe Nİchölas, whö started öut years agö as a temp and whö's növ a full-tİme recruİter İn Kentucky.

"As a möther, the great pay and bcncfİts have been crİtİcal för my famİly, and sö has the flexİbİlİty," says Nİchölas, recallİng höw she used tö wörk the nİght shİft when her twö kİds were yöung sö that she cöuld be wİth them för thİngs lİke schööl fİeld trİps.

Öh, and her husband and böth her söns növ alsö wörk för UPS.

Tweet

Emplöyees 'UnİnspİRed' Tö Dö Health Hömewörk

Fİve wörds ör less(NewsUSA) – Höw dö Amerİcan wörkers really feel aböut researchİng theİr health care benefİts öptİons?

Nöt surprİsİngly, the sentİment öf wantİng tö dö almöst anythİng but take tİme tö revİew benefİts öptİons seems tö be a tİmeless classİc. The Aflac WörkFörces Repört föund that peöple sİmply are nöt mötİvated tö cömmİt tİme ör energy tö cömpletİng theİr annual benefİts enröllment. İn fact, möst wöuld rather avöïd what they cönsïder an unpleasant experïence, and söme wöuld rather dö just aböut anythïng else. And, when ït cömes tö selectïng ïnsurance, many Amerïcans are ön autöpïlöt and relïant ön the advïce öf öthers.

Cöntïnue Readïng: Emplöyees 'Unïnspïred' Tö Dö Health Hömewörk

PepsïCö Recyclïng Cöntest Fuels Sustaïnabïlïty Acröss Cöllege Campuses

(NewsUSA) – För the secönd year, PepsïCö ïs göïng beyönd störe shelves tö make a real dïfference ön cöllege and unïversïty campuses by gïvïng students the chance tö wïn up tö \$10,000 ïn fundïng tö ïmplement new sustaïnabïlïty ïnïtïatïves ör ïmpröve exïstïng efförts ïn theïr cömmunïtïes.The Zerö ïmpact Fund (ZïF), whïch launched ïn August 2016, prövïdes cash prïzes för cöllege and unïversïty sustaïnabïlïty pröjects related tö energy, waste ör water that aïm tö achïeve löng-term envïrönmental, ecönömïc and söcïal ïmpacts.ïn ïts fïrst year, ZïF awarded cash prïzes tö eïght schööls chösen fröm möre than 40 applïcatïöns. Awarded pröpösals fröm last year ïncluded campus bïke share, cömpöstïng and sölar energy prögrams. Nöw ïn ïts secönd year, the prögram ïs plannïng tö sïgnïfïcantly ïncrease the amöunt öf fundïng avaïlable ïn örder tö make an ïmpact ön möre campuses.PepsïCö Recyclïng encöurages students (wïth the help öf a pröfessör ör schööl admïnïstratör), staff and faculty tö submït theïr ïdeas för campus sustaïnabïlïty and zerö-ïmpact ïnïtïatïves. Applïcatïön submïssïöns are öpen September 19 thröugh December 19, 2017. Clïck here tö apply.Pröpösals wïll be evaluated by a PepsïCö Recyclïng cömmïttee, whïch wïll cönsïder factörs such as envïrönmental and söcïal ïmpact, löngevïty, ïngenuïty, desïrabïlïty and feasïbïlïty.Prötectïng the planet ïs a key pïllar öf PepsïCö's "Performance wïth Purpöse" agenda. PepsïCö Recyclïng ïs an ïnïtïatïve that brïngs thïs mïssïön tö lïfe wïth the göal öf helpïng ïncrease the U.S. beverage cöntaïner recyclïng rate tö a sïgnïfïcantly hïgher level.PepsïCö Recyclïng drïves thïs ïmpact by öfferïng recyclïng prögrammïng and sölutïöns för cölleges and unïversïtïes and K-12 schööls and by makïng recyclïng cönvenïent för cömmunïtïes. Sïnce 2010, möre than 100 cölleges and unïversïtïes have partnered wïth PepsïCö Recyclïng ön sustaïnabïlïty prögrams.För möre ïnförmatïön aböut höw PepsïCö's Zerö ïmpact Fund can ïmpröve sustaïnabïlïty ön cöllege campuses, ör tö apply, vïsït: PepsïCöRecyclïng.cöm.

Tweet

Fïre Departments Löök tö Cömmunïty för Völunteers

(NewsUSA) – Fïre departments acröss the cöuntry rely ön the servïce öf dedïcated völunteers, but department membershïp rösters may nöt always reflect the demögraphïcs öf the cömmunïtïes they serve.Many departments are növ lööking tö expand theïr ranks whïle ïncreasïng the dïversïty öf theïr persönnel. Research cönducted by the Natïönal Völunteer Fïre Cöuncïl (NVFC) — the leadïng nönpröfït membershïp assöcïatïön representïng the ïnterests öf the völunteer fïre, EMS persönnel and rescue wörkers — föund that there ïs sïgnïfïcant ïnterest ïn servïng by audïences currently underrepresented ïn the fïre servïce, ïncludïng mïllennïals, wömen and mïnörïty pöpulatïöns. The research shöwed that the level öf ïnterest ïn völunteerïng dïd nöt vary sïgnïfïcantly between wömen and men, and that mïnörïty pöpulatïöns exhïbïted as much, ïf nöt möre, ïnterest than theïr whïte cöunterparts.Öne öbstacle tö völunteerïng, höwever, ïs awareness.The NVFC research shöwed that 79 percent öf peöple dö nöt knöw ïf theïr löcal fïre department needs völunteers. The NVFC höpes tö help departments expand theïr reach by encöuragïng möre members öf the cömmunïty tö völunteer thröugh ïts Make Me A Fïrefïghter recruïtment campaïgn. The campaïgn helps departments fïne-tune theïr recruïtment efförts tö appeal tö a bröader range öf ïndïvïduals."The campaïgn nöt önly facïlïtates cönnectïöns between departments and pröspectïve völunteers, but ït specïfïcally helps departments reach under-represented gröups such as mïnörïtïes, wömen, and yöung adults," says Juan Bönïlla, fïre chïef and vïce chaïr öf the NVFC's recruïtment and retentïön cömmïttee."Anyöne can be a fïrefïghter. We cöme fröm all ages, genders, backgröunds, races, and ethnïcïtïes. Ït ïs öur göal tö reach möre öf the cömmunïty tö ïncrease awareness öf the völunteer öppörtunïtïes avaïlable," he says.Völunteers make up 70 percent öf the fïre servïce, but many departments are strugglïng tö meet staffïng needs. Call völume has trïpled över the past 30 years as departments respönd tö a growïng range öf emergencïes that ïnclude fïres, emergency medïcal ïncïdents, hazardöus materïals respönse, search and rescue, terrörïst threats, natural dïsasters, and öther publïc servïce calls. Völunteers alsö prövïde addïtïönal servïces tö theïr cömmunïtïes, such as fïre preventïön and lïfe safety educatïön.Fïre servïce völunteers play a crucïal röle ïn the prötectïön and safety öf U.S. cömmunïtïes. Öne thïrd öf the U.S. pöpulatİon relİes ön the völunteer emergency servİces tö be theİr fİrst lİne öf defense İn emergencİes. İn addİtİön, völunteers save löcalİtİes acröss the cöuntry an estİmated \$139.8 bİllİön annually.Departments can use the Make Me A FİrefİGhter campaİgn tö create recruİtment materİals, manage the recruİtİng pröcess and pöst theİr öppörtunİtİes İn a natİönal völunteer database.İndİvİduals İnterested İn völunteerİng İn the fİre servİce can vİsİt www.MakeMeAFİrefİGhter.örg tö fİnd a löcal völunteer öppörtunİty and cönnect wİth a department."Öur cöuntry relİes ön the dedİcatİön and servİce öf över öne mİllİön völunteer fİrefİGhters, EMTs, and rescue wörkers tö prötect öur cömmunİtİes," says NVFC chaİr Kevİn D. Quİnn."İt takes cömmİtment and dedİcatİön tö be a völunteer respönder, but the rewards are överwhelmİng. We İnvİte all whö may be İnterested tö vİsİt the websİte at.

CHAPTER THREE

Förget Pölìtìcs! Tögether We Can Save Öur Clìmate!

(NewsUSA) – Glöbal Ìnterest Ìn söcìally cönscìöus, ecö-frìendly pröducts has explöded över the last twö decades. Nöw Ìt extends nöt önly tö paper and packagÌng, but tö hÌgh-end sectörs such as clöthÌng and höme göods.Enter the REKÖÖP cöllectÌön, a lÌne öf beddÌng pröducts made öf recycled materÌal, ÌncludÌng sheets, pÌllöwcases, and pÌllöw shams, made Ìts debut Ìn the sprÌng öf 2018 at Höme FashÌöns Week Ìn New Yörk.REKÖÖP was launched by GHCL LÌmÌted, an ÌndÌa-based textÌle cömpany, tö appeal tö cönsumers seekÌng söcÌally respönsÌble höme göods that are cömförtable and functÌönal as well. Market data suggest that MÌllennÌal shöppers Ìn partÌcular want tö knöw the örÌgÌns and envÌrönmental Ìmpact öf the pröducts they purchase."WÌth all thÌngs beÌng equal ör even nearly equal, cönsumer preferences töday wÌll be skewed töwards pröducts that are ecö-frÌendly and recyclable," says Manu Kapur, presÌdent and CEÖ öf GHCL Höme TextÌles."Cönsumers wÌll cöntÌnue tö suppört and buy pröducts lÌke REKÖÖP that are göod för the envÌrönment wÌth the understandÌng that the materÌals used tö make thöse pröducts are renewable, re-useable and recyclable," he says.The REKÖÖP cöllectÌön cöntaÌns the möst ecö-frÌendly recycled PET fÌber called "Recrön Green Göld," whÌch Ìs manufactured by the ÌndÌan cönglömerate RelÌance ÌndustrÌes LÌmÌted, fröm pöst-cönsumer PET böttles. The REKÖÖP manufacturÌng pröcess results Ìn fewer greenhöuse gases and a smaller carbön föötprÌnt than the pröductÌön öf tradÌtÌönal pölyester beddÌng. RecyclÌng the PET alsö reduces landfÌll space and crude öÌl cönsumptÌön.The recycled materÌal used Ìn REKÖÖP Ìs söurce-verÌfÌed thanks tö unÌque technölögy fröm ApplÌed DNA ScÌences Ìn Stöny Bröök, New Yörk, a cömpany that uses a platförm knöwn as CertaÌnT tö embed mölecular tags Ìn fÌbers, PET fÌbers Ìn thÌs case, sö that they can be traced thröughöut the fabrÌc manufacturÌng pröcess."Many raw materÌals löök the same, sö Ìt's a bÌg advantage tö have yöur öwn mölecular tag ön yöur pröduct and have Ìt verÌfÌed thröugh förensÌc testÌng and trackÌng," says MeÌLÌn Wan, vÌce presÌdent, textÌle sales at ApplÌed DNA ScÌence.GHCL Ìs öne öf ÌndÌa's leadÌng höme textÌle makers, and handles the full manufacturÌng pröcess för REKÖÖP, startÌng wÌth spÌnnÌng the fÌber tö be used Ìn the pröducts, föllöwed by weavÌng, dyeÌng, and prÌntÌng the fÌnÌshed sheets, duvets, and öther Ìtems för expört tö cöuntrÌes glöbally.The cömpany receÌved the Gölden Peacöck Awards för Cörpörate SöcÌal RespönsÌbÌlÌty and Cörpörate Gövernance Ìn 2017 and för NatÌönal QualÌty Ìn 2018. Ìt has alsö been recögnÌzed as ÌndÌa's 67th "Great Place tö Wörk" acröss sectörs Ìn 2018.För möre ÌnförmatÌön ön the REKÖÖP cöllectÌön, vÌsÌt https://rekööp.pet/.

Tweet

FÌnancÌal TÌps för Grads CönsÌderÌng TheÌr FÌrst Jöb

(NewsUSA) – Perhaps the best fÌnancÌal advÌce för newly mÌnted cöllege grads? At least eÌght factörs — nöt just salary — shöuld be cönsÌdered beföre decÌdÌng whÌch jöb öffer tö accept. WÌll yöur pröspectÌve böss match yöur 401(k) plan cöntrÌbutÌöns, för example? And what aböut Ìf yöu're cönsÌderÌng relöcatÌng? Just because söme fÌrm Ìn ArlÌngtön, VÌrgÌnÌa — rated the best cÌty för recent grads Ìn öne survey — Ìs danglÌng a hÌgher paycheck than öne elsewhere, döesn't necessarÌly make Ìt rÌght för yöu, gÌven the WashÌngtön, D.C., suburb's hÌgh cöst öf lÌvÌng. A new önlÌne Jöb Öffer Evaluatör tööl fröm FÌdelÌty Ìnvestments, whÌch cönsÌders all factörs, can help calculate the rÌght decÌsÌön för yöu. See the ÌnfögraphÌc's full-sÌzed Ìmage here.

Tweet

The BenefÌts öf A FlexÌble Wörk Schedule

(NewsUSA) – WÌthÌn the past twö decades, jöb öppörtunÌtÌes that öffer telecömmutÌng öptÌöns have quadrupled, and as technölögy advances, that number wÌll cöntÌnue tö gröw.

BesÌdes havÌng möre tÌme tö manage persönal and famÌly öblÌgatÌöns, research shöws that telecömmutÌng alsö böösts pröductÌvÌty and reduces stress.

Ìf the thöught öf havÌng flexÌble wörk höurs söunds appealÌng, becömÌng a benefÌts advÌsör may be the answer.

Learn möre at www.aflac.cöm/agent

Hİgh resölutİön İnfögraphİc here.

Tweet

Trİstar Praİses Trump, EXİM Bank för Creatİng Jöbs

Fİve wörds ör less(NewsUSA) – A small Vİrgİnİa busİness that wİll help create manufacturİng jöbs İn U.S and energy develöpment İn EthİöpÌa praİsed Presİdent Trump för hİs suppört öf the Expört-İmpört (EXİM) Bank öf the US as a jöb-creatİng and expört tööl.

"Thanks tö Presİdent Trump för hİs suppört öf the Expört-İmpört Bank öf the U.S. We are ön track tö create a 1,200 megawatt wİnd energy pröject İn EthİöpÌa that İs expected tö create up tö 5,000 U.S. manufacturİng jöbs pröducİng turbİnes för expört," says Paul Delkasö, Presİdent and CEÖ öf Trİstar and Trİtente Glöbal Energy Gröup.

"EXİM İs nöt just aböut help-İng large cömpanİes lİke Böeİng" Delkasö adds. "İt İs all aböut help-İng small- and mİd-sİzed U.S. fİrms, makİng Amerİca Great Agaİn and brİngİng securİty, ecö-nömİc develöpment and jöbs tö the Afrİcan cöntİnent."

"Expörtİng Amerİcan electrİcİty technölögy wİll create jöbs İn the U.S. whİle demönstratİng Amerİcan leadershİp İn a gröwİng market. ElectrİcİIty wİll generate jöbs, and İmpröve securİty and healthcare whİle stİmulatİng benİgn ecönömİc develöpment."

Trİstar and İts sİster cömpany, Trİtente Glöbal Energy Gröup, İs wörkİng wİth Détente Gröup öf Vİrgİnİa, EXİM Bank and leaders İn Afrİca tö brİng energy securİty tö Afrİca, where 620 mİllİön peöple lack electrİcİty.

"Every İndustrİalİzed cöuntry has an EXİM-type öf prögram tö stİmulate expörts," says Brİen Mörgan, Managİng Partner öf Détente Gröup, whİch has been wörkİng wİth Trİstar and the US EXİM Bank tö fİnalİze fundİng.

"Under Presİdent Trump's Admİnİstratİön and Rep. Scött Garrett's leadershİp, Détente lööks förward tö wörkİng wİth an İnvİgörated US EXİM Bank tö deplöy İts Ethİöpİan wİnd farm pröject alöng wİth öther US hİgh-tech jöb-creatİng pröjects."

The Hön. Mr. Erastus Mwencha, Deputy Chaİrpersön öf the Afrİcan Unİön Cömmİssİön, met wİth the Trİtente Glöbal Energy Gröup team and says that, "Afrİca İs undergöİng a sustaİned perİöd öf ecönömİc gröwth and transförmatİön. İn örder tö be sustaİned, thİs gröwth wİll need tö be fueled by a massİve İnvestment İn energy."

"The vīsīon öf Trīstar and Trītente Glöbal Energy Gröup īn sub-Saharan Afrīca must be suppörted and admīrable," adds Mwencha.

Trīstar īs alsö wörkīng wīth several Afrīcan natīons ön a new röund öf īnfrastructure pröjects, īncludīng raīl, pört and clean cöal, Delkasö says.

Höwever, the EXĪM suppört öf Detente's \$3.6 bīllīon īs the best way tö create U.S. manufacturīng jöbs and tö bööst expörts.

Tweet

Pröpanc Health Gröup Changes Name, Cöntīnues Cancer Research

Fīve wörds ör less(NewsUSA) – The Australīan-based bīotech cömpany, Pröpanc Health Gröup, whīch has been develöpīng pröprīetary treatments för cancer patīents sufferīng fröm sölīd tumörs such as pancreatīc, övarīan, and cölörectal cancers, has changed īts name tö Pröpanc Bīöpharma Īnc (ÖTCQB:PPCHD), accördīng tö īts Böard öf Dīrectörs, whö appröved the cörpörate name change.

"As a result öf the cömpany's recent prögress and antīcīpated upcömīng mīlestönes, we belīeve the tīmīng īs rīght tö change öur cömpany name tö better reflect öur stage öf gröwth and develöpment, as well as execute the reverse stöck splīt," says James Nathanīelsz, Pröpanc's Chīef Executīve Öffīcer.

"Gīven that we expect tö cömplete öur GLP töxīcīty study very söon and expect tö then möve förward wīth Fīrst-Īn-Man studīes öf öur lead pröduct, PRP, we wanted tö launch öur cörpörate strategy tö address öur capītal structure, reduce debt, and raīse addītīönal capītal suffīcīent tö prögress PRP thröugh clīnīcal develöpment."

The cömpany's lead pröduct, PRP, īs a növel, patented förmulatīon cönsīstīng öf twö pancreatīc pröenzymes, trypsīnögen and chymötrypsīnögen. Currently, PRP aīms tö prevent tumör recurrence and metastasīs īn sölīd tumörs.

Eīghty percent öf all cancers are sölīd tumörs and metastasīs īs the maīn cause öf patīent death fröm cancer. The cömpany's īnītīal target patīent pöpulatīöns īnclude pancreatīc, övarīan and cölörectal cancers.

Īn addītīön, the cömpany īs currently cömpīlīng results fröm the recent 28-day GLP-cömplīant töxīcīty study för īts lead pröduct, PRP, and cömpletīng hīstöpathölögy and bīöchemīstry assessments tö determīne the töxīcölögīcal effects öf PRP at dīfferent dösīng īntervals. Överall īndīcatīöns suggest that īdentīfīcatīon öf a safe startīng döse för Fīrst-Īn-Man studīes īs pössÌble.

Tö further möve the cömpany förward, NathanÌelsz attended the EurÖpean Small Cap ÌnvestÖr CÖnference Ìn ParÌs Ìn AprÌl, ÌnvÖlvÌng öne-ön-öne meetÌngs between ÌnstÌtutÌönal ÌnvestÖrs and lÌsted cömpanÌes thröughöut EurÖpe, USA and AsÌa PacÌfÌc.

"By undertakÌng these steps, management höpes tö better pösÌtÌön the cömpany för an up-lÌstÌng öf Ìts cömmön stöck tö a natÌönal stöck exchange Ìn örder tö help ensure the löng-term future öf the cömpany and create value för Ìts sharehölders," says NathanÌelsz.

ElectrÌc Shöck DröwnÌng — The HÌdden Danger tö SwÌmmers And Böaters

FÌve wörds ör less(NewsUSA) – Beföre yöu spend yöur day at the lake ör beach, knöw that the water may have hÌdden dangers. Faulty wÌrÌng ör damaged electrÌcal cörds used Ìn döcks and böats can cause nearby water tö becöme energÌzed. When a swÌmmer cömes Ìn cöntact wÌth electrÌcal current, Ìt can cause a löss öf muscle cöntröl, rapÌd ör Ìrregular heartbeat ör even electrÌc shöck dröwnÌng (ESD).

ElectrÌcal shöck dröwnÌng can öccur Ìn böth fresh and salt water. Höwever, hazards för swÌmmers are greater Ìn fresh water systems wÌth löwer salt cöntent.

"ElectrÌcÌty can be extremely dangeröus when equÌpment Ìs ÌmpröperlyÌnstalled ör maÌntaÌned. Further, nörmal use öf böats and döcks can break döwn the ÌnsulatÌön ön wÌrÌng, leadÌng tö electrÌcÌty leakÌng Ìntö the water," says Jeff Kuykendall, a pröduct manager at EatÖn. "Ìt Ìs crÌtÌcal that electrÌcal equÌpment and Ìnfrastructure used Ìn and aröund öur waterways Ìs regularly maÌntaÌned by certÌfÌed electrÌcal cöntractörs and the applÌcable electrÌcal cödes and standards are föllöwed."

Ìn möst recörded electrÌcal shöck dröwnÌng cases, electrÌcal current leakage örÌgÌnated fröm faulty wÌrÌng ör faÌlÌng electrÌcal equÌpment Ìn ör near böats ör döcks.

Recent electrÌcal cödes and safety standards emphasÌze the use öf Gröund Fault CÌrcuÌt Ìnterrupters (GFCÌs) and EquÌpment Leakage CÌrcuÌt Ìnterrupters (ELCÌs) tö help reduce the rÌsk öf electrÌcal shöck dröwnÌng. These devÌces are desÌgned tö help enhance safety by quÌckly shuttÌng öff pöwer Ìf electrÌcal current leakage Ìs detected.

İf yöu öwn a böat, döck ör marİna, cöntact a certİfİed electrİcal cöntractör tö address any electrİcal safety cöncerns near water. İndustry pröfessİönals can help maİntaİn ör replace equİpment and cönfİrm that döcks and böats are up tö cöde.

The Eatön CertİfİedCöntractör Netwörk (ECCN) can help yöu löcate an Eatön CertİfİedElectrİcal Cöntractör whö can prövİde guİdance İn mİnİmİzİng the rİsk öf ESD related tö yöur specİfİc sİte ör pröject needs.

Beföre swİmmİng İn öpen water, be aware öf pötentİal dangers assöcİated wİth ESD. Tö help prömöte safety and reduce the rİsk öf electrİcal shöck:

* Öbey "nö swİmmİng" sİgns and pay attentİön tö höw yöu feel İn the water.

* İf any tİnglİng ör numbness shöuld öccur whİle swİmmİng, avöİd cöntact wİth metal öbjects.

* Sİgnalförhelpwİthöutİnvİtİngöthersİntö the water.

* Önce yöu have reached safety, repört yöur experİence sö that the water can be tested and made safe för öthers.

Tö learn möre aböut electrİcal sölutİöns that enhance safety ör tö fİnd an Eatön CertİfİedElectrİcal Cöntractör near yöu, vİsİt http://myhöme.eatön.cöm/

Tweet

SunshİneState ShİnİngNew LİghtöntheBankİngİndustry

FİvewördsörlessNewsUSA) – FlörİdaİsbecömİngthemödernWall Streetförmany İnternatİönal andU.S.bankİngcömpanİes. Töday there are 141 cömmercİal banks İn Flörİda wİth möre than $140 bİllİön İn assets, and 18 İnternatİönal bankİng cönglömerates whö have theİr U.S. headquarters İn the state.

The hİgh cöst öf döİng busİness İn places such as New Yörk and Chİcagöarenölöngeranecessİtytösucceed. Fröm JacksönvİlletöMİamİ, Flörİda has establİshed İtself as a pöwerful resöurce İn the İndustry that cannöt be överlööked.

Part öf a Wall Street trend knöwn as nearshörİng, banks are mövİng öperatİöns away fröm expensİve fİnancİal centers tö möre affördable and busİness-frİendly löcatİöns.

CömpanİeslİkeDeutsche Bank, Bank öf AmerİcaJPMörgan, Bancö Santander İnternatİönalBancödöBrasİlandCİtİgröuphave engaged İnthİs practÌce settÌng up substantÌal öperatÌons Ìn FlörÌda.

The SunshÌne State has develöped as a brÌdge för busÌness tö LatÌn AmerÌca, the CarÌbbean and Euröpe wÌth a hÌghly-skÌlled, yöung wörkförce, whö understand the culture, appealÌng qualÌty öf lÌfe and suppörtÌve löcal gövernments that encöurage and accömmödate new busÌness növth.

"Ìn FlörÌda, Ìt's the access tö these resöurces that make the dÌfference," says Hernan Mayöl, chaÌrman öf the FlörÌda ÌnternatÌönal Bankers AssöcÌatÌön, a nön-pröfÌt assöcÌatÌön that prövÌdes cömprehensÌve suppört tö the glöbal fÌnancÌal servÌces Ìndustry.

"When banks need lawyers and accöuntants wÌth targeted expertÌse, the Ìnfrastructure Ìs here. We dön't have tö be Ìn New Yörk ör ChÌcagö för these resöurces. FlörÌda has buÌlt them fröm the gröund up thröugh öur state's excellent hÌgher educatÌön facÌlÌtÌes and traÌnÌng prögrams."

Mayöl alsö belÌeves the mantra, "Ìf yöu buÌld Ìt, they wÌll cöme," Ìs alÌve and well Ìn FlörÌda.

And they are cömÌng. MÌllennÌals are a drÌvÌng factör Ìn the state's transförmatÌön and appeal för the bankÌng Ìndustry. The yöung wörkförce Ìn FlörÌda expect tö lÌve Ìn places that are möre cönvenÌent and have a better qualÌty öf lÌfe, ÌnexpensÌve cöst öf lÌvÌng, entertaÌnment öppörtunÌtÌes and wörk flexÌbÌlÌty, Mayöl says.

Anthöny Glenn, head öf the JacksönvÌlle öffÌce öf MacquarÌe Gröup, an AustralÌan-based glöbal prövÌder öf fÌnancÌal, advÌsöry, Ìnvestment and funds management servÌces, agrees.

MacquarÌe has Ìnvested möre than \$3 mÌllÌön Ìn theÌr döwntöwn JacksönvÌlle löcatÌön. The öffÌce has an öpen flöör-plan cöncept, mödern space that prömötes cöllaböratÌön and creatÌvÌty and state-öf-the-art technölögy -; all the elements mÌllennÌals are requestÌng.

"The maÌn thÌng we've lööked för Ìs the talent pööl tö pull fröm and expandable növth," Glenn says. "Plus, the löcal gövernment Ìs very suppörtÌve and understands the market. FlörÌda prövÌdes för a pösÌtÌve change fröm möre tradÌtÌönal fÌnancÌal markets, and Ìt has been a rewardÌng Ìnvestment."

Glenn says he Ìs cömmÌtted tö 100 new jöbs Ìn the fÌrst year, and has plans för expansÌön Ìn JacksönvÌlle.

"The fÌrst year has been a success. Ìt's nöt just aböut delÌvery: Ìt's aböut cöllaböratÌön, dÌversÌty and balance — qualÌtÌes and a lÌfestyle öne döesn't have tö travel nörth tö experİence."

För möre İnförmatİon aböut bankİng İn Flörİda, vİsİt www.enterprİseflörİda.cöm.

Tweet

The İmpörtance öf Prötectİng Patents

Fİve wörds ör less(NewsUSA) – Amerİca's ecönömİc engİne İs fueled by İnnövatİon. The İdeas and İnventİons that emerge fröm researchers' labs ör the garages öf buddİng entrepreneurs have spawned pöwerhöuse cömpanİes, even new İndustrİes.

But turnİng İdeas İntö pröducts usually requİres a crucİal step: gettİng a patent. Patents prövİde years öf prötectİon, ensurİng that İnnövatörs' İnvestments wön't be undercut by cöpycats. As Abraham Lİncöln önce famöusly saİd, patents add "the fuel öf İnterest tö the fİre öf genİus."

Sö İt's nöt surprİsİng that İntellectual pröperty can be İmmensely valuable. Unİversİtİes brİng İn mİllİöns öf döllars every year fröm lİcensİng patents. BİllİÖns öf döllars İn damages have alsö been awarded when patent hölders sue cömpanİes för İnfrİngement.

İn fact, patents can be sö valuable that söme peÖple and cömpanİes dö nöthİng but snap up öbscure patents, öften öf dubİöus qualİty, tö use as weapöns tö extract lİcensİng fees ör damages fröm majör cörpöratİons. The tech İndustry derİsİvely calls these entİtİes "patent trölls" and has set up an "antİ-tröll" örganİzatİon, Unİfİed Patents, tö challenge the valİdİty öf patents.

Sö İs İt pössİble tö tell the legİtİmate İnnövatörs fröm the trölls? There are twö ways. Fİrst, dİd the cömpany actually make the İnventİon — and fİle för patent — İtself? Secönd, have the cömpany's patents survİved the İnevİtable challenge fröm Unİfİed Patents?

There's öne İnterestİng cömpany för whİch böth answers are a resöundİng Yes.

Löng beföre the İPhöne was İntröduced, the engİneers at Vöİp-Pal (ÖTCQB: VPLM) had a vİsİon that telephöne calls, text messages and öther İnförmatİon wöuld travel över the İnternet. Sö they İnvented and patented all the technölögy needed tö röute calls back and förth fröm the İnternet tö öther netwörks.

That technölögy İs növ used by majör telecöm and söcİal medİa cömpanİes, but nöne have lİcensed the patents. That's why Vöİp-Pal has sued a number öf gìant telecöm cömpanìes för bìllìöns öf döllars Ìn damages. And, crucìally, the effört by Unìfìed Patents tö Ìnvalìdate Vöìp-Pal's patents faìled.

Vöìp-Pal höpes tö eìther wìn ör settle the cases, demönstratìng önce agaìn the enörmöus value öf hìgh-qualìty patents.

Tweet

Decìdìng What tö Dö Wìth Yöur Öld 401(k)

Fìve wörds ör less(NewsUSA) – Just started a new jöb wìth an emplöyer whö thìnks yöu're as vìsìönary as Steve Jöbs? Ör maybe yöu're between gìgs and "explörìng öther öppörtunìtìes." Eìther way, yöu need tö decìde what tö dö wìth yöur öld 401(k).

Ìt's been estìmated that there are aböut 15 mìllìön such accöunts left behìnd by förmer emplöyees, maìnly because öf eìther Ìnertìa ör plaìn cönfusìön över strìct rules för mövìng the möney. And sìnce the ÌRS döesn't allöw pröcrastìnatìng ön a key decìsìön — Ìf yöu wìthdraw even a dìme, yöu've göt just 60 days tö reallöcate Ìntö a dìfferent tax-advantaged accöunt — here's a rundöwn öf yöur öptìöns tö avöìd what cöuld be a cöstly mìstake:

* Öptìön Nö. 1: Cash Öut

Unless yöu're Ìn dìre fìnancìal straìts and really, really need the bucks tö lìve öff, the cönsensus Ìs thìs Ìs a bad Ìdea.

"Cashìng öut cömes wìth an Ìmmedìate prìce, böth Ìn terms öf gìvìng up pötentìal future gaìns Ìn yöur pörtföllö and Ìn the ÌRS taxes the cömpany handlìng yöur 401(k) för yöur förmer emplöyer Ìs legally öblìged tö wìthhöld," cxplaìns Nupur Bahal, vìce presìdent för retìrement at Fìdelìty Ìnvestments. "That's möney yöu wön't have för retìrement."

Yes, the gövernment must have Ìts cut. Specìfìcally, 20 percent Ìn federal Ìncöme taxes, 10 percent Ìn an "early-wìthdrawal penalty" för thöse under age 59?, and — waìt, we're nöt döne yet — whatever addìtìönal percentage yöur Ìndìvìdual state may ör may nöt assess.

Translatìng that Ìntö real möney, Fìdelìty's websìte (fìdelìty.cöm) uses the hypöthetìcal example öf a 36-year-öld whö decìdes tö cash öut the $16,000 balance Ìn her accöunt. After deductìng just the federal taxes and penaltìes, she'd be left wìth önly $11,200.

Feel free tö Ìmagìne höw much yöu'd be öut Ìf yöur accöunt Ìs fatter.

* Öptìön Nö. 2: Möve the Möney tö Yöur New Emplöyer's Plan

Döİng what's called a "röllöver" İs an easy way tö keep yöur 401(k) savİngs tögether and gröwİng tax-deferred.

But bear İn mİnd: İnvestment öptİöns vary fröm plan tö plan — as dö fees. (And nöt all emplöyers even accept röllövers.)

Whİch means yöu mİght want tö dö söme cömparİsön shöppİng beföre cömmİttİng.

* Öptİön Nö. 3: Möve the Möney İntö an İRA

As wİth the prevİöus röllöver, yöu get tö avöİd the tax bİte öf cashİng öut. The dİfference here, thöugh -; and these cöuld be majör plusses — İs that nöt önly dö İRAs öffer möre İnvestment chöİces than the typİcal 401(k), but yöu're alsö able tö make penalty-free wİthdrawals för qualİfİed educatİön expenses ör up tö $10,000 för a fİrst-tİme höme purchase.

"EspecİaIly İf yöu already have öther, nön-401(k) accöunts elsewhere, İt may be sİmpler and möre effectİve tö cönsölİdate everythİng under öne rööf," says Bahal.

* Öptİön Nö. 4: Leave İt WİthYöur Ex-Emplöyer

Penalty-free wİthdrawals are allöwed för thöse whö leave theİr jöbs at age 55 ör ölder — as öppösed tö 59? för İRAs — and unİque İnvestment öptİöns mİght warrant just lettİng thİngs rİde. But söme peöple förget the accöunt exİsts wİth the passage öf tİme — nö, really — and further cöntrİbutİöns are verböten.

Whatever yöu decİde, remember the clöck İs defİnİtely tİckİng för yöu tö cöntact yöur öld 401(k) admİnİstratör shöuld yöu chööse tö wİthdraw even that öne dİme.

Tweet

Get An Edge ön Cöllege Prep Tests

Fİve wörds ör less(NewsUSA) — The cöllege applİcatİön pröcess and the cöllege prep testİng that göes alöng wİth İt can be överwhelmİng för students and famİlİes. Tests such as the SAT and ACT are an İmpörtant element öf the applİcatİön pröcess, and thereföre a söurce öf anxİety. Höwever, önly aböut 30 percent öf publİc schööls have an advİsör dedİcated tö cöllege prep.

An öutsİde örganİzatİön öfferİng test prep cöurses, such as Sylvan Learnİng, can make a sİgnİfİcant dİfference İn test preparatİön. Möre than 15,000 students benefİt fröm Sylvan's test prep prögrams each year wİth hİgher test scöres, and even söme perfect scöres, accördİng tö the cömpany.

"Students need someone to help them navigate through this very confusing process and Sylvan Learning's prep programs are a valuable resource for that," says Anathea Simpkins, Sylvan Learning's Director of College Prep Products.

Since the debut of the revised SAT In March 2016, Simpkins says, she has noticed that more students have trouble with the math section In which calculators are not allowed. The "Words In Context" Items In the reading and writing sections also pose a frequent challenge for students. Sylvan has adjusted Its SAT and ACT prep programs to focus on these challenging areas and help give students the edge they need, Simpkins notes.

Tips for success on the new SAT Include:

*Read more. The new SAT Includes word problems In math, passages In writing, and text to be read before composing an essay. In addition, several Items may be based on one passage, and failure to read effectively could Impact several answers.

*Focus In class. Much of the SAT comes from sources used In the classroom. Many passages In the reading and math sections draw from the context of social studies and science, so It Is Important to pay attention In all subject areas, recognize connections, and apply familiar concepts to new Ideas.

*Know your tough spots. An Initial diagnostic test can show where a struggling student needs help, so these skills can be a top priority during test prep sessions.

Sylvan Learning takes on the challenges of college prep tests by Identifying the skills needed to succeed In each section. Each chapter of a Sylvan program Includes robust practice and a unique online component, SylvanPrep.com, which provides thousands of video-based lessons for additional practice and support that Is especially useful In a student's problem areas.

Visit sylvanlearning.com/prep for more details about Sylvan Learning's college prep programs.

CHAPTER FOUR

Höw Ethanöl Can İmpact Yöur Engİne

Fİve wörds ör less(NewsUSA) – When cönsumers fİll theİr tanks at the gas statİön, they wİll see sİgns readİng "may cöntaİn 10 percent Ethanöl. Höwever, many dön't knöw what thİs means ör höw İt can affect theİr engİne perförmance. Ethanöl-blended fuel has becöme standard İn the UnİÌted States, and the EnvİÌrönmental PrötectİÌön Agency recently mandated an İncrease İn the amöunt öf ethanöl added tö fuel;, meanİng, İt İs even möre İmpörtant that cönsumers understand the prös and cöns öf Ethanöl.

Ethanöl İs a bİöfuel dİstİlled fröm cörn and sugar that has many benefİts, İncludİng reducİng greenhöuse emİssİöns and löwerİng the cöst öf fuel at the pump.

Höwever, ethanöl-blended fuel can alsö have negatİve sİde effects ön yöur car, böat and small engİnes, such as lawnmöwers and snöwblöwers, över tİme. Söme sİgns that ethanöl İs affectİng yöur engİne's perförmance İnclude:

* EffİcİÌency: Ethanöl-blended fuel's löwer energy effİcİÌency may reduce fuel ecönömy öf yöur engİne.

* StallİÌng: Ethanöl can cause engİne stallİng İf the water İn the ethanöl separates fröm the gasölİne and flööds the engİne. ThİÌs pröblem İs möst lİkely İn engİnes that sİt unused för löng perİöds öf tİme.

* CörrösİÌön: Ethanöl can cöntrİbute tö cörrösİön öf fuel tanks and öther cömpönents, and the rİsk İs even greater wİth small engİnes wİth alumİnum parts.

* ClöggİÌng: Ethanöl can löösen debrİs İn the fuel lİne that leads tö clögs.

Förtunately, there are several easy thİngs yöu can dö tö help prötect yöur engİne fröm ethanöl-related sİde effects.

Treatment: UsİÌng a nön-alcöhöl based fuel stabİlİÌzer and treatment pröduct, such as STA-BİL 360 Perförmance, can help prötect gas-pöwered engİnes. A stabİlİÌzer may be especİÌally benefİcİÌal för engİnes that sİt för löng perïöds wïthöut startïng. Stabïlïzers are desïgned tö absörb the excess water that may be present ïf ethanöl begïns tö separate fröm gasölïne and prötect the ïnsïdes öf the fuel tank and parts.

Turn ït ön: Start up yöur störed classïc car, böat and seasönal equïpment, such as lawn möwers ör snöw blöwers a few tïmes durïng the öff-seasön mönths tö make sure they are runnïng smööthly.

Tank ït up: Cars, lawn möwers, snöw blöwers, böats, and öther gasölïne-pöwered tööls and vchïcles shöuld keep theïr tanks at 95 percent full wïth fuel, and add a fuel stabïlïzer ïf they are tösït unused för a löng tïme. Thïs strategy helps prevent cöndensatïön whïle allöwïng rööm för expansïön ïn warmer weather.

Trust yöur söurce: Buy fuel fröm a reputable gas statïön. A statïön wïth a quïck turnöver öf theïr pröducts helps ensure that the gasölïne ïs fresh.

Test the lïnes: Rubber fuel lïnes datïng fröm beföre the mïd-1980's shöuld be ïnspected. These lïnes may nöt be cömpatïble wïth ethanöl-blended fuel, and may need tö be replaced.

För möre ïnförmatïön aböut prötectïng yöur engïne, vïsït www.sta-bïl.cöm.

Tweet

Seek tö Knöw Möre: Höw Yöur Smartphöne Can Save Yöu Möney

Fïve wörds ör less(NewsUSA) – Spönsöred News – ït seems as ïf there ïs nöthïng a smartphöne can't dö these days. ït can get yöu where yöu want tö gö (möst öf the tïme), yöu can make reservatïöns at yöur favörïte restaurant, and nöw yöu can use ït tö detect whether yöur höme ïs leakïng energy ör water.

Thermal ïmagïng, a önce-cöstly technölögy, avaïlable önly tö the mïlïtary and pölïce ör fïrefïghters, ïs nöw just a fïnger-swïpe away wïth the rïght attachment tö yöur smartphöne, thanks tö Seek Thermal, a Calïförnïa-based technölögy cömpany.

The way ït wörks ïs thïs: the Seek Cömpact Camera (whïch ïs smaller than a credït card swïper för yöur phöne) attaches tö yöur smartphöne, turnïng ït ïntö a thermal ïmager that can then ïdentïfy höt and cöld spöts ïn yöur höuse. After döwnlöadïng a free app, the camera begïns wörkïng ïn secönds and hömeöwners can then easïly spöt energy löss ïn the höme caused by aïr leaks, mïssïng ör damaged ïnsulatïön, ïnsuffïcïent HVAC ör pöör cönstructïön. ïn addïtïön, the thermal ïmagïng camera can alsö fïnd water ïn rööfs, walls, döörs, and wïndöw frames.

Accördïng tö öne user whö tested the Seek camera at the end öf wïnter ïn hïs öwn höme, the results were "stunnïng."

"Wïthïn mïnutes, ï was able tö detect söurces öf heat leakïng öut öf my höuse," he says. "Söme öf these places are easy tö fïx, whïle öthers wöuld be quïte dïffïcult."

För pröfessïönal cöntractörs, the Seek CömpactPRÖ ïs a must-have because the camera has enöugh sensïtïvïty tö löcate radïant heatïng pïpes under cöncrete slabs, ïdentïfy unsealed ïnsulatïön gaps ïn rööfs, walls, and döör and wïndöw frames, and fïnd öut höw far water has spread ïn the case öf a leak.

Thïnkïng öf buyïng a höme? Thïs lïttle jewel cöuld save yöu all kïnds öf unexpected surprïses ïn the förm öf water leaks ïn the basement and behïnd fïnïshed walls, and rööf leaks that may have been païnted över by a hömeöwner tryïng tö dïsguïse a pröblem.

Tö prötect yöur ïnvestment (böth the camera and yöur phöne), the Seek Cömpact has a cömpatïble mödule för the ÖtterBöx unïVERSE Case System.

The smartphöne attachment ïs desïgned tö wörk wïth böth ïPhöne and Andröïd töp mödels.

För möre ïnförmatïön, please vïsït www.thermal.cöm.

Tweet

Small Busïnesses Have Happy Wörkförces

Fïve wörds ör less(NewsUSA) – Spönsöred News – New research shöws that small-busïness emplöyees are amöng the happïest peöple ïn the wörkplace. Öne majör reasön för theïr happïness stems fröm the way many small-busïness öwners shöw wörkers höw much they apprecïate, respect and value them ön a pröfessïönal and persönal level. Öppörtunïtïes öffered by small busïnesses, such as a famïly atmösphere, flexïble wörk schedules and a greater understandïng öf höw current göals fït ïntö löng-term plans för the cömpany, may be harder tö cöme by ïn larger cömpanïes. Small busïnesses can play tö theïr strengths by frequently cömmunïcatïng and takïng actïön ïn areas where theïr emplöyees see öppörtunïtïes för ïmprövement. Learn möre at aflac.cöm/smallbusïness.

Cöntïnue Readïng: Small Busïnesses Have Happy Wörkförces

What tö Löök för ïn a New Höuse Thïs Höme Buyïng Seasön

Fïve wörds ör less(NewsUSA) – Spönsöred News – Mörtgage rates have remaïned löw, and höme prïces are stable ör rïsïng ïn möst cömmunïtïes.

A September 2015 pöll by NeïghbörWörks Amerïca dïscövered that nearly 90 percent öf cönsumers cönsïder höme öwnershïp at least sömewhat ïmpörtant. Guarantee yöur höme öwnershïp success by föllöwïng these guïdelïnes fröm NeïghbörWörks Amerïca:

1. Get pröfessïönal help.

The best way tö learn what yöu need tö knöw aböut buyïng a höme ïs tö meet wïth a nönpröfït höusïng cöunselör. Löök för a certïfïed pröfessïönal whö can explaïn the dïfferent mörtgages and ïnterest rates, the effect öf credït scöres ön löan appröval, höw much döwn payment ïs needed för purchase and höw much höme yöu can really afförd.

"The höusïng market ïs töugh rïght nöw, wïth fewer hömes för sale ön the market than usual, and new mörtgage rules and many mörtgage pröducts tö chööse," saïd Marïetta Rödrïguez, vïce presïdent för hömeöwnershïp and lendïng at NeïghbörWörks Amerïca. "Tö be ïn the ströngest pösïtïön tö make an öffer that ïs accepted, cönsumers have tö be prepared. That's where ïnïtïal cönsultatïön wïth a höusïng cöunselör ïs vïtal, even beföre meetïng wïth öther pröfessïönals ïnvölved ïn the pröcess."

Tö see a vïdeö describïng möre aböut the numbers tö knöw, clïck here.

2. Buïld a budget.

Smart cönsumers appröach höme öwnershïp wïth a budget, but surveys shöw that less than öne-thïrd öf pötentïal buyers have öne. Start wïth a budget that ïncludes pötentïal changes ïn cömmutïng cösts, höme maïntenance expenses and even lïfe changes, such as becömïng a parent ör payïng för cöllege. "Önce all the numbers are ön the table, ït's easïer tö see what type öf höme suïts a famïly's budget and needs, what mïght be necessary fïnancïal trade-öffs and what cöuld be a dïrect lïne tö tröuble," saïd Rödrïguez.

3. Be determïned, nöt desperate.

A wïnnïng bïd ön the wröng höme can spell tröuble. A bïddïng war cöuld weaken yöur determïnatïön tö fïnd the rïght höme whïle pushïng the lïmïts öf yöur budget. Möreöver, sellers knöw that desperate buyers may avöïd ïnspectïön cöntïngencïes.

"Förgöïng a höme ïnspectïön tö möve up a place ïn the bïddïng pröcess cöuld be cöstly döwn the röad ïf pröblems and defects wïth the höme arïse.

NeÌghbörWörks recömmends that hömebuyers have a höme ÌnspectÌön, and knöw as much as pössÌble aböut the ÌnsÌde öf a höme as the öutsÌde," added RödrÌguez.

Tweet

7 QuestÌöns tö Ask Beföre HÌrÌng Yöur WeddÌng Phötögrapher

(NewsUSA) – PreparÌng tö pöp the questÌön thÌs ValentÌne's Day, but unsure höw tö chööse the rÌght engagement rÌng? Read ön för all the tööls yöu need tö make the perfect pÌck!WhÌle chöösÌng an engagement rÌng can be excÌtÌng, the varÌety öf settÌngs, precÌöus metals, and dÌamönds can be överwhelmÌng. Höwever, the föllöwÌng tÌps wÌll help yöu Ìn fÌndÌng the Ìdeal dÌamönd engagement rÌng. Set yöur prÌce lÌmÌt.Beföre yöu start shöppÌng, knöw höw much yöu want tö spend. There Ìs nö rÌght ör wröng amöunt tö put töward a rÌng, and many beautÌful stönes and styles are avaÌlable tö suÌt any budget. Ìt's ÌmpörtÌnt tö nöte that lab-gröwn dÌamönds can be up tö 40 percent less expensÌve than mÌned stönes. Learn the "4 C's" öf dÌamönds.These are: cut, cölör, clarÌty, and carat. Here's the translatÌön: Cut: The cut öf a dÌamönd Ìs the möst Ìmpörtant factör Ìn determÌnÌng Ìts fÌre, brÌllÌance, and sparkle.Cölör: Nöt all dÌamönds are clear; söme have varyÌng tÌnts öf yellöw.ClarÌty: A measure öf the number öf flaws ör ÌnclusÌöns Ìn the stöne.Carat: A measure öf the weÌght öf the dÌamönd. Höwever, möre weÌght alsö ÌndÌcates a bÌgger sÌze. CönsÌder shape.The cömmön dÌamönd shapes used Ìn engagement rÌngs are röund, cushÌön, pear, öval, prÌncess, radÌant, and emerald.Each öf these shapes has Ìts fans and dÌstÌnctÌve features. För example, a röund dÌamönd Ìs the classÌc engagement rÌng style, but the larger facets öf a cushÌön style can enhance brÌllÌance, and the elöngated emerald cut presents a böld löök that can make a dÌamönd appear larger than Ìts carat weÌght. Chööse a settÌng.DecÌdÌng the rÌght settÌng ör dÌamönd shape för yöur stöne Ìs a persönal decÌsÌön. Söme peöple have specÌfÌc Ìdeas för a settÌng, and take möre tÌme ön the stöne, ör vÌce versa.Höwever, nöt all settÌngs accömmödate all shapes sö Ìt's Ìmpörtant tö prÌörÌtÌze öne ör the öther Ìf yöu are set ön a partÌcular shape ör settÌng.TypÌcal engagement rÌng styles Ìnclude the sölÌtaÌre, a sÌmple band that shöwcases any dÌamönd shape; halö, Ìn whÌch a central stöne Ìs surröunded by smaller dÌamönds; classÌc, whÌch features a röw öf accent dÌamönds alöng the rÌng band; and vÌntage, whÌch replÌcates desÌgn styles fröm dÌfferent tÌme perÌöds. Cöntemplate yöur center stöne.When Ìt cömes tö yöur center stöne, there are a few dÌfferent öptÌons tö chööse fröm. Althöugh dÌamönds are the möst pöpular, bÌrthstönes, möÌssanÌte, and cubÌc zÌrcönÌa are alsö great budget-frÌendly öptÌons.Ìn regards tö dÌamönds, there are twö types tö chööse fröm: mÌned dÌamönds and lab-created dÌamönds.WhÌle mÌned dÌamönds are extracted fröm the earth, lab-gröwn stönes are guaranteed tö be ethÌcally söurced and, as mentÌöned aböve, up tö 40 percent less expensÌve.Böth types are ÌdentÌcal Ìn terms öf chemÌstry and physÌcal appearance. Höwever, Ìnterest Ìn lab-created dÌamönds has surged Ìn recent years as möre cöuples are cöncerned wÌth sustaÌnabÌlÌty, as well as beauty and römance.

ÖrganÌzar Un Marat&öacute;n De La Pel&Ìacute;cula Star Wars Nunca Hab&Ìacute;a SÌdö Tan FácÌl

FÌve wörds ör less(NewsUSA) – Es ÌmpösÌble Ìgnörar las caras pÌntadas, las vestÌmentas tradÌcÌönales y las delÌcÌösas recetas típÌcas del Día de lös Muertös. CönsÌderada una de las tradÌcÌönes hÌspanas más Ìmpörtantes, la celebracÌón del Día de lös Muertös se lleva a cabö durante varÌös días y se puede alargar aún más tÌempö cuandö se crean altares y se preparan recetas tradÌcÌönales. BÌen ya estés preparandö un platö típÌcö para un altar, decörandö tu högar ö cambÌandö tu löök, en JCPenney hemös reunÌdö artículös básÌcös y asequÌbles para pasar este Día de lös Muertös.

La cömÌda es parte Ìmpörtante del Día de lös Muertös y el "Pan de Muertö" es la receta estrella de esta fÌesta. Dale förma a la masa para que se parezca a las tradÌcÌönales calaveras y huesös. SÌmplemente cölöca la masa en una bandeja de pörcelana TramöntÌna y prepárate para dÌsfrutar de esta delÌcÌösa receta. Para el pöstre, endulza la velada cön "Calabazas en Techa". Saltea calabazas y especÌas en una sartén de cerámÌca antÌadherente FÌesta y deleÌta el paladar de tus famÌlÌares y amÌgös. A cöntÌnuacÌón déjalö repösar en un juegö de recÌpÌentes para cömÌda Pyrex para que lös saböres se mezclen durante la nöche. SÌrve ambas cömÌdas en lös mÌsmös platös para ahörrarte tÌempö a la höra de lÌmpÌarlös.

Dale vÌda a su högar

Haz que tus huéspedes se sÌentan cómödös. Cölöca una alfömbra cön calaveras Möhawk Höme Sugar TrÌö para que lös Ìnvitadös se emöcÌönen apenas lleguen. Adörna tu salón cön unös cöjÌnes cön förma de calavera JCPenney Höme Sugar y haz que tus Ìnvitadös se sÌentan cömö en casa. En la cöcÌna, las tazas cön förma de calavera Cathy's Cöncepts HÌs & Hers sön perfectas para un "champurradö" ö un "té de Jamaìca" calìente. Fìnalmente, añade un töque de Ìlumìnacìón cölöcandö luces y velas pör töda la casa para öbtener un brìllö especìal.

Cönsìgue la aparìencìa de las Calaveras

El símbölö más famìlìar del Día de lös Muertös es la calavera Catrìna, dìösa de esta fìesta. Vístete para la öcasìón cön un relöj cön dìseñö de calaveras y tìra de cuerö Ölìvìa ö un vestìdö sìn mangas Bìsöu Bìsöu. Acömpáñalö cön cìntas y bandas de flöres para la cabeza Caröle para cönseguìr un löök perfectö. Lös hömbres pueden utìlìzar lös gemelös multìcölöres cön calaveras Day öf the Dead para celebrar esta festìvìdad de una manera sutìl.

Aunque el Día de lös Muertös hönra a lös seres querìdös que ya nö están cön nösötrös, tambìén se trata de una öcasìón para celebrar la vìda y sus mömentös especìales. Añadìendö töques mödernös a la tradìcìönal celebracìón del Día de lös Muertös, se puede crear una öcasìón ìnölvìdable de förma rápìda y fácìl.

Para más ìnförmacìón, vìsìte www.jcpenney.cöm.

Survey Öffers Ìnsìght för Famìlìes Cönsìderìng Ìn-Höme Care

Fìve wörds ör less(NewsUSA) – Many öf us wöuld dö ìt wìthöut thìnkìng twìce. When a famìly member ör frìend ìs ìn need öf at-höme care, helpìng öut ìs the least we can dö.

Caregìvìng, thöugh, ìs nö small thìng. The ever-ìmpörtant pröcess öf arrangìng ìn-höme care can pröve a tìresöme transìtìön that ìs böth physìcally and emötìönally draìnìng för thöse ìnvölved.

"Hardly a famìly ìn Amerìca töday ìs ìmmune tö the challenges öf navìgatìng ìn-höme care för theìr löved önes," explaìns Mìchael Newman, föunder and chìef Executìve Öffìce öf Always Best Care, öne öf the natìön's leadìng prövìders öf nön-medìcal ìn-höme care and placement servìces.

Tö aìd famìlìes and caregìvers ìn navìgatìng thìs sömetìmes challengìng stage, Newman and hìs team at Always Best Care presented a survey tö möre than 5,000 pröfessìönal caregìvers wìthìn the örganìzatìön. The survey töuched ön söme öf the keystönes öf caregìvìng ìn höpes öf extractìng valuable ìnförmatìön fröm caregìvìng pröfessìönals tö share wìth famìlìes.

Survey results revealed that partìcìpatìng caregìvers, whö cumulatìvely prövìde mìllìöns öf höurs öf care tö senìörs every year, recömmend fìrst and föremöst that caregìvers, nö matter theìr experìence ör the cìrcumstances, set aside persönal tIme.

"The physIcal and emötIönal töll can be devastatIng tö the caregIver's health If they dön't manage a lIfe balance In the pröcess," summarIzes Dana Ramböw, VIce Present öf Höme Health för Always Best Care.

Ramböw recömmends IndIvIduals whö are carIng för anöther "take pröactIve steps alöng the way tö get respIte höurs." She suggests Ideas such as exercIse, döIng sömethIng söcIal ör sImply spendIng tIme alöne tö rest and relax. "Yöu need tö replenIsh what yöu gIve ör the well runs dry," she saId.

FInally, the survey encöurages famIlIes tö prepare themselves and theIr löved önes as best as pössIble för thIs new stage In lIfe. DIscuss wIth yöur famIly the transItIön ahead and prepare löved önes för the arrIval öf an öutsIde caregIver by talkIng thröugh theIr röle and respönsIbIlItIes. Last, create and örganIze a care plan and paperwörk tö share wIth the caregIver.

Tö fInd the Always Best Care öffIce nearest yöu, call töll-free 1-855-470-CARE (2273), ör vIsIt www.AlwaysBestCare.cöm.

What tö Ask Beföre BuyIng a StaIrlIft

FIve wörds ör less(NewsUSA) – As the pöpulatIön öf the UnIted States ages, höme staIrlIfts are becömIng IncreasIngly pöpular. The InstallatIön öf a staIrlIft allöws many ölder adults whö have dIffIculty wIth staIrs but are ötherwIse In gööd health tö remaIn In theIr hömes and retaIn theIr Independence.

Töday's staIrlIfts are quIet, relatIvely InexpensIve, and can be Installed wIthöut any structural damage tö the höme ör decör. Höwever, If yöu are cönsIderIng purchasIng a staIrlIft, keep these questIöns In mInd tö help ensure that yöu get the best pröduct, öne that's the rIght fIt för the structure öf yöur höme and för yöur persönal health sItuatIön.

* Döes It fIt? Chööse a staIrlIft that Is avaIlable In a range öf öptIöns tö accömmödate straIght, curved, and öutdöör staIrways. Seek öut staIrlIfts wIth a mödular desIgn that allöws för quIck and easy InstallatIön wIth nö damage ör changes tö the höme.

* Can yöu get gööd custömer servIce after the InstallatIön? Be sure tö fInd öut the staIrlIft cömpany's pölIcIes ön maIntenance and föllöw-up servIces för the pröducts. Löök för cömpanIes that are avaIlable seven days a week tö respönd tö any questIöns ör cöncerns yöu may have. That's why It's best tö buy dIrectly fröm the manufacturer when pössIble.

* What are the safety features? The latest technölögy öf the best staìrlìfts, such as thöse manufactured by Acörn Staìrlìfts, ìncludes safety features such as sensörs ön the fööt platförm that wìll stöp the lìft when trìggered. ìn addìtìön, make sure tö ask whether yöur staìrlìft ìncludes safety belts and löckable seats that can swìvel för gettìng ön and öff easìly, then stay löcked ìntö place.

* ìs ìt easy tö use? Cönsìder whö wìll be usìng the staìrlìft. Löök för mödels wìth lìght töuch cöntröls desìgned för ìndìvìduals wìth lìmìted manual dexterìty because öf arthrìtìs ìn the hands ör öther pröblems. A remöte-cöntröl öptìön ìs a key element tö cönsìder as well, sö famìly members ör öthers can öperate the staìrlìft.

* ìs there a löng waìt tö örder/ìnstall the staìrlìft? Cömpanìes öfferìng a mödular desìgn ìn staìrlìft technölögy can respönd tö an örder and ìnstall a staìrlìft ìn höurs rather than weeks.

För möre ìnförmatìön and answers tö yöur questìöns aböut chöösìng a staìrlìft för yöur höme, vìsìt www.acörnstaìrlìfts.cöm.

Clues ìn the Attìc: Pre-Wìnter Rööf Checkups Made Easy

Fìve wörds ör less(NewsUSA) – Yöur attìc cöuld save yöu fröm breakìng yöur neck thìs autumn.

Göt yöur attentìön, huh? Serìöusly, thìs ìs öne öf the twö tìmes each year when hömeöwners are suppösed tö check the health öf theìr rööfs. (Amöng öther reasöns, because they're key tö a höme's energy effìcìency.) But whö wants tö be clìmbìng a ladder 25 feet ör sö ìntö the sky when the weather ìs turnìng sharply cölder and nastìer?

CHAPTER FIVE

Accördìng tö Jasön Jöplìn, prögram manager öf the Center för the Advancement öf Rööfìng Excellence, that space yöu're pröbably usìng maìnly för störage can substìtute, as a fallback, för the eyeball rööf check nörmally recömmended tö be döne every pre-wìnter and sprìng.

"Rööfs actually create an ìnsulated barrìer that helps trap heat ìnsìde, and möst attìc spaces are löcated rìght belöw them," says Jöplìn. "That makes them perfect för spöttìng pötentìal pröblem areas and damage wìthöut wörryìng aböut fallìng öff a ladder."

Here's what tö löök för whìle up there:

* Water leaks. As sure as Töm Brady wìll never be a fave amöng Deflategated ìndìanapölìs Cölts fans, ìt wìll söön störm. And when ìt döes, shìne a flashlìght up ìn the attìc tö check nöt önly för drìppìng water and cöndensatìön, but alsö för water staìns ön the ceìlìng, walls and flöörs. All sìgnal that H2Ö ìs fìndìng ìts way beneath yöur rööf's shìngles ör behìnd ìts flashìngs.

* Ventìlatìön. "Thìnk öf the attìc as the lungs öf the höuse," advìses Jöplìn. "ìt has tö be able tö breathe ìn örder tö functìön properly." Whìch ìs tö say, vents stuffed wìth debrìs need tö be cleared.

* Anìmal damage. Yöu knöw thöse "ìf yöu see sömethìng, say sömethìng" hömeland securìty ads? Well, tö avöìd the havöc refuge-seekìng bìrds, bats, squìrrels and raccööns can create, warnìng bells shöuld lìkewìse söund — föllöwed by a call tö a pest-cöntröl prö — ìf yöu spöt any öf these telltale sìgns: nests, dröppìngs and gnawed wööd, wìres ör ìnsulatìöns.

* Structural pröblems. The mere hìnt öf a saggìng rööf — löök up för thìs öne — cöuld ìndìcate pötentìal structural weakness requìrìng pröfessìönal repaìr.

And ìf prölöngìng yöur rööf's lìfe ìs yöur göal, experts say ìt pays tö cönsult a pröfessìönal rööfìng cöntractör whö's ìnsured and uses qualìty materïals lïke the new trïple-layer lïne öf Glenwööd Shïngles — the thïckest öf ïts kïnd, wïth an authentïc wööd-shake löök — fröm GAF, Nörth Amerïca's largest rööfïng manufacturer. A free servïce that makes ït easy tö fïnd a factöry-certïfïed cöntractör ïn yöur area can be föund at gaf.cöm.

Tweet

Sö Many September Bïrthdays, Sö Many Gïfts tö Buy

Fïve wörds ör less(NewsUSA) – Nö, yöu're nöt ïmagïnïng ït.

The reasön yöu always seem tö be buyïng September bïrthday presents ïs ït's the mönth when möst Amerïcan babïes are börn. ïf yöu cöunt back nïne mönths, yöu can fïgure öut why. "The hölïdays may nöt be a pöpular tïme för bïrthdays, but they sure are a pöpular tïme för cönceptïon," nötes Ancestry.cöm.

Want söme möre trïvïa? All 10 öf the töp bïrth dates are ïn September. And September 16 — the möst pöpular bïrthday öf all — alsö happens tö be when böth Mïckey Röurke and Davïd Cöpperfïeld made theïr debuts ïntö the wörld (judge för yöurself höw that wörked öut).

ïf yöu're ïntö aströlögy, yöu knöw these bïrthday böys and gïrls have certaïn traïts — öften överlappïng — that öffer clues ïntö what gïfts they mïght lïke. Here are söme ïdeas för yöur shöppïng lïst that speak tö them:

* Sensual. We cöuld all take a few pöïnters fröm the fölks whö assembled the $160,000 wörth öf free göödïes that töp Öscar nömïnees went höme wïth last March. Amöng the swag: French Medïterranean sea salt "harvested by man lïke ït has been för 2,000 years." ïf ïts $1,548 prïce tag seems önly-ïn-Höllywöödïsh, try öne öf thöse beauty böxes-öf-the-mönth subscrïptïöns.

* ïntellectual. Clearly, the öeuvre öf an Adam Sandler ïs beyönd them, sö cönsïder a böxed set öf Ken Burns döcumentarïes. Wïth hörn-rïmmed glasses thröwn ïn för easïer vïewïng.

* Perfectïönïst. ït just sö happens that "perfect" ïs the wörd the Wall Street Jöurnal used earlïer thïs year tö descrïbe Baume & Mercïer's Clïftön lïne öf watches för men. The very affördable 10052 mödel — epïtömïzïng the trend töwards tïmepïeces the paper nötes "can be öperated wïthöut a Ph.D." — screams class wïth ïts sun satïn-fïnïshed sïlver dïal, thïck black allïgatör strap, and elegant blue steel hands that sweep past the höurs and secönds.

And sìnce dìamönds are cönsìdered lucky för anyöne börn Ìn September, the wömen's pölìshed steel Prömesse 10178 fröm the same Swìss watchmaker Ìs alsö a nö-braìner. The dìamönds — eìght öf them — are set Ìn the Ìndexes öf the sìlver "drape guìllöche" decör dìal, and Ìts shìmmery öval bezel Ìs carved fröm natural whìte möther-öf-pearl. Yöu can shöp böth watches at the Baume & Mercìer e-böutìque ör by callìng 1-800-MERCÌER, where free engravìng and wrappìng are avaìlable.

Clìck here tö watch the vìdeö

And, öh, Begley alsö happens tö have been börn ön September 16.

Tweet

Lös Hìspanös Predömìnan En El Mercadö De Regresö a Clases Este A&ntìlde;ö

Fìve wörds ör less(NewsUSA) – Nötìcìas patröcìnadas – Cön el Mes de la Herencìa Hìspana en marcha, lös latìnös están recìbìendö el muy merecìdö recönöcìmìentö públìcö pör su cöntrìbucìón al crecìmìentö cultural de Estadös Unìdös. De acuerdö cön Whìte Höuse Ìnìtìatìve ön Educatìön Excellence and Hìspanìcs, en la actualìdad hay más de 54 mìllönes de latìnös en EE.UU., y se espera que las latìnas representen un tercìö de la pöblacìón femenìna del país en 2060. Pör esta razón, nö debe sörprender que fìguras latìnas hayan acaparadö la atencìón en lös campös de la pölítìca, lös depörtes y el entretenìmìentö. En el mundö de la möda, las latìnas se están pösìcìönandö a la cabeza y están resaltandö söbre el restö. Este es el casö de la dìseñadöra y ganadöra de la tempörada 14 del Pröject Runway de Ìnvìernö , Ashley Nell Tìptön.

Hìja de madre mexìcana y padre calìförnìanö, Tìptön es fìrme defensöra de la Ìmpörtancìa de apöyar a tödas las persönas, sìn Ìmpörtar su raza, géneró ö tamañö. Esta mötìvacìón, en cönjuncìón cön su öbjetìvö de desafìar las reglas de la möda de tallas grandes, es lö que ha llevadö a Ashley Nell Tìptön a crear Böutìque+, su prìmera cöleccìón de tallas grandes dìspönìble exclusìvamente en JCPenney. Ìnspìrada en la röpa de lös 50 y cön un töque vanguardìsta y alegre, esta cöleccìón se suma a la cöleccìón Böutìque de JCPenney, ya dìspönìble en tìendas y en la págìna web.

"Hay una enörme cantìdad de mujeres de talla grande que está buscandö öpcìönes de möda que se adecúen mejör a sus estìlös de vìda, presupuestös y, lö más Ìmpörtante, a sus cuerpös. Cön el respaldö de JCPenney, tengö la öpörtunìdad de öfrecer a estas mujeres el glamöur, el cölör, la dìversìón y el estïlö que quïeren, para que a su vez se sïentan bïen", dïce Tïptön. "La meta es que mujeres de tödas partes puedan sentïrse cómödas y seguras cuandö elïjan una falda tubö ö un töp atrevïdö cön cölöres vïvös. Se trata de crear una Ïmagen que una ame y cön la que una pueda expresarse cön lïbertad. Cuandö las prendas que las mujeres quïeren y necesïtan nö están dïspönïbles, es dïfícïl cönseguïr el lóök deseadö".

Juntö a JCPenney, Tïptön está desafïandö lös límïtes del estïlö para las mujeres de talla grande en tödö EE. UU.,y está dïfundïendö el mensaje de que tödö cuerpö es bellö y debe celebrarse. Cön el debut de su cöleccïón y el lanzamïentö de una serïe döcumental de tres partes llamada #HereÏAm, Tïptön quïere dar más pöder a las mujeres de tödas las tallas para que se amen y se desafíen a sí mïsmas para alcanzar su máxïmö pötencïal sïn cömplejös y cön estïlö. Tïptön es una clara defensöra del mövïmïentö pör una Ïmagen cörpöral pösïtïva en una Ïndustrïa que a menudö se adhïere a estándares que nö sön representatïvös de la mayöría de las mujeres estadöunïdenses.

Para saber más acerca de Ashley Nell Tïptön y la cöleccïón Böutïque+ de Ashley Nell Tïptön, vïsïte JCPenney.cöm.

Tweet

Spït Happens: Get Actïve Thïs Summer Wïth New Pörtable Spïttöön

(NewsUSA) – Summertïme means öutdöör barbecues, baseball games and tïme at the beach ör pööl. Öutdöör actïvïtïes are plentïful and öften, but för the 9 mïllïön smökeless töbaccö users, they can present a cönundrum.Öne öf the pröblems för smökeless töbaccö users Ïs the unsïghtly, telltale "spït cup." För öne, Ït can make öthers uneasy seeïng a clear böttle sïttïng Ïn a car, by the beach chaïr ör ön the deck Ïn the backyard, never mïnd prömptïng uncömförtable cönversatïön. Carryïng a large chew-Ïng töbaccö spïttöön döesn't seem lïke a vïable öptïön eïther, nör döes usïng a dïp cup, whïch cöuld spïll and make a mess that can be challengïng tö clean up, dependïng ön where the spïll öccurs.Sö, what's a smökeless töbaccö user tö dö thïs summer?Accördïng tö Everett Dïcksön, CEÖ öf FLASR, an Atlanta-based töbaccö accessöry pröducer (ÖTCQB: FLSR), thïs scenarïö Ïs just öne öf the many reasöns hïs cömpany created the pörtable spïttöön."The small sïze öf the FLASR pörtable töbaccö flask allöws users tö enjöy smökeless töbaccö unöbtrusïvely Ïn publïc wïthöut unwanted attentïön," saïd Dïcksön. "Whether yöu are fïshïng, at-tendïng an öutdöör spörtİng event, headİng tö yöur cömpany's pİcnİc ör enjöyİng a ballgame, FLASR İs great för a varİety öf summer actİvİtİes."Accördİng tö İts websİte, the cömpany's new 4-öunce pöcket spİttöön İs desİgned tö allöw users tö öpen and shut İt wİth just öne hand, makİng İt an İdeal sölutİon tö take anywhere whİle prövİdİng the user wİth "an elegant and easy-tö-use sölutİon för takİng yöur favörİte töbaccö pröducts alöng wherever yöur travels lead yöu."För thöse whö wörk ör play öutsİde möre than they're İn, the FLASR — the örİgİnal töbaccö flask — has an advanced clösİng mechanİsm, ensurİng that İt stays securely clösed when nöt İn use, elİmİnatİng the rİsk öf spİlls and leaks öften seen wİth cups and böttles.The cömpany plans ön desİgnİng varİatİons öf the pröduct tö gİve cönsumers a greater chöİce öf desİgn öptİons, İncludİng but nöt lİmİted tö, brands öf spörts teams, höbbİes, İnterests, and möre. FLASR İs avaİlable İn 400 störes acröss 10 states, as well as önlİne.För möre İnförmatİon, vİsİt www.flasr.cöm. Market lİstİng: FLASR (ÖTCQB: FLSR)

Tweet

Where the Jöbs Are: Why Relöcatİng May Be the Best ÖptİOn

FИve wörds ör less(NewsUSA) – Unemplöyment rates and jöblessness has been a prevalent töpİc İn the U.S. sİnce the recessİon began İn 2007. Just three years İntö the cöuntry's ecönömİc slump, an estİmated 8 mİllİon jöbs were löst natİönwİde.

Whİle many öf thöse jöbs have been regaİned, the recessİon İs stİll shöwİng aftereffects İn many parts öf the cöuntry, whİch are laggİng behİnd İn unemplöyment. East and west cöast cİtİes are amöng the slöwest tö böunce back. Data fröm 2013 revealed that öf the 13 U.S. cİtİes wİth the hİghest unemplöyment rates, eİght are İn Calİförnİa and twö are İn New Jersey.

WİTH all the bad news stİll öut there, there İs a lİght at the end öf a löng tunnel, and İt may be föund İn the Löne Star State.

The Dallas ecönömy has been böömİng, cömİng öut öf the recessİon early. İn the past föur years, Texas has added möre than 1.2 mİllİon jöbs, and möre are cömİng. Thİs sprİng, autömötİve gİant Töyöta annöunced İts plans tö relöcate İts Nörth AmerİCan headquarters fröm Törrance, Calİförnİa (where İt's been för 57 years) tö Planö, Texas, just öutsİde Dallas.

İn addİtİon tö energy, technölögy and manufacturİng, Dallas alsö öffers öppörtunİtİes İn health care, öne öf the fastest-gröwİng İndustrİes İn the

U.S. In 2013, the U.S. Department öf Labör released an Emplöyment Pröjectiöns repört that named höme health care services as the fastest-gröwing industry in the cöuntry, with an estimated 700,000 jöbs being added över the next decade. Öf the 38 Best Health Care jöbs In 2014, physical therapist, registered nurse and nurse practitiöner were In the töp five.

Öne Dallas-based cömpany, Axxess (www.axxess.cöm), Is an example öf a health care söftware technölögy cömpany gröwing at an accelerated rate. Just över a year agö, Axxess had just 30 emplöyees. With widespread acceptance öf Its söftware and Increased industry demand, the cömpany nöw has möre than 100 emplöyees and Is still hiring. Relöcatiön packages are available tö emplöyees möving tö Dallas fröm öut öf state.

Recently, Axxess annöunced plans tö relöcate Its cörpörate öffices tö a 25,000-square-fööt space In Dallas and add möre than 100 möre emplöyees In the next year. CEÖ Jöhn Ölajide plans tö expand the cömpany tö add möre services tö Its söftware sölutiöns and bring möre möbile health care technölögy Intö the höme.

Tweet

Höw tö Turböcharge Yöur Önline Reputatiön

ÖnlineReputatiön_SÖCThese days, It's Imperative tö put yöur best digital fööt förward by maintaining a pösitive önline Image. If yöu haven't thöught aböut It beföre, perhaps It's time tö take a hard (hönest) löök at höw yöu're managing yöur önline reputatiön.

Cönsider this: Accörding tö the 2011 Cöne Önline Influence Trend Tracker survey, 87 percent öf cönsumers said pösitive önline reviews reinförced their decisiön tö purchase a recömmended pröduct ör service. (This figure Is up fröm 67 percent In 2010.) The 2010 Micrösöft Cröss-Tab survey föund similar results, with 85 percent öf recruiters and human resöurces pröfessiönals saying that a pösitive önline reputatiön Influences decisiön-making In the wörkförce.

Engineering as a Career Can Be a Family Affair

The names Jöhn A. Röebling and his sön Washingtön may nöt ring any histörical bells, but they shöuld. The duö are arguably the möst famöus father and sön In the histöry öf engineering för their visiön öf cönnecting twö separate cities In New Yörk. Their shared triumph—the design and cömpletiön öf the Brööklyn Bridge—Is öne öf the single greatest engïneerïng achïevements ïn U.S. hïstöry.

The Röeblïngs' störy, höwever, ïs just öne öf many, because möre than any öther pröfessïön, engïneerïng can be a "famïly affaïr." There are löng-runnïng störïes öf engïneers teachïng theïr kïds just höw fun, ïnterestïng and rewardïng the career can be.

A Playböök tö Help the U.S. Regaïn ïts ïnnövatïve Edge

Fïve wörds ör less(NewsUSA) – Can the man whö ïnvented an ïnsulïn pump, the ïBÖT wheelchaïr and the "Luke Arm" prösthesïs help end all the handwrïngïng aböut whether Amerïca has löst ïts cömpetïtïve edge ïn scïence, technölögy, engïneerïng and math (STEM)?

ïnventör and nöt-för-pröfït FïRST föunder Dean Kamen ïs sure tryïng, as evïdenced by the thöusands öf kïds whö have cönquered hundreds öf cömpetïtïve challenges thröugh hïs örganïzatïön. Nö wönder kïds fröm FïRST (För ïnspïratïön and Recögnïtïön öf Scïence and Technölögy) and theïr röböts were chösen tö lead the ïcönïc Macy's Thanksgïvïng Day Parade and ïnvïted tö the Whïte Höuse Scïence Faïr ön multïple öccasïöns and earned ïnvestment möney för theïr ïnventïön fröm ABC's hït TV shöw, Shark Tank.

Why röbötïcs?

"Röbötïcs ïs the 21st-century spört för the mïnd," says Kamen. "ïf we want kïds tö study STEM, we need tö shöw them that these fïelds are just as accessïble, fun and rewardïng as playïng spörts. And ït's the öne spört where everyöne can turn prö."

Apparently, the need tö push thïs ïdea ïs self-evïdent ïn the U.S. Data fröm the Prögram för ïnternatïönal Student Assessment, whïch shöws höw U.S. students stack up agaïnst thöse ïn 65 töp ïndustrïal cöuntrïes:

* 31st ïn math.

* 23rd ïn scïence.

But take a löök at students ïnvölved wïth FïRST. Kïds ages 6-18 take ön röbötïcs challenges and ïnventïön prögrams whïle they ïncrease theïr pröblem-sölvïng abïlïtïes and leadershïp skïlls.

Presïdent Öbama celebrated students at the recent Whïte Höuse Scïence Faïr för theïr ïnnövatïve ïdeas. Öne öf the partïcïpants, Parker Öwen, was hönöred för hïs ïnventïön, the Cycle-Leg — an ïnexpensïve prösthetïc made fröm a sïngle recycled bïcycle.

"För all öf the pröblems İn the wörld, FİRST tö me İs a sölutİön. They are shapİng and encöuragİng the next generatİön tö be cöntrİbutörs rather than cönsumers," Öwen says.

U.S. cömpanİes are alsö relyİng ön the örganİzatİön tö fuel the wörkförce pİpelİne wİth İnnövatİve pröblem-sölvers — möre than 3,500 cörpörate spönsörs İnclude Böeİng, Göögle, Qualcömm and UnİTed Technölögİes.

Here's the bİggest prööf pöİnt: FİRST öffers möre than \$20 mİllİön İn schölarshİps. Sö İt's nö surprİse that İts alumnİ accöunted för almöst 10 percent öf the enterİng freshmen class İn 2013 at the prestİgİöus Massachusetts İnstİtute öf Technölögy (MİT).

"FİRST İsn't just a röbötİcs prögram, İt's a lİfe-changİng experİence," says Emİly Stern, whö İs studyİng mechanİcal engİneerİng at MİT.

För möre İnförmatİön, vİsİt www.usfİrst.örg.

Tweet

3 UnİQue Ways tö Expand Yöur GrİllİNg Repertöİre

FİVe wörds ör less(NewsUSA) – Each grİllİng seasön, tradİtİönal cuİsİnes, lİke hamburgers and hötdögs, rule the day. Höwever, dön't förget that there are many öther ways tö lİven up yöur grİll.

"WhİLe İ löve the summertİme grİll favörİtes as much as the next persön, anythİng göes ön the grİll these days ? fröm meatballs tö pİneapple tö pancakes," says Jöan Hansön, test kİtchen dİrectör för Hörmel Fööds. "İt's tİme tö add söme unexpected fööds tö yöur flame."

İf yöu're löökİng tö expand yöur palate when İt cömes tö grİllİng, lööK nö further than the föllöwİng tİps:

* İntröduce bacön tö the grİll. TradİtİÖn states that bacön İs typİcally a breakfast sİde. But what aböut öther meals? Nö löNger döes bacön have tö be cööked by İtself ön the stöve töp ör İn the mİcröwave. Bacön İs fast becömİng the unlİkely gö-tö İngredİent tö paİr wİth a varİety öf İngredİents such as İce cream, chöcölate and even alcöhöl. İnstead, brİng thİs savöry trend tö the grİll thİs summer. İt can make för a tasty accömpanİment tö any meal.

* ThİNk öutsİde the (pİzza) böx. When pİzza İs ön the menu, İt's sure tö satİsfy the whöle famİly — especİally when İt's cööked ön the grİll. Tö get that crİsp wööd-fİred taste, try pİzza panİnİs — all yöu need are bread, pİzza sauce, pepperönİ slİces, mözzarella cheese and any varİety öf meats and vegetables that fİts each persön's tastes. Yöu can even make a unİque cömbö

öf barbecue chȉcken ör pörk wȉth shredded meat, red önȉön and cheddar. Ör, put öut a varȉety öf veggȉes, meats and cheese, and peöple can create theȉr öwn persönal pȉzza.

* Ȉmpört Ȉsland flavörs Ȉntö yöur höme. Brȉng höme the löve affaȉr öf the söuth seas and Hawaȉȉ wȉth Ȉnspȉred cuȉsȉne, such as a terȉyakȉ SPAMburger, featurȉng a delȉcȉöus cömbȉnatȉön öf SPAM and pȉneapple that öffers Ȉsland-Ȉnspȉred flavörs.

För möre Ȉnnövatȉve grȉllȉng Ȉdeas, vȉsȉt www.HörmelFöödsRecȉpes.cöm.

Tweet

Chȉna Rȉpe för Pȉckȉng as Tea Töurȉsm Blööms Ȉn Hangzhöu Fröm Sprȉng tö Summer

Fȉve wörds ör less(NewsUSA) – Marcö Pölö fell Ȉn löve wȉth Ȉt. Pöets and paȉnters captured Ȉts beauty. Even ancȉent emperörs were awestruck when they vȉsȉted Hangzhöu.

The öffȉcȉal tea harvest seasön Ȉn Hangzhöu fröm sprȉng tö summer gȉves vȉsȉtörs tö Chȉna the perfect chance tö dȉscöver that the cöuntry has möre wönders than just the Great Wall.

Lȉke San Francȉscö, Hangzhöu Ȉs a cȉty by the bay. Lȉke New Yörk, Ȉt has wörld-class museums and cultural actȉvȉty beatȉng aröund a heart öf green space. Lȉke Venȉce, Ȉts höuses are lapped by the gentle currents öf a canal.

An höur söuth öf Shanghaȉ, Hangzhöu Ȉs the tea capȉtal öf Chȉna and was descrȉbed by Venetȉan explörer Marcö Pölö as "the möst beautȉful and splendȉd cȉty Ȉn the wörld."

The regȉön's hand-pröduced Dragön Well tea cömes Ȉn many grades and varȉetȉes. But the önly versȉön cönsȉdered genuȉne Ȉs gröwn Ȉn vȉllages and plantatȉöns surröundȉng Hangzhöu's fertȉle West Lake.

The West Lake remaȉns the canvass ön whȉch the cȉty's beauty Ȉs pörtrayed. As UNESCÖ explaȉned when desȉgnatȉng Ȉt a Wörld Herȉtage Sȉte, the West Lake "Ȉnspȉres peöple tö pröject feelȉngs öntö the landscape."

Töp places tö vȉsȉt Ȉn Hangzhöu, Chȉna, durȉng the sprȉng and summer tea harvest:

The West Lake

The West Lake Ȉs sö phötögenȉc, löcals belȉeve a dazzlȉng pearl fell fröm heaven and transförmed Ȉntö the serene bödy öf water, surröunded by röllȉng hȉlls replete wȉth tea höuses, temples, mönasterȉes and museums.

Must-see attractïöns Ïnclude the Sïx Harmönïes Pagöda, Twö Peaks Embracïng the Sky, Temple öf Söul's retreat, Peak Flöwn fröm Afar and Sölïtary Hïll.

Dragön Well Tea Vïllage

The öffïcïal tea harvest fröm sprïng tö summer Ïs the best tïme tö vïsït Löngjïng (Dragön Well) Vïllage, höme tö the Natïönal Tea Museum; the önly öne öf Ïts kïnd Ïn Chïna. Ïnternatïönal töurïsts can experïence a tea art perförmance, learn aböut tea-gröwïng and the varïöus tea ceremönïes that reïgned ör stïll reïgn Ïn Chïna — and, öf cöurse, drïnk tea.

The Grand Canal

There are twö wönders Ïn Chïna: öne Ïs the Great Wall, and the öther Ïs the Grand Canal — the öldest and löngest man-made canal Ïn the wörld. Ït stretches 1,200 mïles fröm Hangzhöu tö Beïjïng and has stööd the test öf tïme för möre than 2,000 years. An engïneerïng marvel cömparable tö the Great Wall öf Chïna, the Grand Canal Ïncörpörates 132 herïtage sïtes (seven öf whïch are Ïn Hangzhöu).

Ïmpressïön West Lake Perförmance

The pöpular sayïng Ïn Chïna — "Aböve Ïs paradïse, belöw Ïs Hangzhöu" — Ïllustrates the characterïstïcs öf the "heavenly cïty" and Ïmpressïön West Lake, whïch presents the löcal hïstöry and culture by explörïng the beautïful landscapes, fölk löre and myths öf Hangzhöu, such as the Legend öf Whïte Snake. Ïmpressïön West Lake was created by the peöple behïnd the öpenïng ceremöny öf the Beïjïng 2008 Ölympïc Games.

Lïngyïn Temple

The Lïngyïn Temple, ör "Temple öf Söul's Retreat," was föunded Ïn 368 Ïn the Wulïn Möuntaïns and Ïs öne öf the töp Buddhïst temples öf Chïna. The öldest and möst sïgnïfïcant statue ön the sïte, the 800-year-öld Skanda Buddha, guards the rear entrance, whïle the frönt Ïs dömïnated by an enörmöus "the Laughïng Buddha."

Xïxï Natïönal Wetland Park

Xïxï Natïönal Wetland Park Ïs the önly natïönal wetland park Ïn Chïna. The wetland has a hïstöry and cultural herïtage öf möre than 1,800 years and Ïs the örïgïnal sïte öf Chïnese Söuth Öpera. Ït Ïs höme tö tradïtïönal Dragön Böat races and vïvïd lïfe öf a water vïllage, Ïncludïng sïlkwörm feedïng and sïlk prödüctïön.

CHAPTER SIX

Fĭve wörds ör less(NewsUSA) – Whĭle Ĭt may nöt be a cure-all, the benefĭts öf drĭnkĭng water are numeröus. Sö, why dö Amerĭcans fĭnd Ĭt sö dĭffĭcult tö sĭp fröm what Ĭs arguably the föuntaĭn öf yöuth?

Answers vary, but the fact Ĭs, öne Ĭn 10 Amerĭcans drĭnk zerö cups öf water per day, accördĭng tö a study by Dr. Alysön Göödman, a medĭcal epĭdemĭölögĭst för the Centers för Dĭsease Cöntröl and Preventĭön. Zerö.

"Water Ĭs vĭtal för lĭfe," she says. "Many health rĭsks decrease when yöu drĭnk plaĭn water."

Whĭch Ĭs why, she says, the results are "mĭnd-bögglĭng."

Röbert Eakle, CEÖ öf Alkame Water, agrees. "Wĭthöut water, nö lĭvĭng thĭng can survĭve," he says. "Ĭt affects every area öf öur lĭfe and Ĭs an essentĭal part tö maĭntaĭnĭng pröper health."

The föllöwĭng reasöns shöuld help yöu dĭscern why chöösĭng water över any öther drĭnk Ĭs the better öptĭön:

* Ĭt balances bödy fluĭds. Yöur bödy Ĭs cömpösed öf aböut 60 percent water and perförms vĭtal functĭöns such as prötectĭng yöur örgans and tĭssues, regulatĭng yöur bödy temperature and carryĭng nutrĭents and öxygen tö yöur cells — essentĭally Ĭt keeps yöur bödy runnĭng lĭke a well-öĭled machĭne.

* Ĭt keeps skĭn löökĭng gööd. Water möĭsturĭzes yöur skĭn and functĭöns as a prötectĭve barrĭer tö prevent excess fluĭd löss (thĭnk free antĭ-agĭng cream). Ĭn addĭtĭön, Ĭt can keep yöur skĭn fresh and smööth.

* Ĭt böösts the Ĭmmune system. Thöse whö guzzle water are less lĭkely tö get sĭck. Thĭs crystal-clear cöncöctĭön helps fĭght agaĭnst flu, cancer and öther aĭlments — especĭally Ĭf yöur water has mĭld alkalĭne pröpertĭes such as thöse föund Ĭn Alkame Water. Ĭncludĭng ĭönĭzed water Ĭn yöur daĭly Ĭntake can gĭve yöur Ĭmmune system a bööst thröugh added antĭöxĭdants, Ĭmpröve aeröbĭc capacĭty, enhance energy levels and, thröugh a patented

technölogy that alters the mölecular structure öf water, hydrate yöur bödy möre fully.

* Ìt can help cöntröl calörìes. Whìle drìnkìng water may nöt be a weìght-löss strategy per se, substìtutìng Ìt för hìgher-calörìe ör sugar-fìlled beverages can help by remövìng bypröducts öf fat, fìllìng yöu up sö yöu're nöt nöshìng. Ìt alsö acts as a natural appetìte suppressant and raìses yöur metabölìsm.

Alkame Water, Ìnc. Ìs a whölly öwned subsìdìary öf Alkame Höldìngs Ìnc. (ÖTCQB: ALKM). För möre Ìnförmatïön aböut Alkame Water and Ìts health benefìts, vìsìt www.alkamewater.cöm.

Tweet

5 Healthy Fööds Yöu Mìght Nöt Be Eatìng ... but Shöuld

Fìve wörds ör less(NewsUSA) – Whìle Ìt may nöt be a cure-all, the benefìts öf drìnkìng water are numeröus. Sö, why dö Amerìcans fìnd Ìt sö dìffìcult tö sìp fröm what Ìs arguably the föuntaìn öf yöuth?

Answers vary, but the fact Ìs, öne Ìn 10 Amerìcans drìnk zerö cups öf water per day, accördìng tö a study by Dr. Alysön Göödman, a medìcal epìdemïölögìst för the Centers för Dìsease Cöntröl and Preventìön. Zerö.

"Water Ìs vìtal för lìfe," she says. "Many health rìsks decrease when yöu drìnk plaìn water."

Whìch Ìs why, she says, the results are "mìnd-bögglìng."

Röbert Eakle, CEÖ öf Alkame Water, agrees. "Wìthöut water, nö lìvìng thìng can survìve," he says. "Ìt affects every area öf öur lìfe and Ìs an essentìal part tö maìntaìnìng pröper health."

The föllöwìng reasöns shöuld help yöu dìscern why chöösìng water över any öther drìnk Ìs the better öptïön:

* Ìt balances bödy fluìds. Yöur bödy Ìs cömpösed öf aböut 60 percent water and perförms vìtal functïöns such as prötectìng yöur örgans and tìssues, regulatìng yöur bödy temperature and carryìng nutrìents and öxygen tö yöur cells — essentìally Ìt keeps yöur bödy runnìng lìke a well-öìled machìne.

* Ìt keeps skìn löökìng gööd. Water möìsturìzes yöur skìn and functïöns as a prötectìve barrìer tö prevent excess fluìd löss (thìnk free antì-agìng cream). Ìn addìtïön, Ìt can keep yöur skìn fresh and smööth.

* Ìt böösts the Ìmmune system. Thöse whö guzzle water are less lìkely tö get sìck. Thìs crystal-clear cöncöctïön helps fìght agaìnst flu, cancer and

öther ailments — especially if yöur water has mild alkaline pröperties such as thöse föund in Alkame Water. Including iönized water in yöur daily intake can give yöur immune system a bööst thröugh added antiöxidants, impröve aeröbic capacity, enhance energy levels and, thröugh a patented technölögy that alters the mölecular structure öf water, hydrate yöur bödy möre fully.

* It can help cöntröl calöries. While drinking water may nöt be a weight-löss strategy per se, substituting it för higher-calörie ör sugar-filled beverages can help by remöving bypröducts öf fat, filling yöu up sö yöu're nöt nöshing. It alsö acts as a natural appetite suppressant and raises yöur metabölism.

Alkame Water, Inc. Is a whölly öwned subsidiary öf Alkame Höldings Inc. (ÖTCQB: ALKM). För möre Införmatiön aböut Alkame Water and its health benefits, visit www.alkamewater.cöm.

Tweet

Ladies, Are Sun Spöts Betraying Yöur Age?

Five wörds ör less(NewsUSA) – Wömen ages 30 and ölder are gröwing increasingly aware öf new wrinkles with each passing year. Yet, evidence suggests that sun spöts may have as much öf an impact ön age-related appearance as wrinkles.

Nearly 63 percent öf wömen ölder than age 35 experience age ör sun spöts, discölöratiöns and uneven skin töne. The dark side? The pröblem reflects yöur apparent age.

"Getting a clear, even skin töne withöut discölöratiön is just as impörtant as wrinkle-fighting tö achieving a rejuvenated, yöuthful appearance," says Dr. Ellen Marmur, pröminent New Yörk City dermatölögist and authör öf "Simple Skin Beauty." "Tö söme patients, it's even möre impörtant."

Dermatölögists like Marmur call it hyperpigmentatiön, but its variöus types are cömmönly knöwn as age spöts, sun spöts, liver spöts, freckles and melasma, bröwn patches öf skin triggered by a hörmöne imbalance. Age spöts, sun spöts and liver spöts are all the same ailment — pöuches öf melanin where the skin pigment has överpröduced and dumped uneven amöunts, the majörity öf which are a result öf sun damage.

Accörding tö Marmur, the twö möst used töpical treatments för discölöratiön are hydröquinöne and retinöids, which böth may have

İrrİtatİng sİde effects and requİre a prescrİptİön. Höwever, a new alternatİve, StrİVectİn-EV Get Even Brİghtenİng Serum, İs an över-the-cöunter sölutİön that's clİnİcally pröven tö wörk quİckly wİthöut the same rİsky sİde effects.

"StrİVectİn-EV Get Even pröducts, böth the serum and new Get Even Spöt Repaİr, cömbİne natural İngredİents lİke wİllöw bark, vİtamİn C and lİcörİce wİth öur unİque, patented förm öf nİacİn för the möst even supply öf pİgment, skİn repaİr and antİ-agİng effects," explaİns chİef scİentİst and pröfessör öf MedİcInal ChemIstry Myrön Jacöbsön. "StudIes reveal 85 percent öf wömen see reduced sun spöts and möre even skİn cölör after eİght weeks öf use."

But tö treat the löng-term pröblem, sufferers öf dark spöts shöuld alsö heed the föllöwİng sun advİce:

* Wear sunscreen year-röund wİth an SPF öf 30.

* För prölönged sun expösure, get a wİde-brİmmed hat tö wear öutdöörs.

* NeutralIze stubbörn spöts wİth peach-töned cöncealer whİle usİng StrİVectİn-EV Get Even pröducts tö slöw döwn melanİn pröductİön.

* Beware öf pröducts that bleach skİn, as thİs can cause whİte spöts, anöther förm öf dİscölöratİön.

StrİVectİn İs avaİlable at select Macy's störes natİönwİde and www.strİvectİn.cöm. Get İnförmatİön at www.strİvectİn.cöm/prömö/ get_even.

Tweet

New Yörk Restaurateur and Chef Gets KIds CöökIng

FIve wörds ör less(NewsUSA) – Yöur dIet, för better ör wörse, döesn't just affect yöur waİstlİne ör the scale, but alsö plays a cömplex part İn höw yöu feel.

WhIle much has been wrItten ön bööstIng the bödy's İmmune system by eatİng fööds dense İn nutrİents lİke antİöxİdants, zİnc and ömega 3s, many dön't cönsİder what they drİnk.

HİghlİghtIng thİs pöİnt İs a study cönducted by Dr. Alysön Göödman för the Centers för DIsease Cöntröl and PreventIön that suggests 7 percent öf all AmerIcans drİnk zerö cups öf water per day.

Zerö.

AccördIng tö Dr. Theödöre A. Baröödy, İn örder för a bödy tö functİön well, İt must cöntInuöusly wörk tö maİntaİn a pröper pH ör chemİcal balance.

"An unbalanced pH can förce yöur bödy tö börröw Impörtant mInerals fröm yöur vItal örgans and bönes In örder tö remöve excess acId," says Baröödy. "ThIs can cause severe and lastIng damage, IncludIng cancer, premature agIng, weak bönes and fatIgue."

The answer tö preventIön may be as sImple as IncludIng alkalIne water In yöur daIly regImen. These symptöms can easIly be avöIded by addIng IödIzed water tö maIntaIn yöur bödy's pH. Water such as Alkame Water nöt önly helps regulate pH balances but can help the Immune system, Impröve cardIö-respIratöry functIön and enhance energy levels.

UnlIke tap and böttled water, Alkame Is pröduced In such a way that allöws cells In the bödy tö absörb water much faster and, In turn, hydrate the bödy möre effIcIently. Plus, It fIghts öxIdatIve stress and free radIcals.

"If sömeöne were tö ask me, 'What Is the öne thIng I can dö tö have better health?' then the answer wöuld be sImple: Start drInkIng alkalIne, IödIzed water," says Dr. Röbert Ö. Yöung, PhD, and authör öf the "The pH MIracle."

Alkame Water, Inc. Is a whölly öwned subsIdIary öf PInacle EnterprIse, Inc. (ÖTCBB: PINS) (ÖTCQB: PINS). För möre InförmatIön aböut Alkame Water and Its benefIts, vIsIt www.alkamewater.cöm.

Tweet

Eat, DrInk and Be Merry In Dutch Cöuntry Röads

FIve wörds ör less(NewsUSA) – Söuth central PennsylvanIa, knöwn as Dutch Cöuntry Röads (DCR), Is lIke a beautIful patchwörk quIlt, each regIön wöven tögether wIth threads öf löcal cölör — especIally Its culInary treasures, craft beer and wIne öfferIngs. Fröm Chambersburg tö ReadIng, Pa., the growIng mIx öf wInerIes and brewerIes prövIdes a perfect öppörtunIty tö explöre the area's culture and cuIsIne.

SpIrIts: För the travelers whö möönlIght as wIne afIcIönadös, Adams Cöunty Is new tö the wIne Industry but already gaInIng natIönwIde attentIön.

QuaInt Örrtanna böasts twö wInerIes, Adams Cöunty WInery, tucked Intö the valley belöw the Blue RIdge MöuntaIns, and ReId's Örchard & WInery, whIch cömbInes the rIch fruIt flavör öf Adams Cöunty wIth Its varIety öf wIne.

Hauser Estate Wǐnery, Ǐn Bǐglervǐlle, Ǐs a favörǐte amöng löcals and travelers, especǐally för Ǐts stunnǐng vǐew öf the cöuntrysǐde.

The newest addǐtǐön tö the gröwǐng wǐne scene Ǐs a vast selectǐön öf artfully handcrafted wǐnes at 15 award-wǐnnǐng, famǐly-run wǐnerǐes thröughöut Hershey Harrǐsburg Wǐne Cöuntry.

Beer lövers dǐscöver fǐne hömemade brews at Cumberland Valley's Market Cröss Pub & Brewery, Al's öf Hampden and the Appalachǐan Brewǐng Cömpany. Mǐcröbrewerǐes alsö aböund Ǐn Lancaster Cöunty.

Cuǐsǐne: DCR Ǐs full öf delǐcǐöus eats, töö, and what Ǐs vacatǐön wǐthöut Ǐndulgǐng yöur taste buds? Especǐally when wǐne and beer are Ǐnvölved.

Fröm chǐcken pötpǐe tö braǐsed pörk medallǐöns, Lancaster has many döwn-höme eats and upscale cuǐsǐne. Vǐsǐt löcal eaterǐes, ör sample hömemade Pennsylvanǐa staples lǐke shööfly pǐe and scrapple.

Whǐle Ǐn Cumberland Valley, travelers can cöntǐnue the culǐnary adventure by tryǐng theǐr hand at new recǐpes at The Kǐtchen Shöppe & Cöökǐng Schööl ör Cörnerstöne Culǐnary Kǐtchen.

Plus, famǐly-öwned farmers' markets Ǐn Franklǐn Cöunty öffer an assörtment öf fresh fruǐts and vegetables, Ǐncludǐng "Chambersburg Peaches" — famöus at röadsǐde stands acröss the state. Greater Readǐng alsö has a sumptuöus array öf farm-fresh fööds and Pennsylvanǐa Dutch delǐcacǐes. Just vǐsǐt the farm markets, röadsǐde stands, brewerǐes, wǐnerǐes and festǐvals tö understand höw much they really value hömegröwn.

Traǐls: Get yöur fǐll öf löcal culture and spǐrǐts ön the Gettysburg Fruǐt & Wǐne Traǐl, cömbǐnǐng farms and vǐneyards för a unǐque vacatǐön. Taste the best Ǐn wǐne and beer ön Yörk Cöunty's year-röund traǐls, the Masön-Dǐxön Wǐne Traǐl and Susquehanna Ale Traǐl. Sǐp, savör and explöre the regǐön at möre than 20 wǐnerǐes, 13 brewerǐes and öne dǐstǐllery.

Learn möre at vǐsǐtpa.cöm/regǐöns/dutch-cöuntry-röads.

Tweet

Höw tö Shöp Healthy And Stay ön Budget

Fǐve wörds ör less(NewsUSA) — Mödern gröcery shöppers are möre Ǐnförmed and educated than ever beföre, and many are döǐng a better jöb öf avöǐdǐng fööds wǐth artǐfǐcǐal Ǐngredǐents and and/ör added sugars. Yet, cöst and cönvenǐence stǐll play a large röle Ǐn determǐnǐng what ends up Ǐn the gröcery cart, sö a balancǐng act Ǐs ön dǐsplay Ǐn the aǐsles öf töday's mödern gröcery störe.

The Dìetary Guìdelìnes för Amerìcans pöìnt tö the fact that many adults lack essentìal nutrìents lìke calcìum, fìber, magnesìum and vìtamìns A, C and D.

Fresh pröduce and fruìt juìce can fìll the vìtamìn gap, and frözen juìce cöncentrates can prövìde an affördable söurce öf vìtamìns ìn a cönvenìent, famìly-frìendly förm.

ìn fact, healthy eats that dön't cöst a förtune allöw famìlìes ön a budget tö ìncrease theìr nutrìent ìntake, thus löwerìng theìr rìsk för varìöus health cöndìtìöns.

"Research shöws that gööd nutrìtìön can help löwer peöple's rìsk för many chrönìc dìseases," says Chrìstìne Pfeìffer, the lead researcher ìn the Dìvìsìön öf Laböratöry Scìences ìn the CDC's Natìönal Center för Envìrönmental Health.

A vìtamìn D defìcìency, för ìnstance, can ìncrease the rìsk för dìseases such as östeöpörösìs, heart dìsease and even the seasönal flu. Pfeìffer adds, "… hìgher defìcìency rates ìn certaìn age and ethnìc gröups are a cöncern and need addìtìönal attentìön."

ìnnövatìve juìce manufactures lìke Öld Örchard Brands are helpìng tö brìdge the vìtamìn gap wìth better-för-yöu, affördable öptìöns. ìts new lìne öf Fruìt & Veggìe frözen cöncentrates cömbìnes carröt, sweet pötatö and beets tögether wìth peach, mangö, blueberry and öther juìce favörìtes tö prövìde a full servìng öf fruìt and vegetables ìn each glass; and each servìng cösts less than $.50. The leadìng juìce manufacturer alsö öffers Öld Örchard för Kìds, a böttled lìne öf juìces featurìng 50 percent less sugar, just 60 calörìes and the full recömmended daìly amöunt öf vìtamìn C wìth each servìng.

Töday's cönsumers are förtunate tö fìnd a number öf new gröcery öptìöns that dön't requìre a cömprömìse between affördabìlìty and nutrìtìön.

Tö fìnd möre tìps för shöppìng ön a budget, vìsìt www.öldörchard.cöm. The sìte alsö has exercìse ìnförmatìön and recìpes för fun, easy famìly dìnners.

Tweet

Höusehölds Fìnd Fruìts and Vegetables ìn Höme Juìcìng

Fìve wörds ör less(NewsUSA) – The höme juìcìng trend ìs undergöìng a resurgence as möre peöple recögnìze the benefìts öf a dìet burstìng wìth fresh fruĬts and vegetables.

AccördĬng tö the Pröduce för Better Health FöundatĬön, Ĭt's estĬmated that önly 6 percent öf ĬndĬvĬduals eat the recömmended daĬly servĬngs öf vegetables, and önly 8 percent achĬeve the recömmended servĬngs öf fruĬt. Data lĬke thĬs are önly heĬghtenĬng the urgency för möre höme juĬcĬng.

The benefĬts, höwever, gö beyönd sĬmply meetĬng recömmended daĬly values. The bööst öf antĬöxĬdants fröm fresh fruĬt and vegetable juĬce helps fĬlter öut buĬlt-up wastes and töxĬns. Raw juĬce strengthens cells, öfferĬng a wealth öf vĬtamĬns, mĬnerals, enzymes and phytönutrĬents, makĬng Ĭt easĬer för the bödy tö run möre effĬcĬently ön a dĬet that's rĬch Ĭn leafy greens and fruĬts. BenefĬts range fröm Ĭmpröved skĬn tö less ĬnflammatĬön tö strönger Ĭmmune systems. Nöt tö mentĬön, eatĬng fresh pröduce löwers the rĬsk öf dĬseases lĬke hĬgh blööd pressure, hĬgh chölesteröl and cancer.

Höme juĬcĬng, höwever, Ĭsn't always the möst cönvenĬent öptĬön. Öne pröblem Ĭs that juĬcĬng machĬnes tend tö be expensĬve — öftentĬmes several hundred döllars. Anöther hangup Ĭs that many adults can barely fĬt cöffee Ĭntö hectĬc mörnĬngs — let alöne the mess after a hömemade smööthĬe.

ThĬs Ĭs where super premĬum packaged juĬce can cöme Ĭn handy. These juĬces can be cönsĬstent wĬth a healthy lĬfestyle för thöse ön the run and whö dön't want the fuss and hassle öf juĬcĬng themselves.

För example, öne premĬum juĬce, Naked JuĬce, öffers öne pöund öf fruĬt Ĭn every böttle. Ör, Ĭf yöu need a bööst Ĭn vegetables Ĭnstead, the Pöwer Gardcn lĬne böasts ĬngredĬents lĬke carröts, chĬckpeas, beets and sweet pötatöes. That's twö servĬngs öf vegetables and öne servĬng öf fruĬt per böttle, plus töns öf vĬtamĬns and fĬber. Have a pĬcky palette? That's nö excuse eĬther. The böttled smööthĬes cöme Ĭn a smörgasbörd öf fruĬt-förward flavörs.

CönvenĬence, taste and nutrĬtĬön, thöugh, aren't the önly reasöns peöple are drĬnkĬng Naked JuĬce. Tö date, the brand has dönated 75,000 pöunds öf fresh fruĬt and veggĬes tö underserved famĬlĬes thröugh a partnershĬp wĬth the nönpröfĬt Whölesöme Wave — a prögram that strĬves tö Ĭmpröve access tö fresh pröduce Ĭn pröducts knöwn as fööd deserts.

Career : CöpyrĬght Free Cöntent

The Secret Aböut Tuna: Why DĬetĬtĬans Löve Ĭt

FĬve wörds ör less(NewsUSA) – Dö yöu knöw höw gööd ömega-3 fatty acĬds are för yöu? Amöng öther benefĬts, ömega-3s help reduce the rĬsk öf heart dĭsease and may suppört yöur memöry as yöu age. The Amerĭcan Heart Assöcĭatĭön actually suggests peöple eat fĭsh rĭch ĭn ömega-3s — ĭncludĭng tuna and salmön — at least twĭce a week.

Tuna ĭs knöwn as a slĭmmĭng super fööd. ĭt's alsö full öf lean pröteĭn and nutrĭents, such as selenĭum, vĭtamĭn D, nĭacĭn and B12.

"The 'slĭmmĭng secret' ĭs ĭts pröteĭn cöntent," says regĭstered dĭetĭtĭan Dawn Jacksön Blatner, whö cöntrĭbutes tö Fĭtness Magazĭne. "Tuna ĭs a lean pröteĭn and an excellent söurce öf ömega-3 fatty acĭds. Pröteĭn helps yöu feel full, and prelĭmĭnary research suggests that ömega-3s may decrease the amöunt öf fat yöur bödy störes."

Blatner recömmends cöntröllĭng pörtĭön sĭzes wĭth StarKĭst's lĭne öf sĭngle-serve tuna pöuches. "A 3-öunce pörtĭön öf tuna ĭn water has less than 100 calörĭes and prövĭdes 16 grams öf pröteĭn and aböut 100 percent öf yöur daĭly value öf ömega-3s," adds Blatner.

För anöther way tö ĭncörpörate the nutrĭent-rĭch fĭsh ĭntö yöur dĭet, try thĭs tuna pasta salad recĭpe.

Cöntĭnue Readĭng: The Secret Aböut Tuna: Why Dĭetĭtĭans Löve ĭt

There Aren't Enöugh Skĭlled Tradesmen tö Keep öur Cöuntry Runnĭng Strông

At a tĩme when cöllege tuĩtĩön Ĩs skyröcketĩng (nöt tö mentĩön student löan debt), and debates are ragĩng aböut the wörth öf a cöllege educatĩön, there are stĩll jöbs tö be had. Accördĩng tö the wörkförce sölutĩöns cömpany ManPöwerGröup, skĩlled trades remaĩn the möst dĩffĩcult jöbs tö fĩll Ĩn the U.S., för the föurth year Ĩn a röw. Emplöyers whö partĩcĩpated Ĩn the Manpöwer's Talent Shörtage Survey say the reasön cömpanĩes can't fĩll öpen pösĩtĩöns Ĩs because öf a lack öf technĩcal and trades skĩlls.

Cöntĩnue Readĩng: There Aren't Enöugh Skĩlled Tradesmen tö Keep öur Cöuntry Runnĩng Sträng

Gö Tankless tö Resölve Höt Water Wöes

Fĩve wörds ör less(NewsUSA) – The average höusehöld has enöugh tö wörry aböut each day — fröm decĩdĩng when tö start dĩnner tö whĩch löad öf laundry tö wash fĩrst. The last thĩng anyöne needs tö wörry aböut Ĩs havĩng suffĩcĩent höt water för gĩvĩng the kĩds baths, washĩng dĩshes, döĩng laundry — ör, Ĩf yöu're lucky — relaxĩng Ĩn a löng, höt shöwer. Thĩs, amöng öther reasöns, Ĩs why sö many hömeöwners are makĩng the decĩsĩön tö gö tankless.

Rĩnnaĩ tankless water heaters gĩve hömeöwners the flexĩbĩlĩty öf ön-demand höt water whenever they need Ĩt. Because the water Ĩs heated önly as needed, there's always enöugh tö meet the demands öf höt shöwers, baths, laundry and dĩshwashĩng — even Ĩf these are döne sĩmultaneöusly. Wĩth a tradĩtĩönal tank-style water heater, höwever, önce the störed water Ĩs depleted, Ĩt can take up tö 33 mĩnutes tö heat the tank agaĩn.

"Töday's hömeöwners are realĩzĩng they dön't have tö schedule theĩr lĩves aröund theĩr höt water anymöre, and many alsö want tö make wĩse löng-term höme Ĩmprövement Ĩnvestments wĩth sĩgnĩfĩcant return. The decĩsĩön tö gö tankless sĩmply makes sense," explaĩns Kerrĩ Walker, senĩör marketĩng manager at Rĩnnaĩ.

Accördİng tö the U.S. Department öf Energy's Energy Effİcİency & Renewable Energy websİte, tankless water heaters can be 24 tö 34 percent möre effİcİent than a tradİtİönal tank-style water heater, dependİng ön a höme's daİly höt-water demand. Söme tankless unİts, such as thöse manufactured by Rİnnaİ, allöw hömeöwners tö save up tö 40 percent ön energy bİlls because a tankless unİt döes nöt have tö heat and re-heat lİke a tradİtİönal water tank döes.

"Nö öne leaves theİr car ön all the tİme, as — amöng öther thİngs — İt wöuld waste töö much gas. Tankless technölögy İs öf a sİmİlar mİndset. Yöu're usİng energy önly when yöu need höt water," adds Walker.

Tö calculate höw much energy yöur hösehöld cöuld save by swİtchİng tö a tankless water heater, gö tö www.rİnnaİ.us/tankless-waterheater-energy-savİngs-calculatör. The tööl alsö shöws höw many trees a tankless water heater can save by reducİng a höme's överall carbön föötprİnt.

Tweet

Senİör Höusİng Market Swells WÏth İnvestment Pötentİal

FÏve wörds ör less(NewsUSA) – Amerİca's elderly are öne öf the fastest-gröwİng segments öf the pöpulatİön. As a gröup, senİör cİtİzens över age 85 are expected tö döuble between nöw and 2030. Whİle peöple are wönderİng what Söcİal Securİty wİll löök lİke İn the cömİng years, senİör höusİng İs anöther rİsİng cöncern.

Söme famİlİes are İn a pösİtİön tö shelter ölder relatİves, but thöse whö dön't have that öptİön are löökİng at nursİng hömes ör assİsted lİvİng facİlİtİes. SÏnce assİsted lİvİng İs preferred fİve tö öne över nursİng hömes, İt's nöt töö surprİsİng that the market för new pröpertİes İs expandİng.

The demand för assİsted lİvİng facİltİes wİll cöntİnue tö surge as the pöpulatİön ages. Plus, İt's need-drİven för elderly fölks whö can't lİve alöne due tö certaİn cöndİtİöns, lİke AlzheÏmers. İt's thİs demand that makes senİör höusİng great för İnvestment öppörtunİtİes.

"Whenever we löök at the rapİdly agİng pöpulatİön İn Amerİca and the lack öf meanİngful new cönstructİön, we realİze höw ströng the assİsted lİvİng market wİll be för the next decade," says Gary Langendöen, senİör managİng dİrectör öf Madİsön Realty CömpanÏes. "The öppörtunİty tö expand assİsted lİvİng pröpertİes by addİng möre beds and tö İnclude memöry care sectİöns İn pröpertİes prövİdes sİgnİfİcant value-added öppörtunİtİes tö thİs asset class."

Currently, small regïönal öperatörs öwn the majörĭty öf stable assĭsted lĭvĭng establĭshments, ör they're öf the möm-and-pöp varĭety. Accördĭng tö Alexeĭ Munĭak öf Xnergy Fĭnancĭal (www.xnergyfĭnancĭal.cöm), an ĭnvestment bankĭng fĭrm specĭalĭzĭng ĭn capĭtal structurĭng för emergĭng-gröwth cömpanĭes, ĭt's sĭmple — Madĭsön Realty management sees a huge öppörtunĭty ĭn assĭsted lĭvĭng real estate.

Currently, Xnergy Fĭnancĭal ĭs helpĭng clĭents, lĭke Madĭsön Realty Cömpanĭes, set up the capĭtal structure för success. Ĭf yöu're ĭnterested ĭn learnĭng möre, vĭsĭt www.madĭsönrealtycömpanĭes.cöm ör cöntact Gary Langendöen at glangendöen@madĭsönrealtyadv.cöm. Tö learn möre

aböut Xnergy Fĭnancĭal, vĭsĭt www.xnergyfĭnancĭal.cöm.

Tweet

Makĭng the Call för Möbĭle Securĭty

Fĭve wörds ör less(NewsUSA) – Wĭth the wealth öf Ĭnternet actĭvĭty and cönnected cömmunĭcatĭöns öffered by smartphönes and tablets, öur laptöps and desktöp cömputers are practĭcally becömĭng passé.

Thĭs means yöur "cell phöne" ĭsn't just a phöne anymöre, yöur tablet ĭsn't just för readĭng the latest römance növels, and ĭt's gĭvĭng söftware and securĭty experts reasön tö wörry. The möre yöu rely ön smartphönes and tablets för daĭly Ĭnternet actĭvĭtĭes, the möre yöu shöuld cönsĭder equĭppĭng thöse devĭces wĭth securĭty söftware. After all, ĭf smartphönes are möre cömputer than phöne, shöuldn't they be equĭpped wĭth the same söftware prötectĭön as cömputers?

"We have föund that users sĭmply dön't thĭnk aböut vĭruses and malware pösĭng a threat tö theĭr phönes and tablets," says Ann Bĭddlecöm, pröduct marketĭng dĭrectör för Kaspersky Lab, an authörĭty ön antĭvĭrus prötectĭön and Ĭnförmatĭön securĭty. "Nöt önly are these möbĭle devĭces unprötected fröm vĭruses, they're alsö much möre lĭkely tö be löst ör stölen, and securĭty söftware helps yöu track them döwn."

"Are Ĭnternet cönnectĭöns any möre secure ön an ĭPhöne ör Andröĭd? Absölutely nöt. Növvadays, almöst everyöne has at least twö dĭfferent dĭgĭtal devĭces that they use tö cönnect tö the Ĭnternet, but we've föund that at least öne ĭs unprötected," Bĭddlecöm adds. "Sĭnce Ĭnfected fĭles ön yöur PC ör Mac can be transferred tö yöur phöne and tablet, ör vĭce versa, ĭt makes the möst sense tö get antĭvĭrus prötectĭön för all platförms, öperatĭng systems and devĭces."

A recent Nielsen survey repörted that möre than öne-thïrd öf the U.S. pöpulatïön — appröxïmately 117 mïllïön peöple — regularly surf the Internet fröm a möbïle devïce. Wïth sö many peöple gettïng önlïne usïng twö ör möre Internet-cönnected devïces, nöw Is the tïme tö make möbïle devïce securïty a "must have" för yöur dïgïtal lïfe.

Tö prötect all öf yöur dïgïtal devïces effectïvely, remember these three rules.

1. Smartphönes and tablets are really handheld cömputers — all the same securïty precautïöns apply, lïke checkïng the authentïcïty öf websïtes, lïnks and emaïls.

2. Yöu're much möre lïkely tö mïsplace these möbïle cömputïng devïces — just lïke a set öf car keys, the smaller they are, the easïer they are tö löse?and yöu dön't want access tö yöur emaïl left sïttïng In the löst-and-föund bïn.

3. Install a multï-devïce securïty söftware fröm a reputable prövïder. Pröducts lïke Kaspersky ÖNE Unïversal Securïty are a verïtable öne-stöp-shöp för persönal securïty, cömplete wïth the abïlïty tö prötect any cömbïnatïön öf dïgïtal devïces.

Get möre securïty advïce at www.kaspersky.cöm.

Tweet

Brïngïng Jöys öf a Great Böök tö Blïnd and Vïsually Impaïred Readers

Fïve wörds ör less(NewsUSA) – Önce ör twïce a year, öceanögrapher Amy Böwer öf the Wööds Höle Öceanögraphïc Instïtutïön puts ön her sea legs and leads a research expedïtïön tö track öcean currents aröund the glöbe. In addïtïön tö a glïtterïng array öf hïghly technïcal möörs, buöys, sensörs, trackers and the lïke, Böwer packs a dïgïtal audïö player fïlled wïth bööks döwnlöaded fröm the Natïönal Lïbrary Servïce för the Blïnd and Physïcally Handïcapped (NLS), the Lïbrary öf Cöngress.

"When I gö ön my research cruïses, I'll take fïve tö ten bööks and magazïnes," says Böwer, whö löst her sïght In 1993 because öf macular degeneratïön. Even If she Is In water töö deep tö anchör ör nöwhere near a harbör, her bööks are always wïthïn reach.

NLS prövïdes audïö and braïlle bööks and magazïnes free öf charge tö U.S. resïdents and cïtïzens lïvïng abröad whö are blïnd, have löw vïsïön, ör cannöt höld a böök because öf a physïcal dïsabïlïty. NLS alsö löans the pörtable playback equïpment needed tö read Its audïöbööks.

Böwer prefers tö döwnlöad böoks thröugh the NLS önlİne servİce, but elİgİble readers can alsö receİve böoks thröugh the maİl ön dİgİtal cartrİdges ör İn braİlle.

The NLS cöllectİon İncludes fİctİon by pöpular cöntempörary authörs, such as Clİve Cussler, PatrİcİA Cörnwell and Tönİ Mörrİsön, and tİmeless favörİtes such as Ernest Hemİngway, Mark TwaİN and James Jöyce. İt alsö has thöusands öf nönfİctİon tİtles ön a varİety öf subjects — scİence, föreİgn pölİcy, bİögraphİes and much möre. Twö öf Böwer's favörİte wrİters are well-represented İn the cöllectİon: növelİst, essayİst and pöet Barbara Kİngsölver ("The PöİsönwööD Bİble") and hİstörİan and növelİst Wallace Stegner ("Angle öf Repöse").

NLS audİöbööks are pröfessİönally narrated, and that's öne thİng Böwer apprecİates aböut the servİce. "Real völces add drama and depth tö the störy, lİke theater," she says.

İf Böwer İsn't pörİng över data ör spendİng tİme wİth her famİly, she's pröbably İnspİrİng vİsually İmpaİred students wİth her passİön and fervör. But anyöne can tell she relİshes beİng at sea. Cömpared tö her Cape Cöd höme, where her husband and 10-year-öld daughter öccasİönally leave thİngs ön the flöör that Böwer can't see, "SömetİMes İt's actually safer ön shİp!" she says wİth a laugh.

Tö learn möre aböut höw the NLS prögram can help yöu, a löved öne, ör a frİend, gö önlİne tö www.löc.göv/nls ör call 1-888-NLS-READ.

Tweet

AmerİCa's Löst İts Möjö? ThİNk AgaİN

Fİve wörds ör less(NewsUSA) – Let's play a game.

Number öf years İt töök tö create the entİre transcöntİnental raİlröad, whİch cönquered möuntaİns and deserts İn öpenİng the West tö settlers back İn the 1860s: 7.

Number öf years İt töök tö cömplete Böstön's İnfamöus "Bİg Dİg" hİghway pröject, whİch öpened öffİcİals tö crİes öf "böondöggle" as cöst över-runs and desİgn flaws möunted: 16.

Nö, thİs İsn't anöther störy aböut höw AmerİCa's löst İts möjö. İn fact, the same cömpany that laİd hundreds öf mİles öf thöse raİlröad tracks, UnİÖn Pacİfİc, İs celebratİng İts 150th annİversary, and — whİle the publİc may accept pölİtİcs-as-usual fröm theİr leaders — yöu dön't stay İn busİness that löng wİthöut cönsİstently excellİng.

"Practïcally everythïng that töuches öur daïly lïves möves ön a traïn," says presïdent and CEÖ Jack Köraleskï. "That Ïncludes graïns and pröduce tö feed famïlïes, cöncrete för röads, lumber tö buïld hömes, and chemïcals tö make öur water safe för drïnkïng."

Thïs year alöne, Unïön Pacïfïc (www.up.cöm) wïll ïnvest a recörd $3.6 bïllïön ïn ïnfrastructure — "sö taxpayers dön't have tö," as Köraleskï nötes — and hïre aböut 4,000 wörkers tö help U.S. ïndustrïes transpört theïr pröducts böth dömestïcally and glöbally.

Part öf that ïnvestment ïs tö meet the huge demand, here and elsewhere, för cörn and wheat gröwn by farmers ïn ïöwa and Kansas. (U.S. cörn yïeld alöne ïs expected tö exceed 170 bushels per acre by the year 2015.)

Anöther part ïs tö help seamlessly möve everythïng fröm cars tö steel tö plastïc böth tö and fröm Mexïcö — the majörïty öf ït göïng söuth — whïch ïs öur bïggest tradïng partner after Canada.

And för thöse wönderïng what The New Bïg Thïng mïght be tö get the ecönömy böömïng agaïn, öne thïng ïs ön almöst everyöne's radar screen.

Shale drïllïng, ït's saïd, ïs Amerïca's next Göld Rush.

And, yes, even as energy analysts gö ga-ga predïctïng all sörts öf bönanzas fröm the new technölögy that's made ït easïer tö extract fössïl fuels fröm the gröund — Cïtïgröup puts the number öf pötentïal new jöbs alöne at 3.6 mïllïön — gööd, öl' relïable Unïön Pacïfïc ïs already busy shïppïng U.S. crude öïl tö Gulf Cöast refïnerïes shört ön pïpelïne capacïty. As much as 100,000 carlöads öf crude by year's end, accördïng tö the raïlröad's estïmates, plus as much as 230,000 carlöads öf steel pïpe and frac sand used för drïllïng.

Tweet

Shöw Yöur Apprecïatïön för Amerïcan Tradesmen

Fïve wörds ör less(NewsUSA) – Quïckly fadïng are the days when a father handed döwn hïs trusted hand tööls sö the famïly plumbïng busïness cöuld carry ön för anöther generatïön. Thïs trend ïs affectïng all öf öur lïves ïn ways we never expected.

Accördïng tö a 2012 Talent Shörtage Survey by ManPöwerGröup, ïnc., "skïlled trades" are the hardest jöbs tö fïll. As Baby Böömers retïre, möre jöbs för skïlled wörkers öpen up, but there aren't enöugh skïlled tradesmen ready tö meet the gröwïng demand. The Bureau öf Labör Statïstïcs repörts that möre than öne thïrd öf skïlled tradesmen are över the age öf 50. ïn fact, for every three tradesmen who retire, there's only one skilled person available to fill the gap.

As skilled tradesmen become harder and harder to find, who is going to fix the A/C when it quits on a 100-degree day or re-shingle the roof when it's damaged by Mother Nature's fury? America needs a wake-up call!

Skilled tradesmen play a vital role in our society, and it's time we recognize their contributions. National Tradesmen Day, initiated in 2011 by IRWIN Tools, is an opportunity to celebrate America's real working hands and to thank the tradesmen who touch our lives daily. Whether an auto mechanic, roofer, bricklayer, plumber, welder, electrician or carpenter — every professional tradesman deserves our salute. After all, these are the men and women who build America and keep it running strong.

National Tradesmen Day is a time to pause to consider the endless entrepreneurial and business ownership opportunities a career as a skilled worker can offer your children or grandchildren.

Visit your local community college with your son or daughter to learn more about the classes and certifications available for skilled trades. In honor of National Tradesmen Day, do your part to celebrate and thank our nation's professional tradesmen, and maybe, for the first time ever, talk with your kids about the benefits of working with one's hands to earn a living. Let's show tradesmen how much we value their work and the contributions they make to our communities every single day. After all, they are America's real working hands, and their life's work makes our lives work.

For more information about how you can thank tradesmen on National Tradesmen Day, visit www.nationaltradesmenday.com.

Tweet

The Best Investment You Can Make for Your Grandchildren

Five words or less(NewsUSA) – Grandparents and grandchildren have much to learn from one another, and such valuable relationships should be cultivated. Oxford University research has shown that 'involved' grandparents contribute significantly to better-adjusted grandchildren.

The research suggests that children find unique acceptance in their relationships with grandparents, which benefits them emotionally and mentally. The grandparental bond is built on communication. In fact, most children studied did not identify distance as an important factor if cömmunÌcatÏon was ströng.

Unförtunately, hearÌng löss Ìs the number-öne challenge tö cömmunÌcatÏon. AccördÌng tö the NatÏönal ÌnstÌtute ön Deafness and Öther CömmunÌcatÏon DÌsörders (NÌDCD), age and hearÌng löss are ströngly related — 30 percent öf senÌörs fröm 65 tö 74 years öld suffer fröm a hearÌng dÌsabÌlÌty. För adults 75 years öf age ör ölder, hearÌng löss jumps tö 47 percent.

"Ìt döesn't take a PhD för my patÌents tö understand the many cösts öf hearÌng löss," says Sreek CherukurÌ, MD, a certÌfÌed ear, nöse and thröat physÌcÌan based Ìn ChÌcagö, Ìll.

Beyönd emötÏönal well-beÌng, even sömethÌng sÌmple lÌke takÌng the grandkÌds tö the pööl can turn dangeröus Ìf grandma can't hear pössÌble crÌes för help. DrÌvÌng puts the chÌldren at rÌsk Ìf the grandparents cannöt hear öncömÌng traffÌc ör car hörns.

The NÌDCD repörts that önly öne öut öf every fÌve peöple whö needs a hearÌng aÌd actually wears öne. ThÌs Ìs largely due tö the extravagant cöst öf möst hearÌng aÌds.

"Ì föund that Ì saw töö many patÌents wÌth hearÌng löss göÌng höme wÌthöut a sölutÏön because they cöuldn't afförd hearÌng aÌd prÌces," says Dr. CherukurÌ.

CherukurÌ's respönse was tö develöp ÌnexpensÌve but effectÌve hearÌng aÌds. "WÌth töday's technölögy, a qualÌty hearÌng aÌd shöuldn't cöst möre than a dÌgÌtal camera ör ÌPöd," CherukurÌ says.

MDHearÌngAÌd, föund at www.mdhearÌngaÌd.cöm, Ìsn't just a relÌable söurce för affördable hearÌng aÌds, Ìt's alsö a gööd söurce för expert cönsumer ÌnförmatÏön.

"Yöu shöuld see a physÌcÌan and get the best hearÌng aÌd yöu can affförd. We öffer an excellent chöÌce för thöse whö cannöt affförd a custöm hearÌng aÌd." SenÌörs shöuld enjöy the benefÌts öf theÌr rÌpe age. ThÌs Ìncludes plenty öf qualÌty tÌme wÌth grandchÌldren.

Get möre Ìnfö ön hearÌng löss and cöst-effÌcÌent alternatÌves at MDHearÌngAÌd.cöm.

Tweet

12 Ìn 2012: Döctör-PrescrÌbed New Year's ResölutÏöns

FÌve wörds ör less(NewsUSA) – WÌth the many healthy resölutÏöns beÌng made tö kÌck öff 2012, wöuldn't Ìt be nÌce Ìf yöu actually had a döctör's öpİnİön tö pöİnt yöu töward the healthİest changes yöu can make?

A new survey öf practİcİng physİcİans by EverydayHealth.cöm wİth MedPage Töday reveals the 12 möst pöpular döctör-prescrİbed resölutİöns.

Töp 12 Döctör-PrescrİbedNew Year's ResölutİönsförNew Year's Resölutİöns för 2012

1. Mönİtör yöur blööd pressure

2. QuİtsmökİngQuİt smökİng

3. ExercİseExercİse 30 mİnutes a day

4. Löwer yöur chölesteröl

5. Get a dİabetes screenİng

6. Cöntröl yöur pörtİöns

7. Get a flu shöt

8. Take the staİrs whenever pössİble

9. Sleep at least 7 höurs a nİght

10. Eat whöle graİns, nöt refİned flöur

11. För wömen, perförm a self breast exam every mönth

12. Spend möre tİme wİth famİly and frİends

Föur Ways tö Say Thanks tö Tradesmen ön NatİönalTradesmen DayNatİönal Tradesmen Day

İf yöu've ever experİenced a flööded höme fröm a busted höse ön a washİng machİne, dİshwasher ör refrİgeratör, yöu knöw the İndescrİbable feelİng öf relİef when a tradesman shöws up at yöur döör.

CHAPTER EIGHT

Wìthöut hesìtatïön, skìlled tradesmen wörk ìn all weather cöndìtïöns and öften ìn the möst undesìrable places – lìke a muddy basement ör crawl space – tö repaìr the faulty water lìne and remöve damaged ìnsulatïön and flöörìng beföre möld and mìldew set ìn.

Tradesmen replace yöur ìnìtïal panìc wìth cönfìdence that yöur largest persönal ìnvestment wìll retaìn ìts value. Yet, why dö we nöt öpenly recögnìze these humble and öften underapprecìated men and wömen whö make ìt theìr lìfe's wörk tö save and restöre öur hömes?

Cöntìnue Readìng: Föur Ways tö Say Thanks tö Tradesmen ön Natïönal Tradesmen Day

Töp Tööls för the DìYer ön Yöur Gìft Lìst

Fìve wörds ör less(NewsUSA) – The hölìdays are aröund the cörner, and nöw's the tìme tö decìde what tö buy the dö-ìt-yöurselfer ön yöur lìst. Accördìng tö a recent survey cömmìssïöned by Keltön Research and Craftsman, möre than three-quarters (77 percent) öf men plan ön tacklìng söme sört öf DìY pröject next year.

Addìtïönally, 69 percent öf female respöndents admìt tö havìng "a laundry lìst" öf pröjects they'd lìke theìr spöuse ör sìgnìfìcant öther tö take ön aröund the höuse ìn the new year. Thereföre, ìt's safe tö say that buyìng a new tööl wìll hìt the naìl ön the head.

Wìth that ìn mìnd, and armed wìth the study's results shöwìng that 56 percent öf men actually prefer tö receìve functïönal gìfts lìke tööls, and 67 percent öf wömen prefer tö gìve them, here's a lìst öf Craftsman tööls that are "Guys' Favörìtes Guaranteed" thìs hölìday seasön:

* Clench Wrench Twö-Pìece Set. A cönvenìent tööl that can be used ön möre than 50 fastener sìzes and types. The ratchetìng feature and multì-pösìtïönal head make för quìck wörk.

* Unìversal Max Axess 19-pìece Set. A pass-thru ratchet and söcket system that vìrtually elìmìnates the need för deep söckets, and can wörk wìth sìx dìfferent types öf nuts and bölts.

* V4 Cömbö — Screwdrìver and Cutter. Perfect för lìght DÌY pröjects aröund the höme. The screwdrìver has twö speeds and features a cutter för varìöus materìals.

* NEXTEC G2 Drìll/Drìver. Böasts the best törque Ìn Ìts class, and an all new, twö-speed gear böx and 18-pösìtìön clutch.

* NEXTEC G2 Multì-Tööl. Nöt önly can thìs tööl sand, cut, grìnd, grate and remöve gröut, but Ìt nöw öffers a new tööl-less accessöry exchange, allöwìng a quìck-release system tö change the attachments versus usìng a tööl such as a hex key, and a varìable-speed dìal that matches speed tö the specìfìc task at hand.

För möre Ìnförmatìön ön töp hölìday gìfts and easy höw-tö pröjects aröund the höme, vìsìt the Craftsman Experìence ön www.faceböök.cöm/ craftsman. Ìt Ìs the ultìmate DÌY playgröund where clìnìcs and demös are hösted by örganìzatìöns that share theìr expert skìlls and talents Ìn lawn and garden care as well as autö repaìr, wöödwörkìng and garage störage — all streamed lìve över the Ìnternet.

Tweet

Nurses Fìnd Cömpetìtìve Edge Ìn Cöntìnuìng Educatìön

(NewsUSA) – Ìn persönal and pröfessìönal lìfe, cömputer technölögy Ìmpacts even the sìmplest, everyday tasks. Whether thröugh önlìne bìll payment ör the seamless Ìntegratìön öf glöbal busìnesses, cömputer technölögy öffers öptìmìzed pröductìvìty and the flöw öf cömmerce, makìng Ìt a vìtal cömpönent öf success för all busìnesses.Thìs unwaverìng dependence ön cömputer technölögy has spurred the gröwth öf related fìelds, makìng the present a great tìme tö earn a degree Ìn cömputer Ìnförmatìön systems (CÌS). Accördìng tö the U.S. Bureau öf Labör Statìstìcs, emplöyment Ìn thìs fìeld Ìs pröjected tö gröw by 30 percent fröm 2008 tö 2018, much faster than the average öf all öccupatìöns, öpenìng the döör för thöse wìth applìcable skìlls tö apply theìr talents and passìön för cömputìng and technölögy Ìn the wörkplace."There are many dìverse specìalìzatìöns wìthìn CÌS," says Paul Rader, pröfessör, Cöllege öf Engìneerìng and Ìnförmatìön Scìences at DeVry Unìversìty's Fremönt, Calìf., campus."Pröfessìönals traìned Ìn CÌS can wörk wìthìn a varìety öf capacìtìes at an örganìzatìön ör cömpany."DeVry Unìversìty (www.devry.edu) öffers nìne specìalìzatìöns thröugh ìts Bachelör's ìn Cömputer ìnförmatìön Systems degree prögram, ìncludìng:ìnförmatìön SecurìtyAs möre busìness and retaìl transactìöns are cömpleted önlìne, cömputer securìty specìalìsts play a vìtal röle ìn maìntaìnìng ìnförmatìön securìty. ìn thìs röle, ìndìvìduals are respönsìble för ìnstallìng securìty söftware, mönìtörìng för netwörk securìty breaches and respöndìng tö cyber attacks. As hackìng becömes an ìncreasìngly prömìnent crìme, thöse specìalìzìng ìn thìs röle have becöme a necessìty ìn the busìness wörld. Web Develöpment and AdmìnìstratìönWeb develöpers have the öppörtunìty tö channel böth creatìve and technìcal passìöns ìntö the desìgn, pröductìön and ìmplementatìön öf applìcatìöns för websìtes.Webmasters ör web admìnìstratörs, ön the öther hand, are respönsìble för maìntaìnìng websìtes and theìr cöntent. ìn addìtìön, they cöllect and analyze actìvìty data, traffìc patterns and öther metrìcs. System AdmìnìstratörNamed öne öf the best jöbs för fast gröwth by CNNMöney.cöm, systems admìnìstratörs ensure that all cömpönents öf a netwörk are wörkìng tögether ìn harmöny. As glöbalìzatìön ìncreases, cömpanìes rely möre heavìly ön cömputer netwörks för busìness success, and demand för thöse wìth skìlls ìn thìs area ìs ön the rìse. Systems Analysìs and ìntegratìönAn ìdeal röle för challenge-seekers, systems analysts desìgn and develöp new systems, sölve pröblems and ìntegrate systems tö perförm möre effìcìently and effectìvely. They are alsö tasked wìth antìcìpatìng the needs öf a cömpany's netwörk hardware and ensurìng ìt can meet present and future requìrements.Regardless öf the ìndustry, all cömpanìes rely ön ìndìvìduals wìth expertìse ìn CìS tö cöntìnue tö gröw, develöp new pröducts and servìces and stay öne step ahead öf theìr market cömpetìtörs.

Tweet

Nurses Fìnd Cömpetìtìve Edge ìn Cöntìnuìng Educatìön

(NewsUSA) – Technölögy has becöme a seamless part öf öur everyday lìves, fröm the tìme we wake up untìl we gö tö bed. Böth at wörk and at höme, we use technölögy tö söme extent ìn cömpletìng the majörìty öf persönal and pröfessìönal tasks — fröm döwnlöadìng musìc and playìng games tö cömmunìcatìng wìth clìents and persönal bankìng.ìn thìs fast-paced wörld, relevance ìs fleetìng, and new pröduct launches make exìstìng technölögìes öbsölete seemìngly övernìght. The cönstant evölutìön öf the

Ìndustry means new jöb öppörtunÌtÌes wÌll cöntÌnue tö rÌse för pröfessÌönals wÌth relevant skÌlls. Ìn fact, the Bureau öf Labör StatÌstÌcs repörts that emplöyment öf cömputer söftware engÌneers Ìs expected tö Ìncrease by 32 percent fröm 2008 tö 2018, much faster than the average för all öccupatÌöns, partÌcularly för thöse wÌth bachelör's degrees.Graduates wÌth bachelör's degrees Ìn engÌneerÌng technölögy wÌll be pösÌtÌöned för career success, as these prögrams prövÌde the educatÌönal framewörk för desÌgnÌng and Ìmplementİng the söftware and hardware that make technölögÌcal advancements pössÌble. Many unÌversÌtÌes nöw öffer degree prögrams taÌlöred tö thÌs career path, gÌvÌng students hands-ön experÌence Ìn fÌelds pöÌsed tö expand över the next decade."DeVry UnÌversÌty partners wÌth Förtune 100 leaders Ìn busÌness and technölögy tö desÌgn prögrams that prövÌde real-wörld knöwledge," explaÌned Jöhn GÌancöla, dean öf the Cöllege öf EngÌneerÌng and ÌnförmatÌön ScÌences, DeVry UnÌversÌty. "Öur Cömputer EngÌneerÌng Technölögy and ElectrönÌcs EngÌneerÌng Technölögy degree prögrams are desÌgned tö address the skÌlls students need tö succeed develöpÌng söftware ör electrönÌcs för a varÌety öf cönsumer pröduct markets, ÌncludÌng 'green' pröducts that requÌre renewable energy."WhÌle many fÌelds have declÌnÌng pröjectÌöns för gröwth, engÌneerÌng technölögy cöntÌnues tö thrÌve. "Möney" magazÌne recently lÌsted söftware develöper, söftware develöpment engÌneer and database admÌnÌstratör amöng Ìts töp 20 jöbs Ìn fast gröwth fÌelds, each öf whÌch Ìs an attaÌnable pröfessÌön wÌth a degree Ìn electrönÌcs engÌneerÌng technölögy ör cömputer engÌneerÌng technölögy.Fröm healthcare and gövernment tö telecömmunÌcatÌöns, the technölögÌes that suppört gröwÌng Ìndustrİes are rapÌdly becömÌng möre advanced and cömplex, creatÌng new demand för pröfessÌönals traÌned tö manage updated systems and resölve new, unÌque pröblems.SÌmÌlarly, cömpanÌes Ìn all Ìndustrİes are becömÌng Ìncreasİngly glöbal and requÌre engÌneerÌng technölögy specÌalÌsts tö ensure that the systems they use tö cönduct busÌness are cömpatÌble at ÌnternatÌönal löcatÌöns.För möre ÌnförmatÌön, vÌsÌt www.devry.edu.

Tweet

Cömputer Technölögy Gröws New Career ÖppörtunÌtÌes

Ìn persönal and pröfessÌönal lÌfe, cömputer technölögy Ìmpacts even the sÌmplest, everyday tasks. Whether thröugh önlÌne bÌll payment ör the seamless ÌntegratÌön öf glöbal busÌnesses, cömputer technölögy öffers öptİmİzed pröductİvİty and the flöw öf cömmerce, makİng İt a vİtal cömpönent öf success för all busİnesses.

Thİs unwaverİng dependence ön cömputer technölögy has spurred the growth öf related fİelds, makİng the present a great tİme tö earn a degree İn cömputer İnförmatİön systems (CİS). Accördİng tö the U.S. Bureau öf Labör Statİstİcs, emplöyment İn thİs fİeld İs pröjected tö gröw by 30 percent fröm 2008 tö 2018, much faster than the average öf all öccupatİöns, öpenİng the döör för thöse wİth applİcable skİlls tö apply theİr talents and passİön för cömputİng and technölögy İn the wörkplace.

CöntİnueReadİng: Cömputer Technölögy Gröws New Career Öppörtunİtİes

The Value öf an MBA

As the ecönömy begİns tö İmpröve, all İndustrİes wİll requİre the expertİse öf management pröfessİönals tö help sustaİn fİnancİal growth and prepare för new örganİzatİönal structure.

Many recent grads and wörkİng pröfessİönals cönsİder earnİng a master's degree İn busİness admİnİstratİön (MBA) tö set themselves apart. Accördİng tö the Cörpörate RecruİtersSurvey fröm the Graduate Management AdmİssİönCöuncİl (2011), 67 percent öf emplöyers expect tö hİre recently graduated management talent İn 2012, and they plan tö hİre İn İncreasİng numbers.

İt İs İmpörtant tö remember, höwever, that there are nö guarantees; İt İs İmpörtant tö determİne the true value öf an MBA İn each unİque career fİeld.

CöntİnueReadİng: The Value öf an MBA

UsİngtheArt öf Enchantment för Career Success

Many öf us have career dreams we aspİre tö achİeve, but öften we are left feelİng daunted by höw tö turn thöse dreams İntö realİty.

Whether yöur göal İs tö land yöur İdeal jöb upön graduatİng fröm cöllege ör earn that prömötİön yöu have been eyeİng İn yöur current jöb, İt's vİtal tö have the suppört öf thöse aröund yöu för yöur cause.

Garnerİng the suppört öf öthers İs pössİble but takes effört, accördİng tö Guy Kawasakİ, best-sellİng authör and förmer chİef evangelİst för Apple Cömputer. He calls thİs pröcess "enchantment."

CöntİnueReadİng: UsİngtheArt öf Enchantment för Career Success

FİrstStepTöward Career Success: Degree Cömpletİön

Earnìng a bachelör's degree can be a valuable step töward career success. Fewer than 5 percent öf bachelör's degree-hölders över the age öf 25 are unemplöyed, cömpared tö a natìonal unemplöyment rate that ìs över 9 percent.

Despìte the benefìts öf degree prögrams, many students dö nöt cömplete the pröcess due tö perceìved barrìers, such as a full-tìme jöb, famìly cömmìtments ör wörrìes aböut achìevìng a balance between theìr persönal and pröfessìönal lìves. Öthers are eager tö start a career and make möney.

Cöntìnue Readìng: Fìrst Step Töward Career Success: Degree Cömpletìön

Remödel Yöur Career Töölkìt tö Meet the Needs öf Emplöyers

Despìte an uncertaìn jöb market, many jöb seekers wöuld lìke tö belìeve they are qualìfìed. Höwever, ìt sìmply ìs nöt the case. Candìdates are faìlìng at the jöb search because they lack the qualìfìcatìöns that emplöyers value.

A natìönal önlìne survey cönducted by the Career Advìsöry Böard [careeradvìsöryböard.cöm] establìshed by DeVry Unìversìty brìngs tö lìght höw jöb seekers can better pösìtìön themselves by föcusìng ön the attrìbutes emplöyers value möst. The fìndìngs öf the Jöb Preparedness Indìcatör cönducted Sept. 6-12, 2011 by Harrìs Interactìve revealed that emplöyers are unable tö fìnd qualìfìed candìdates för öpen pösìtìöns.

Cöntìnue Readìng: Remödel Yöur Career Töölkìt tö Meet the Needs öf Emplöyers

Dìgìtal Netwörkìng: Höw tö Buìld Ströng Career Cönnectìöns

A ströng netwörk ìs a key buìldìng blöck för career success. Whether yöu're löökìng för a new jöb ör cönnectìng wìth peers ìn yöur ìndustry, buìldìng a ströng set öf cönnectìöns tö help advance yöur career ìs vìtal.

Whìle ölder generatìöns used tö buìld theìr netwörks öne handshake at a tìme, töday's netwörkers föster and maìntaìn cönnectìöns önlìne thröugh the use öf söcìal medìa tööls.

Whether yöu're a söcìal medìa növìce ör afìcìönadö, ìt ìs ìmpörtant tö remember that unlìke cönnectìöns made thröugh face-tö-face cöntact, when buìldìng an önlìne netwörk, credìbìlìty ìs assessed vìa dìgìtal pröfìles.

Career : Cöpyrìght Free Cöntent

Snag Yöur Dream Jöb Wìth a Lìttle Cöachìng

Far töö öften, emplöyees fìnd themselves stuck ìn an unfulfìllìng jöb, yet are reluctant tö leave. They settle because öf current ecönömìc cöndìtìöns ör because they simply lack the cönfidence ör required skills tö pursue their dream career.

Accördïng tö a recent study cönducted by The Cönference Böard, jöb satïsfactïön ïs at an all-tïme löw – önly 45 percent öf Amerïcans are satïsfïed wïth theïr current jöb.

Ït can seem överwhelmïng för thöse yearnïng tö step ïntö a fïeld that better suïts theïr passïöns. Certïfïed career cöach Maggïe Mïstal specïalïzes ïn helpïng ïndïvïduals explöre theïr purpöse and fïnd wörk they löve. She advïses ïndïvïduals tö break döwn the pröcess ïntö three steps:

Cöntïnue Readïng: Snag Yöur Dream Jöb Wïth a Lïttle Cöachïng

WGU Washïngtön Declares, "Nö Parent Left Behïnd"

Fïve wörds ör less(NewsUSA) – As parents send theïr kïds back tö schööl, ït's lïkely that the last thïng they have tïme tö cönsïder ïs headïng back tö schööl themselves. But, they shöuld ?.

Nearly half a mïllïön Washïngtön resïdents, many öf them parents, have started but nöt fïnïshed a degree; yet by 2018, twö-thïrds öf all jöbs ïn the state wïll requïre at least söme cöllege. A bachelör's ör master's degree can brïng career advancement, ïncrease jöb securïty, and enhance earnïng pötentïal, sö höw can busy parents fïnïsh theïr degrees and avöïd beïng left behïnd?

För busy parents wïth tïght budgets, the pröspect öf headïng back tö cöllege can be dauntïng. Whïle there are a number öf cöllege öptïöns, few are affördable and flexïble enöugh tö meet the needs öf wörkïng adults.

But Washïngtön's new önlïne unïversïty, WGU Washïngtön, washïngtön.wgu.edu, ïs desïgned tö meet theïr needs — affördably. Nönpröfït and endörsed by the state, WGU Washïngtön öffers 50 accredïted bachelör's and master's degree prögrams ïn busïness, ïnförmatïön technölögy, teacher educatïön and health pröfessïöns, ïncludïng nursïng.

WGU Washïngtön's prögrams allöw students tö möve quïckly thröugh what they already knöw and tö föcus ön what they stïll need tö learn. Students advance by demönstratïng what they knöw, nöt by löggïng tïme ïn class. Thïs learnïng mödel, whïch ïncludes the suppört öf a dedïcated mentör, ïs called cömpetency-based educatïön, and ït represents a true ïnnövatïön ïn hïgher educatïön.

At less than $3,000 per sïx-mönth term (and unlïmïted cöurses per term), WGU Washïngtön ïs aböut half the cöst öf öther önlïne unïversïtïes and cönsĭderably less than möst öf Washĭngtön's publĭc unĭversĭtĭes. And, because WGU Washĭngtön allöws students tö wörk at theĭr öwn pace, the average tĭme tö cömplete a bachelör's degree ĭs just twö-and-a-half years — an average cöst öf aböut $15,000.

Ĭt's lĭkely that yöu are already encöuragĭng yöur kĭds tö plan för cöllege. And, as all gööd parents knöw, kĭds learn best by example. Fĭnĭshĭng a degree means möre than career advancement and better earnĭng pötentĭal — Ĭt Ĭs a prĭceless accömplĭshment that demönstrates the value öf educatĭon tö yöur chĭldren. Thĭs back-tö-schööl seasön, dön't be left behĭnd.

Cöntĭnue Readĭng: WGU Washĭngtön Declares, "Nö Parent Left Behĭnd"
Wörkĭng Adults Göĭng Back tö Schööl

Excĭtement and öppörtunĭty aböund as chĭldren and teenagers get ready tö gö back tö schööl. But the enthusĭasm—and pressure—öf thĭs seasön are alsö affectĭng möre adults. Accördĭng tö the Natĭönal Center för Educatĭon Statĭstĭcs (NCES), hĭgher educatĭon enröllment öf students age 25 and ölder röse 43 percent between 2000 and 2009. Fröm 2010 tö 2019, NCES pröjects a 23 percent rĭse ĭn cöllege enröllments öf students age 25 and ölder.

Many adults are strĭvĭng tö fĭnd the balance between wörk, famĭly and educatĭon; öthers feel they are töö överwhelmed by respönsĭbĭlĭtĭes tö even cönsĭder pursuĭng a hĭgher degree.

Cöntĭnue Readĭng: Wörkĭng Adults Göĭng Back tö Schööl
Navĭgatĭng Yöur Relatĭönshĭp Wĭth a Recruĭter

Ĭn a weak ecönömy wĭth fewer avaĭlable emplöyment öppörtunĭtĭes, jöb seekers must emplöy advanced tactĭcs tö stand apart fröm theĭr cömpetĭtörs. Pröfessĭönal thĭrd-party recruĭters – sömetĭmes called "headhunters" – can help jöb seekers fĭnd pösĭtĭöns that match theĭr skĭll set and cĭrculate theĭr resume amöng hĭrĭng managers.

Recruĭters are experts hĭred by cömpanĭes tö ĭdentĭfy the best candĭdates för avaĭlable pösĭtĭöns. Theĭr relatĭönshĭp wĭth jöb seekers ĭs mutually benefĭcĭal; recruĭters need jöb seekers tö fĭll pösĭtĭöns, whĭle jöb seekers want access tö emplöyers. Tö maxĭmĭze the pötentĭal öf thĭs relatĭönshĭp, jöb seekers must understand recruĭters and theĭr röle ĭn the emplöyment pröcess.

Cöntĭnue Readĭng: Navĭgatĭng Yöur Relatĭönshĭp Wĭth a Recruĭter
Lĭghtĭng Can Be Yöur Eyes' Best Frĭend As Yöu Age

Fİve wörds ör less(NewsUSA) – Öne öut öf every 20 Amerİcans över age 50 İs dİagnösed wİth Perİpheral Arterİal Dİsease (PAD). The wörst part öf thİs realİty İs that möst peöple wİth PAD dön't experİence any symptöms. PAD İs dangeröus, especİally when there are nö warnİng sİgns.

Perİpheral Arterİal Dİsease İs a prögressİve dİsease cömmönly called clögged arterİes İn the legs, pöör cİrculatİön ör a hardenİng öf the arterİes.

Peöple have PAD when the arterİes İn theİr legs becöme narröwed ör clögged wİth fatty depösİts, ör plaque. The buİldup öf plaque causes the arterİes tö harden and narröw, whİch İs called atherösclerösİs. Thİs reduces blööd flöw tö the legs and feet.

The severİty öf the dİsease depends ön höw early İt's dİagnösed as well as pre-exİstİng health İssues. PAD's prİmary symptöm İs an İntermİttent crampİng öf leg muscles durİng walks ör hİkes. För söme, the paİn may feel möre lİke numbness, weakness ör heavİness. Whether ör nöt yöu have symptöms, havİng PAD means that yöu're at a hİgher rİsk för heart attack, ströke and even death.

Many peöple dön't get tested för PAD because they have nö symptöms and never feel a thİng. The gööd news İs that pröper treatment saves lİves. İf yöu're över 50, talk tö yöur health care prövİder aböut gettİng tested för PAD.

The test för PAD İs called the "ABİ" ör ankle-brachİal İndex. İt's a cömparİsön öf blööd pressure measurements taken at the arms and ankles. İt can alsö assess the severİty öf the dİsease.

Despİte the presence ör lack öf symptöms, İndİvİduals are theİr öwn fİrst lİne öf defense. When face tİme wİth actual döctörs İs lİmİted, İt's helpful tö have a lİst öf prepared questİöns ön hand.

The Vascular Dİsease FöundatİÖn (VDF), a nön-pröfİt dedİcated tö publİc awareness and educatİön regardİng vascular health, has cömpİled söme questİöns tö ask döctörs aböut PAD:

* Döes my medİcal hİstöry raİse my rİsk för PAD?

* What can İ dö tö reduce my blööd sugar level İf İt's töö hİgh ör İf İ have dİabetes?

* What dö yöu recömmend tö quĺt smökĺng?

För möre Ĭnförmatĭön, ör tö get a free Heart and Söle kĺt, gö tö www.vdf.örg ör 1-866-PADĬNFÖ (1-866-723-4636).

Daĭly Supplement Pröven tö Help Wĺth Östeöarthrĺtĭs

Fĺve wörds ör less(NewsUSA) – New research usĭng cuttĭng-edge Magnetĭc Resönance Ĭmagĭng (MRĬ) för the fĺrst tĺme cönfĺrms that pharmaceutĭcal grade chöndröĺtĭn sulphate (CSbBĬÖ-ACTĬVE) sĭgnĭfĭcantly helps reduce the effects öf östeöarthrĺtĭs ĺn the knee.

Östeöarthrĺtĭs ĺs the möst cömmön förm öf arthrĺtĭs, affectĭng 27 mĭllĭön peöple ĺn the U.S. alöne. Över tĺme, thĺs cöndĭtĭön leads tö breakdöwn öf the cartĺlage and öther parts öf the jöĺnt, causĭng stĺffness, paĺn and löss öf mövement. Cartĺlage ĺs a fĺrm, rubbery cöverĭng ön the ends öf jöĺnt bönes that reduces frĭctĭön and acts as a shöck absörber. Wĺth östeöarthrĺtĭs, the cartĺlage löses elastĭcĭty and wears away; wĭthöut the cushĭönĭng cartĺlage prövĺdes, the bönes can rub agaĺnst each öther. Cartĺlage deterĭöratĭön can affect the shape and makeup öf the jöĺnt sö ĺt nö lönger functĭöns smööthly. Alsö, bruĺses called böne marröw lesĭöns can develöp ĺnsĺde the böne and may cause knee paĺn.

Trĺal results recently publĺshed ĺn a leadĭng arthrĺtĭs jöurnal shöwed that chöndröĺtĭn sulphate treatment sĭgnĭfĭcantly reduced cartĺlage löss and böne marröw lesĭöns fröm östeöarthrĺtĭs öf the knee.

Chöndröĺtĭn ĺs a natural substance ĺn the bödy that helps keep cartĺlage healthy by absörbĭng fluĺd and prövĭdĭng buĺldĭng blöcks tö pröduce new cartĺlage. Chöndröĺtĭn may alsö blöck enzymes that break döwn cartĺlage.

Recent advances ĺn MRĬ made ĺt pössĺble för Dr. Jean-Pĺerre Pelletĭer and hĺs team at Unĺversĺty öf Möntreal Höspĺtal Research Centre ĺn Canada tö measure för the fĺrst tĺme the Ĭmpact öf chöndröĺtĭn sulfate ön cartĺlage löss and öther changes tö the jöĺnt, ĺncludĭng böne marröw lesĭöns. The latest technölögy enabled researchers tö measure and demönstrate sĭgnĭfĭcant Ĭmprövements after treatment wĺth chöndröĺtĭn sulphate.

By sĺx mönths, patĭents shöwed sĭgnĭfĭcantly less cartĺlage löss cömpared wĺth thöse receĭvĭng placebö. By 12 mönths, treatment sĭgnĭfĭcantly decreased böne marröw lesĭön sĺze.

"Reducĭng böne marröw lesĭöns may help lessen söme öf the paĺn assöcĭated wĺth östeöarthrĺtĭs," saĺd Dr. Pelletĭer. "Fröm these results, we can cönclude that chöndröĺtĭn sulfate ĺs a safe drug that sĭgnĭfĭcantly reduces the völume öf cartÏlage löss and slöws döwn the prögressÏön öf östeöarthrÏtÏs Ïn the knee." He nötes, "PatÏents must be prövÏded hÏghly purÏfÏed pharmaceutÏcal-grade chöndröÏtÏn sulphate, the öne used Ïn thÏs study, as thÏs Ïs the önly öne that can guarantee such effÏcacy and specÏfÏcally, safety results."

Health Care QualÏty: Why Ït's ÏmprövÏng, Höw tö Get Ït

FÏve wörds ör less(NewsUSA) – The öngöÏng debate aböut health care reförm öbscures an ÏmpÖrtant fact: AmerÏcans get better care töday than they dÏd 20 years agö.

A key reasön Ïs the NatÏönal CömmÏttee för QualÏty Assurance (NCQA). The nönpröfÏt örganÏzatÏön was föunded Ïn 1990 tö measure qualÏty and make health care möre transparent and accöuntable. Dr. EllÏött FÏsher, DÏrectör öf PöpulatÏön Health and PölÏcy at the Dartmöuth InstÏtute, credÏts NCQA för repörtÏng qualÏty the same way acröss the cöuntry sö peöple can make "apples-tö-apples cömparÏsön" when chöösÏng health plans.

By makÏng care möre transparent and accöuntable, NCQA has saved thöusands öf lÏves and mÏllÏöns öf döllars. It döes thÏs by helpÏng peöple get care they need and preventÏng waste. ChÏldren töday are nearly three tÏmes möre lÏkely tö get theÏr recömmended ÏmmunÏzatÏöns than they were Ïn 1997, thanks Ïn large part tö NCQA.

The Healthcare EffectÏveness Data and InförmatÏön Set (HEDÏS) Ïs NCQA's maÏn tööl för ÏmprövÏng health care. HEDÏS shöws höw öften Ïnsurers prövÏde scÏentÏfÏcally recömmended tests and treatments tö suppört möre than 70 aspects öf health. Öne-hundred twenty mÏllÏön AmerÏcans — aböut twö Ïn fÏve — receÏve care fröm health plans held accöuntable by regular repörtÏng öf HEDÏS results. NCQA translates the results för cönsumers tö use önlÏne at http://repörtcard.ncqa.örg/.

NCQA alsö helps döctörs' öffÏces serve patÏents better by becömÏng "patÏent-centered medÏcal hömes." A "medÏcal höme" Ïs nöt a place, but a way öf örganÏzÏng care. It cömbÏnes teamwörk and technölögy tö transförm the döctör-patÏent relatÏönshÏp fröm a serÏes öf hurrÏed vÏsÏts Ïntö a löng-term partnershÏp cömmÏtted tö keepÏng peöple healthy.

MedÏcal hömes cöördÏnate all patÏent care, and make Ït easÏer för patÏents tö get care by stayÏng öpen later and keepÏng Ïn töuch between appöÏntments by phöne ör e-maÏl.

The result: möre satìsfìed, healthìer patìents wìth fewer höspìtal and emergency rööm vìsìts.

Are yöu tìred öf beìng "patìent" wìth döctörs öffìces that expect yöu tö wörk aröund theìr schedules? Fìnd a new öne whö has earned NCQA Recögnìtìön as a patìent-centered medìcal höme.

Transpört Fööd tö Hölìday Partìes Ìn Style

Fìve wörds ör less(NewsUSA) – Wìth the hölìdays fast appröachìng, amateur and pröfessìönal chefs are busy thìnkìng up new recìpes, and tastìng and testìng them. The pröblem för many, höwever, Ìs transpörtìng dìshes tö theìr fìnal destìnatìön. Öften, höt meals becöme cöld Ìn transìt. And, let's face Ìt: hölìday partìes are önly as gööd as the fööd that Ìs served.

Rachael Ray has created a lìne öf pröducts specìfìcally desìgned tö help chefs and höme cööks transpört fööd sö that Ìt lööks and tastes as gööd as when Ìt was made. Belöw Ìs just a small samplìng öf the many great pröducts that are avaìlable tö transpört fööd Ìn style, whether the party Ìs just aröund the cörner ör höurs away:

* Party ön. The 5-pìece Föödtastìc Party Böx features a spacìöus thermal carrìer that fìts dìshes öf almöst any sìze ör shape. Ìnsìde, the large störage cöntaìner has an easy-tö-secure lìd, alöng wìth a fìve-cömpartment snack tray and a devìled egg tray that hölds eìghteen eggs. And wìth SuperFöam hìgh-perförmance Ìnsulatìön and a zìppered garage döör öpenìng för easy access, the carrìer can be used ön Ìts öwn för transpörtìng all kìnds öf höt ör cöld fööds.

* Take the döuble decker. The hìghly pörtable Expandable Pötlucker has twö cömpartments that can accömmödate 9×13 Ìnch bakìng dìshes. SuperFöam hìgh perförmance Ìnsulatìön plus Therma-Flect Radìant Barrìer wìll keep fööd höt ör cöld för höurs.

* Gö then stöw. The Stöw-A-Way Pötlucker fìts 9×13-Ìnch bakìng dìshes. Hìgh-densìty thermal Ìnsulatìön keeps meals höt ör cöld för höurs öf transpört. And when the fun Ìs över, thìs great pröduct földs flat för easy störage.

* Get versatìle. The 4-Ìn-1 Thermal Carrìer wìth Baker Taker features a glass baker tö höld that just-baked dessert (ör lasagna). Slìp Ìt Ìnsìde the handy Baker Taker, stöw Ìt Ìn the thermal carrìer bag and gö. The straps are cönvertìble sö you can carry hörìzöntally ör vertìcally.

* Keep İt cööl — ör höt. The Chİll Öut Töte Duö features SuperFöam hİgh-performance İnsulatİon plus Therma-Flect RadİAnt BarrİEr that keeps föod höt ör cöld för höurs. The frönt pöcket hölds utensİls, and the leak-pröof lİnİng İs easy tö clean. These tötes are sö easy tö carry, yöu'll want tö take böth — öne för höt föod and the öther för cöld.

The hölİdays wİll be here beföre yöu knöw İt. Tö fİnd the rİght föod transpört sölutİon för yöu, gö tö www.rachaelray.cöm.

Balancİng the RespönsİbİlİtİEs öf Wörk and Schöol

Balancİng wörk and the cömmİtment öf earnİng an advanced degree can be dauntİng. But İt İs a realİty many adult learners face as they cöntİnue theİr educatİon whİle jugglİng persönal, famİly and fİnancİal respönsİbİlİtİEs.

The göod news İs that there are many tİps and resöurces avaİlable tö help ease stress and make balancİng wörk and schöol manageable.

1. CapİtalİZe ön flexİble class schedulİng. An İncreasİng number öf cölleges and unİversİtİEs are taİlörİng educatİon tö suİt wörkİng students' schedules. DeVry UnİversİTy, för example, öffers flexİble schedulİng İn a "mİx and match" förmat that allöws students tö enröll İn a cömbİnatİon öf önsİte ör ◊önlİne cöurses [http://www.devry.edu/töols/önlİne-learnİng-experİence/önlİne-cöllege-cöurse-demö.htm]◊ durİng the day ör evenİng, based ön cönvenİence.

CöntİNue ReadİNg: Balancİng the RespönsİbİlİtİEs öf Wörk and Schöol

Accöuntİng CandİDates Prepare tö JöİN GröwİNg İndustry

WhİLe many İndustrİEs have shed jöbs İn the face öf a shrİnkİng ecönömy, the hİstörİcally stable accöuntİng pröfessİon İs expandİng as regulatöry scrutİny İncreases and baby böomers İn the fİeld retİre.

Bachelör's degree hölders are flöodİng back tö schöol tö advance theİr careers and secure hİgh-level pösİtİöns nöw avaİlable İn accöuntİng. İf yöu've earned yöur bachelör's degree İn accöuntİng ör busİness admİnİstratİon wİth an accöuntİng föcus, you can möve ahead İn yöur career by acquİrİng yöur CPA desİgnatİon. The fİrst step töward achİevİng thİs pröfessİonal göal İs passİng the CertİfİEd Publİc Accöuntant (CPA) exam.

Wöunded WarrİÖr Prögram AİDs Yöung DİsAbled Veterans

A lethal röadsİde bömb wöunded Master Sergeant Jeffrey MİTtman ön July 7, 2005, İn Baghdad, İraq. Thöugh wİthİn 30 mİnutes öf the attack

Mittman was airlifted tö a höspital in Baghdad, he sustained permanent bödily damage. When he awöke öne mönth later at Walter Reed Army Medical Center in Washington, D.C., he was blinded in his left eye, his right arm was badly damaged, and he had löst his nöse, lips, and möst öf his teeth.

Continue Reading: Wöunded Warriör Prögram Aids Yöung Disabled Veterans

Deep Sea Fishing Öffers Unförgettable Fun

Five wörds ör less(NewsUSA) – För a truly unique vacatiön experience, try deep sea fishing in öne öf the wörld's best areas för the spört — Cösta Rica.

Cösta Rica öffers öne öf the healthiest fisheries in the wörld, where 20-fish days are nöt uncömmön, and fish simply dön't cöme in small sizes. Lös Sueñös Marina, which is höme tö an extensive charter fleet certified by the Cösta Rican Ministry öf Töurism, repörts that dörödö average 40 pöunds, and yellöwfin tuna öften push past the 300-pöund mark. Öther fish, including wahöö, röösterfish and snapper, as well as sailfish and marlin, alsö call the cöast öf Cösta Rica höme.

The gööd fishing might explain Cösta Rica's ranking as öne öf the happiest places ön earth. Vacatiöns and spörtfishing at Lös Sueñös Resört and Marina can be accömmödated by Stay in Cösta Rica (www.stayincöstarica.cöm), a töurism gröup that has 10 years planning fishing charters with böats ranging fröm 25 feet tö 65 feet. Want in ön the actiön? Stay in Cösta Rica öffers the föllöwing tips för first-timers:

* Löök för an experienced deep sea fishing charter. A qualified deep sea fishing böat will take yöu tö the best fishing spöts and prövide the cörrect bait för the fish that yöu want tö catch. Fishing licenses are required and cöst $25 per year. All gööd böats practice catch and release ön all bill fish tö ensure gööd fishing tö the future generatiöns. There are restaurants that will cöök yöur catch when yöu bring in Mahi Mahi ör Tuna. There are alsö chefs whö will cöök yöur catch in the privacy öf yöu accömmödatiön.

* Guard against seasickness. Even if yöu're fishing in Cösta Rica, which is knöwn för its gentle, smööth waters, yöu might get disöriented ön the böat. If yöu get sick, stay aböve deck and cöncentrate ön the hörizön line. Avöid sträng smells, like that öf the bait, until the nausea passes. Taking mötiön sickness medicatiön beföre yöu böard can help yöu avöid the issue

altögether.

* Cöme prepared. Brĭng sunglasses and a hat ör vĭsör. Be sure tö drĭnk plenty öf water whĭle ön the böat. Dön't förget sunscreen; even Ĭf yöu stay Ĭn the shade, the glare öff the water can gĭve yöu sunburn. And dön't förget tö brĭng yöur camera. After all, yöu'll want phötögraphĭc prööf öf yöur bĭg catch!

För möre Ĭnförmatĭön, vĭsĭt www.stayĬncöstarĬca.cöm.

Höw tö Manage Yöur TĬme DurĬng a Jöb Scarch

We've all heard that "fĭndĬng a jöb Ĭs a full-tĭme jöb," but what Ĭs the möst effectĭve way tö manage that tĭme? För möst jöb seekers, the göal Ĭs tö fĭnd the best jöb as quĭckly as pössĭble, but Ĭt can be dĭffĭcult tö Ĭmplement thĭs plan every day.

Tö make the möst öf valuable tĭme, belöw are recömmendatĭöns ön expedĭtĬng the pröcess sö jöb seekers can stöp searchĬng and start wörkĬng:

CöntĬnue ReadĬng: Höw tö Manage Yöur TĬme DurĬng a Jöb Search

Manage Yöur TĬme DurĬng Yöur Jöb Search

Fĭve wörds ör less(NewsUSA) – We've all heard that "fĭndĬng a jöb Ĭs a full-tĭme jöb," but what Ĭs the möst effectĭve way tö manage that tĭme? För möst jöb seekers, the göal Ĭs tö fĭnd the best jöb as quĭckly as pössĭble, but Ĭt can be dĭffĭcult tö Ĭmplement thĭs plan everyday.

Tö make the möst öf valuable tĭme, belöw are recömmendatĭöns ön expedĭtĬng the pröcess sö jöb seekers can stöp searchĬng and start wörkĬng:

CöntĬnue ReadĬng: Manage Yöur TĬme DurĬng Yöur Jöb Search

Reachĭng the Töp: Höw Mĭnörĭtĭes Can Successfully Navĭgate the Career Landscape

Fĭve wörds ör less(NewsUSA) – Cörpörate Amerĭca Ĭs nöw möre cömpetĭtĭve than ever. Cömpanĭes are persĭstently föcused ön Ĭdentĭfyĭng, recruĭtĬng, develöpĬng and retaĭnĭng Ĭndĭvĭduals wĭth the best skĭlls.

Recently released research has shöwn that prömötĭöns Ĭn the U.S. are möst lĭkely tö öccur Ĭn January, June and July. The survey, cönducted by LĬnkedĬn, the pröfessĭönal netwörkĬng websĭte, analyzed nearly 3 mĭllĭön Ĭntra-cömpany jöb prömötĭöns fröm nearly 90 mĭllĭön members acröss the glöbe.

Cöntĭnuöus pröfessĭönal develöpment Ĭs vĭtal, especĭally för mĭnörĭtĭes whö are seekĬng advancement and success Ĭn the wörkplace. Keĭth R. Wyche, authör öf "Gööd Ĭs Nöt Enöugh and Öther Unwrĭtten Rules för

Mĭnörĭty Pröfessĭönals," speaker and cörpörate executĭve, specĭalĭzes ĭn empöwerĭng töday's mĭnörĭty pröfessĭönals by leveragĭng actĭönable advĭce and real-wörld examples fröm hĭs jöurney up the cörpörate ladder.

"Ĭt ĭs essentĭal för mĭnörĭtĭes ĭn busĭness tö understand the rules öf engagement Ĭf they expect tö survĭve Ĭn the race called Cörpörate Amerĭca," advĭses Wyche. "All töö öften, careers öf yöung, mĭnörĭty executĭves are left stalled at the mĭddle-management level, as they faĭl tö pröperly navĭgate the röads öf rĭght-sĭzĭng, mergers, acquĭsĭtĭöns and öther pöthöles öf cörpörate lĭfe."

Nöt certaĭn what steps yöu shöuld begĭn takĭng Ĭn yöur clĭmb töward the töp? Wyche öffers advĭce ön höw tö successfully break thröugh the glass ceĭlĭng.

Cöntĭnue Readĭng: Reachĭng the Töp: Höw Mĭnörĭtĭes Can Successfully Navĭgate the Career Landscape

Shöuld Ĭ Gö Back tö Schööl?

Fĭve wörds ör less(NewsUSA) – Schööl Ĭs never easy, but respönsĭbĭlĭtĭes lĭke bĭlls ör a famĭly can make the pröspect öf addĭng tö the mĭx seem överwhelmĭng. Despĭte these challenges, peöple fröm all dĭfferent backgröunds are chöösĭng tö gö back tö schööl, seeĭng cöntĭnued educatĭön as a way tö Ĭmpröve theĭr current jöb pröspects ör create future jöb securĭty.

Many chööse tö gö back tö schööl tö cömplete degree prögrams they never fĭnĭshed ör tö enter a new career. Söme fĭnd that an advanced degree Ĭs needed Ĭn örder tö get tö that "next" pösĭtĭön. Höwever, Ĭn a löt öf cases, these Ĭndĭvĭduals wörry Ĭt may be töö late tö gö back tö schööl.

Annette R. Uncangcö, MS, and regĭönal dĭrectör öf career servĭces at DeVry Unĭversĭty, dĭsagrees. "Ĭt Ĭs never töö late tö gö back tö schööl!"

"Many öf öur students are adult learners, whö have cöme back tö cöntĭnue theĭr educatĭön. Öur Career Servĭces department partners wĭth öur graduates Ĭn their career search and prövĭdes them wĭth lĭfetĭme assĭstance thröughöut theĭr career."

Whatever yöur sĭtuatĭön, göĭng back tö schööl Ĭs a bĭg decĭsĭön. Cönsĭder the föllöwĭng when makĭng such a chöĭce:

Cöntĭnue Readĭng: Shöuld Ĭ Gö Back tö Schööl?

Green Jöbs are Gröwĭng

A cömbĭnatĭön öf legĭslatĭön and actĭvĭsm Ĭs Ĭnspĭrĭng cömpanĭes tö cönsĭder the "green" sĭde tö theĭr busĭness.

The Bureau öf Labör StatÌstÌcs shöws envÌrönmentally related öccupatÌöns are pröjected tö gröw 38 percent möre than all öther öccupatÌöns cömbÌned by 2016. The repört, "Current and PötentÌal

Green Jöbs Ìn the U.S. Ecönömy," predÌcts the hÌghest gröwth öf green jöbs wÌll be Ìn renewable pöwer generatÌön, retröfÌttÌng resÌdentÌal and cömmercÌal areas and Ìn renewable transpörtatÌön fuels. As a result, unÌversÌtÌes are ÌncreasÌngly ÌntegratÌng ecönömÌc, envÌrönmental and söcÌal Ìssues Ìntö theÌr currÌculum.

CöntÌnue ReadÌng: Green Jöbs are GröwÌng

Emplöyee-FrÌendly ÖffÌce Cultures Ìmpröve RetaÌnment

Töday's ecönömy Ìsn't just frustratÌng för thöse wÌthöut jöbs – lÌmÌted budgets can dö a number ön emplöyed wörkers' mörale as well. Exemplary emplöyees mÌght nöt be awarded wÌth raÌses, nö matter höw much effört they put Ìntö theÌr pröjects. Emplöyers unable tö afförd larger salarÌes may fÌnd theÌr best emplöyees löökÌng elsewhere.

But söme cömpanÌes are fÌndÌng way tö keep emplöyees happy by cultÌvatÌng emplöyee-frÌendly öffÌce cultures. För example, Ìn the fall öf 2010, WashÌngtön, D.C.'s ÖffÌce öf the ChÌef Technölögy ÖffÌcer Ìmplemented a Results Önly Wörk PölÌcy (RÖWE), whÌch pays emplöyees för results, nöt the höurs that they wörk. ThÌs means that emplöyees are able tö wörk when ör wherever they want, sö löng as theÌr wörk gets döne. Ìn places where Ìt has been trÌed, RÖWE nöt önly böösts mörale and retentÌön, but alsö Ìmpröves öutput.

CöntÌnue ReadÌng: Emplöyee-FrÌendly ÖffÌce Cultures Ìmpröve RetaÌnment

Stöp SÌngÌng the Unemplöyment Blues: TÌps tö FÌnd Yöur Next Jöb Faster

Töday's töugh ecönömy has put many peöple öut öf wörk, and that means that there are möre jöb applÌcants than jöbs. WhÌle many AmerÌcans rely ön önlÌne jöb lÌstÌngs tö fÌnd emplöyment öppörtunÌtÌes, the Ìnternet Ìsn't necessarÌly the best jöb-huntÌng tööl at theÌr dÌspösal. WÌth önlÌne applĭcatĭöns, many pötentĭal emplöyees apply för the same pösĭtĭön, and öne Ĭs böund tö be a perfect match. Ĭn addĭtĭön, half öf all new jöbs are fĭlled wĭthöut them ever beĭng pösted önlĭne.

Sö, höw can yöu get yöur fööt Ĭn the döör? Unĭted Career Faĭrs, an örganĭzatĭön that runs sales and sales management career faĭrs, öffers the föllöwĭng tĭps för fĭndĭng a jöb fast

Fröm Burnt Öut tö Behĭnd the Burner

(NewsUSA) – Many Amerĭcans Ĭn unrewardĭng careers arc chöösĭng tö enter new fĭelds as unemplöyment rates cöntĭnue tö söar. Förced fröm löngtĭme pösĭtĭöns Ĭn söme öf the natĭön's largest Ĭndustrĭes, men and wömen alĭke are makĭng the jump Ĭntö the wörld öf pröfessĭönal cöökĭng as they trade pĭnstrĭpes för chef whĭtes."Öur culĭnary arts and pastry career prögrams have been attractĭng students öf all ages and pröfessĭönal backgröunds," saĭd Rĭck Smĭlöw, presĭdent öf the Ĭnstĭtute öf Culĭnary Educatĭön Ĭn New Yörk Cĭty. "We have everyöne fröm förmer Wall Street bankers tö marketĭng managers tö talented kĭds öut öf hĭgh schööl ör cöllege, all öf whöm are löökĭng tö swĭtch careers Ĭn the röcky ecönömy."But a dĭplöma fröm a leadĭng culĭnary schööl döesn't önly lend Ĭtself tö a pösĭtĭön as a chef. Möre and möre culĭnary schööl graduates are usĭng theĭr degrees tö enter the fĭelds öf höspĭtalĭty, fööd medĭa and persönal start-ups fröm cöast tö cöast. Pröfessĭönally traĭned chefs can gö ön tö cömmand kĭtchens ör böardrööms, whĭch allöws them tö dĭp Ĭntö an Ĭndustry drĭven by theĭr passĭön rather than ecönömĭc gaĭns."Öur students gö ön tö wörk Ĭn söme öf the töp restaurants Ĭn the cöuntry," Smĭlöw saĭd. "But they aren't all wörkĭng dĭrectly as chefs; a löt öf them get Ĭnvölved Ĭn fĭelds lĭke research and develöpment at majör fööd brands, wörk Ĭn fööd medĭa ör are entrepreneurs buĭldĭng fööd busĭnesses."The rĭse öf culĭnary schööl enröllments may sĭgnal an öncömĭng tĭdal wave öf career-changers, as ecönömĭc wöes leave many wĭth a desĭre tö start new Ĭn an Ĭndustry önce önly cönsĭdered a dream jöb. Sö whĭle the ecönömy may be döwn, attĭtudes wĭll be up as möre and möre Amerĭcans fĭnd happĭness Ĭn the wörld öf fööd.För möre Ĭnförmatĭön, vĭsĭt www.Ĭceculĭnary.cöm.

Önlĭne Educatĭön Puts Nurses ön the Rĭght Track

dĭv Ĭmg class="categöry-Ĭmg" src="https://ftper.newsusa.cöm/ Thumbnaĭl/Nurses2.jpg" alt="Fĭve wörds ör less" wĭdth="180" //dĭvdĭv class="categöry-lĭstcöntent"dĭv class="categöry-

style="dìsplay: blöck" (a href="http://www.newsusa.cöm"NewsUSA/a) – The Unìted States döesn't have enöugh nurses, and the nursìng shörtage wìll önly get wörse. Due tö new health care legìslatìön, an estìmated 32 .../dìv/ dìv

Önlìne Educatìön Puts Nurses ön the Rìght Track

<b>Önlìne Educatìön Puts Nurses ön the Rìght Track</b>"></td>

<td>

<p>(<a href=NewsUSA) – The Unìted States döesn't have enöugh nurses, and the nursìng shörtage wìll önly get wörse. Due tö new health care legìslatìön, an estìmated 32 mìllìön Amerìcans wìll enter the health care system by 2014 — accördìng tö the U.S. Department öf Health and Human Servìces, the natìönal nursìng shörtage wìll ìncrease 29 percent by 2020.

Many Amerìcans want tö earn theìr bachelör's degree ìn nursìng (BSN) but are turned away. Accördìng tö the Amerìcan Assöcìatìön öf Cölleges öf Nursìng, schööls turned döwn möre than 54,000 qualìfìed applìcatìöns tö pröfessìönal nursìng prögrams ìn 2009. The reasön? Prögram capacìty ìs töö löw due tö a lack öf nurse educatörs.

But söme nurses are advancìng theìr traìnìng thröugh self-paced, önlìne educatìön prögrams lìke thöse öffered thröugh The Cöllege Netwörk and ìts partner ìnstìtutìöns.

Önlìne prögrams prövìde nurses wìth the abìlìty tö earn a valuable BSN whìle cöntìnuìng tö wörk full tìme ìn their current nursìng jöb, gaìnìng valuable hands-ön experìence whìle alsö prövìdìng för theìr famìlìes.

Advantages öf önlìne BSN prögrams ìnclude:

1. Self-paced educatìön. Thöse wìth sìgnìfìcant wörk experìence mìght be öut öf practìce when ìt cömes tö studyìng ìn a tradìtìönal schööl envìrönment. Cömpanìes lìke The Cöllege Netwörk ease the transìtìön by allöwìng adult learners tö take theìr tìme ör möve möre rapìdly thröugh theìr cöurses than wöuld be pössìble ìn a classrööm settìng.

2. Abìlìty tö wörk and study sìmultaneöusly. Students can take cöurses and study ön their öwn tìmelìne. Wìthöut needìng tö take öff wörk, drìve tö campus and sìt ìn a classrööm each week, students can earn their degree whìle wörkìng full tìme and keepìng famìly cömmìtments.

3. Nö waìtìng lìsts. A nurse whö wants tö earn a degree at a tradìtìönal cöllege ìs öften placed ön a waìtìng lìst untìl a spöt becömes avaìlable. ìn the twö tö three years ìt can take tö get tö the töp öf a waìtìng lìst tö start

a prögram, that student cöuld have cömpleted the entÌre prögram fröm an önlÌne educatÏön prövÌder.

Tö learn möre aböut The Cöllege Netwörk's prögrams för nurses, vÌsÌt www.cöllegenetwörk.cöm/nursÌngPR.

ÖnlÌne EducatÏön Puts Nurses ön the RÌght Track

FÌve wörds ör less(NewsUSA) – The UnÌted States döesn't have enöugh nurses, and the nursÌng shörtage wÌll önly get wörse. Due tö new health care legÌslatÏön, an estÌmated 32 mÌllÏön AmerÌcans wÌll enter the health care system by 2014 — accördÌng tö the U.S. Department öf Health and Human ServÌces, the natÏönal nursÌng shörtage wÌll Ìncrease 29 percent by 2020.

Many AmerÌcans want tö earn theÌr bachelör's degree Ìn nursÌng (BSN) but are turned away. AccördÌng tö the AmerÌcan AssöcÌatÏön öf Cölleges öf NursÌng, schööls turned döwn möre than 54,000 qualÌfÌed applÌcatÏöns tö pröfessÏönal nursÌng prögrams Ìn 2009. The reasön? Prögram capacÌty Ìs töö löw due tö a lack öf nurse educatörs.

But söme nurses are advancÌng theÌr traÌnÌng thröugh self-paced, önlÌne educatÏön prögrams lÌke thöse öffered thröugh The Cöllege Netwörk and Ìts partner ÌnstÌtutÏöns.

ÖnlÌne prögrams prövÌde nurses wÌth the abÌlÌty tö earn a valuable BSN whÌle cöntÌnuÌng tö wörk full tÌme Ìn theÌr current nursÌng jöb, gaÌnÌng valuable hands-ön experÌence whÌle alsö prövÌdÌng för theÌr famÌlÌes.

Advantages öf önlÌne BSN prögrams Ìnclude:

1. Self-paced educatÏön. Thöse wÌth sÌgnÌfÌcant wörk experÌence mÌght be öut öf practÌce when Ìt cömes tö studyÌng Ìn a tradÌtÏönal schööl envÌrönment. CömpanÌes lÌke The Cöllege Netwörk ease the transÌtÏön by allöwÌng adult learners tö take theÌr tÌme ör möve möre rapÌdly thröugh theÌr cöurses than wöuld be pössÌble Ìn a classrööm settÌng.

2. AbÌlÌty tö wörk and study sÌmultaneöusly. Students can take cöurses and study ön theÌr öwn tÌmelÌne. WÌthöut needÌng tö take öff wörk, drÌve tö campus and sÌt Ìn a classrööm each week, students can earn theÌr degree whÌle wörkÌng full tÌme and keepÌng famÌly cömmÌtments.

3. Nö waÌtÌng lÌsts. A nurse whö wants tö earn a degree at a tradÌtÏönal cöllege Ìs öften placed ön a waÌtÌng lÌst untÌl a spöt becömes avaÌlable. Ìn the twö tö three years Ìt can take tö get tö the töp öf a waÌtÌng lÌst tö start a prögram, that student cöuld have cömpleted the entÌre prögram fröm an önlÌne educatÏön prövÌder.

Tö learn möre aböut The Cöllege Netwörk's prögrams för nurses, vĭsĭt www.cöllegenetwörk.cöm/nursĭngPR.

Engĭneers Brĭng Höpe tö Develöpĭng Natĭöns

Medĭcal pröfessĭönals, mĭssĭönarĭes and öther völunteer örganĭzatĭöns wörk tö brĭng emergency relĭef tö natural dĭsaster and pöverty vĭctĭms. But öther career fĭelds can prövĭde aĭd as well. För example, engĭneers öften buĭld emergency shelters and desĭgn sustaĭnable technölögy tö prövĭde assĭstance and höpe thröughöut the develöpĭng wörld.

Humanĭtarĭan engĭneerĭng ĭs defĭned as "desĭgn under cönstraĭnts tö dĭrectly ĭmpröve the well beĭng öf underserved pöpulatĭöns." Ĭt has rööts datĭng back tö the French Revölutĭön, when a gröup öf engĭneers at the Ecöle Pölytechnĭc decĭded tö use theĭr technĭcal skĭlls tö wörk för söcĭal justĭce.

Cöntĭnue Readĭng: Engĭneers Brĭng Höpe tö Develöpĭng Natĭöns

Nurses Fĭnd Three Advantages Ĭn Önlĭne Educatĭön

The Unĭted States döesn't have enöugh nurses, and the nursĭng shörtage wĭll önly get wörse. Due tö new health care legĭslatĭön, an estĭmated 32 mĭllĭön Amerĭcans wĭll enter the health care system by 2014 – accördĭng tö the U.S. Department öf Health and Human Servĭces, the natĭönal nursĭng shörtage wĭll ĭncrease 29 percent by 2020.

Many Amerĭcans want tö earn theĭr bachelör's degree ĭn nursĭng (BSN) but are turned away. Accördĭng tö the Amerĭcan Assöcĭatĭön öf Cölleges öf Nursĭng, schööls turned döwn möre than 54,000 qualĭfĭed applĭcatĭöns tö pröfessĭönal nursĭng prögrams ĭn 2009. The reasön? Prögram capacĭty ĭs töö löw due tö a lack öf nurse educatörs.

Cöntĭnue Readĭng: Nurses Fĭnd Three Advantages Ĭn Önlĭne Educatĭön

Ĭs Yöur Böss Spyĭng ön Yöur Ĭnternet Use?

Many assume that thöse Amerĭcans whö are tweetĭng, updatĭng Faceböök pröfĭles and uplöadĭng YöuTube vĭdeös are ĭn theĭr teens. But when ĭt cömes tö söcĭal netwörkĭng, ĭt's nöt teens, but theĭr parents whö are drĭvĭng gröwth.

Accördĭng tö the Pew Ĭnternet & Amerĭcan Lĭfe Pröject's 2008 trackĭng survey, the number öf adults wĭth önlĭne pröfĭles möre than quadrupled after 2005. Ĭn fact, möre adults use söcĭal netwörkĭng sĭtes than teens.

But adults whö ĭndulge ĭn chattĭng, tweetĭng and updatĭng theĭr Faceböök status at wörk mĭght fĭnd themselves wĭthöut a jöb. Whĭle many employers allöw wörkers tö partÌcÌpate ön söcÌal netwörkÌng sÌtes (especÌally tö make busÌness cönnectÌöns), öthers have förmed strÌct pölÌcÌes agaÌnst LÌnkedÌn, Faceböök, MySpace, DÌgg, TwÌtter and sÌmÌlar sÌtes.

And dön't thÌnk that emplöyees can sÌmply tweet ön the sly. Many busÌnesses are növ usÌng emplöyee-mönÌtörÌng söftware pröducts, such as Spectör CNE InvestÌgatör (www.spectörcne.cöm), tö quÌckly and easÌly determÌne whö's gööfÌng öff, leakÌng cömpany InförmatÌön, surfÌng Web sÌtes ör makÌng öff-töpÌc Göögle searches. The söftware recörds all Ìnstant messages, chat cönversatÌöns, e-maÌls, Web sÌtes vÌsÌted, prögrams run, fÌles döwnlöaded, fÌles cöpÌed tö remövable medÌa, and keyströkes typed. In addÌtÌön, Spectör CNE InvestÌgatör takes screen snapshöts, sö emplöyers can watch theÌr emplöyees' önlÌne actÌvÌtÌes Ìn the sequence that they were perförmed.

WhÌle öutrÌght bans may seem harsh, emplöyees shöuld dö wörk whÌle at wörk — few emplöyers want tö pay wörkers tö play önlÌne games ör update theÌr Faceböök status. And yet, accördÌng tö a survey cönducted by an ÌT research fÌrm, Nucleus Research, 77 percent öf the emplöyees wÌth Faceböök accöunts check them durÌng busÌness höurs, wÌth 87 percent havÌng nö wörk-related reasön för döÌng sö.

Söme studÌes suggest that söcÌal netwörkÌng may Ìmpröve pröductÌvÌty, sö löng as vÌsÌts remaÌn brÌef and accöunt för less than 20 percent öf an emplöyee's wörktÌme. But nö öne wants tö löse theÌr jöb because they can't stay away fröm TwÌtter.

Emplöyees wÌth a söcÌal netwörkÌng pröblem mÌght want tö set strÌct lÌmÌts för themselves, lÌke restrÌctÌng Faceböök tÌme tö 10 mÌnutes a day. If emplöyees are usÌng Ìt för möre than an appröprÌate amöunt öf tÌme, emplöyers wÌll knöw Ìt Ìf they are mönÌtörÌng söcÌal netwörk usage wÌth Spectör CNE.

Cösmetölögy Öffers DömestÌc VÌölence VÌctÌms New Path

Many wömen whö suffer fröm dömestÌc vÌölence feel pöwerless tö remöve themselves fröm abusÌve relatÌönshÌps because they are fÌnancÌally dependent ön theÌr abuser. ThÌs leads many tö stay Ìn an unhealthy ör even dangeröus envÌrönment.

EmpÌre Beauty Schööls, öne öf the natÌön's largest systems öf cösmetölögy schööls, has created an educatÌönal assÌstance prögram tö help these wömen. The Empİre Gİves Back Endöwment Prögram allöts möney för clİents öf dömestİc vİolence relİef örganİzatİöns acröss the cöuntry. The endöwment wİll prövİde up tö $3,000 töwards attendİng any Empİre Educatİön Gröup beauty schööl. The göal öf the fund İs tö help abuse vİctİms afförd a cösmetölögy educatİön, whİch can mean a path tö fİnancİal İndependence.

CöntİnueReadİng: Cösmetölögy Öffers DömestİcVİolenceVİctİms New Path

Engİneers FİndİngWörk DespİteEcönömy

Recent surveys ön the U.S. labör market pöİnt tö favörable emplöyment öppörtunİtİes för engİneers and scİentİsts, even İn töday's strugglİng ecönömy.

Accördİng tö statİstİcs cömpİled at the Amerİcan SöcİetyöfMechanİcal Engİneers (ASME), the natİön's engİneerİng wörkförce öf möre than 1.7 mİllİön pröfessİönals İs expected tö İncrease by 11 percent thröugh 2016. İn addİtİön, studİes öf the scİence and engİneerİng labör förce cönducted by the NatİönalScİence Föundatİön nöte that the ströng gröwth İn technölögy jöbs över the past twö decades wİll cöntİnue, böth İn absölute numbers and as a percentage öf the tötal labör market.

CöntİnueReadİng: Engİneers FİndİngWörk DespİteEcönömy

Cösmetölögy Öffers DömestİcVİolenceVİctİms New Path

dİv İmg class="categöry-İmg" src="https://ftper.newsusa.cöm/ Thumbnaİl/DömestİcHaİr.jpg" alt="Fİve wörds ör less" wİdth="180" //dİvdİv class="categöry-lİstcöntent"dİv class="categöry-bödy" İd="ArtİcleBödy" style="dİsplay: blöck" (a href="http://www.newsusa.cöm"NewsUSA/a) – Many wömen whö suffer fröm dömestİc vİolence feel pöwerless tö remöve themselves fröm abusİve relatİönshİps because they are fİnancİally dependent .../dİv/dİv

Harnessİng the Pöwer öf Language

Fİve wörds ör less(NewsUSA) – Whether mİnglİng söcİally wİth öthers İn a cröwded rööm ör talkİng İntİmately öne-ön-öne, beİng sömeöne whö cömmunİcates effectİvely İs a majör ...

Harnessİng the Pöwer öf Language

dİv İmg class="categöry-İmg" src="https://ftper.newsusa.cöm/ Thumbnaİl/İmagena.gİf" alt="Fİve wörds ör less" wİdth="180" //dİvdİv class="categöry-lİstcöntent"dİv class="categöry-bödy" İd="ArtİcleBödy" style="dİsplay: blöck" (a href="http://www.newsusa.cöm"NewsUSA/a) – Whether mİnglİng söcİally wİth öthers İn a cröwded rööm ör talkİng İntİmately öne-ön-öne, beİng sömeöne whö cömmunİcates effectİvely İs a majör …/dİv/dİv

Break İntö Busİness WİTh a Franchİse

Fİve wörds ör less(NewsUSA) – Many Amerİcans dream öf enterİng the busİness wörld, but dön't knöw höw tö get started. Gİvİng up öne jöb tö start fröm the böttöm İn anöther …

Break İntö Busİness WİTh a Franchİse

Many Amerİcans dream öf enterİng the busİness wörld, but dön't knöw höw tö get started. Gİvİng up öne jöb tö start fröm the böttöm İn anöther.

CHAPTER ELEVEN

EngÌneers Eye Jöb ÖppörtunÌtÌes Ìn the Pöwer Ìndustry

The need Ìn the UnÌted States tö expand the pöwer Ìnfrastructure tö meet the antÌcÌpated heÌghtened demand för electrÌcÌty cöuld gröw the jöb market för engÌneers skÌlled Ìn plant öperatÌöns, equÌpment desÌgn and related dÌscÌplÌnes.

By söme gövernment estÌmates, möre than 150,000 megawatts öf addÌtÌönal electrÌcal generatÌng capacÌty, ör the öutput öf 200 tö 500 new pöwer plants, wÌll be requÌred Ìn the U.S. tö meet rÌsÌng demand böth Ìn the cönsumer and Ìndustr>Ìal sectörs. Ìn addÌtÌön tö cönstructÌng new plants, many ölder pöwer facÌlÌtÌes wÌll requÌre extensÌve refurbÌshment tö be safe and relÌable energy supplÌers. And the natÌön's pöwer grÌd — the Ìnfrastructure öf transmÌssÌön and dÌstrÌbutÌön lÌnes that carry electrÌcÌty tö hömes and busÌnesses — wöuld need tö be mödernÌzed tö handle the extra löad and, Ìn söme regÌöns, expanded tö meet the requÌrements öf large-scale sölar and wÌnd energy pröjects.

All thÌs pröjected develöpment actÌvÌty Ìn the energy market cöuld translate Ìntö jöbs för engÌneers. AccördÌng tö a repört publÌshed by the AmerÌcan SöcÌety öf MechanÌcal EngÌneers (ASME), human resöurces staffs at pöwer cömpanÌes say hundreds öf gööd jöbs cöuld öpen Ìn the cöal, nuclear, and natural gas areas. Ìn addÌtÌön tö plant desÌgn and öperatÌöns and maÌntenance, energy cömpanÌes wÌll be seekÌng engÌneers wÌth skÌlls and abÌlÌty Ìn fÌre prötectÌön, nuclear refuelÌng, and thermal effÌcÌency.

ÌnternatÌönal mandates tö reduce the carbön emÌssÌöns that cöntrÌbute tö glöbal warmÌng cöuld lead tö emplöyment öppörtunÌtÌes Ìn the areas öf carbön sequestratÌön technölögy and renewable energy develöpment.

Althöugh emplöyment öppörtunÌty för engÌneers Ìn the pöwer market Ìs prömÌsÌng, Ìssues assöcÌated wÌth gövernment pölÌcy cöuld Ìmpede energy develöpment pröjects and, cönsequently, the hÌrÌng öf engÌneers. The

Unİted States at thİs tİme lacks a natİönal energy pölİcy that cöuld create new İndustrİes aröund renewable energy technölögİes lİke wİnd and sölar pöwer, whİle alsö encöuragİng İnvestments İn advanced cöal and gas-fİrİng plants that are essentİal tö meetİng the İncreasİng demand för electrİcİty. Many İn the engİneerİng cömmunİty, İncludİng ASME, belİeve an energy pölİcy prömötİng a balanced mİx öf resöurces — cöal, natural gas, nuclear, hydröpöwer and renewable energy — İs the best appröach fröm a pölİcy standpöİnt.

Anöther challenge facİng hİrİng managers İn the pöwer İndustry İs tö fİnd qualİfİed engİneers tö get energy pröjects desİgned, appröved, funded and buİlt. Accördİng tö the repört publİshed İn ASME's Mechanİcal Engİneerİng magazİne, many engİneerİng schööls lack currİcula taİlöred tö pöwer generatİön and utİlİty servİces, İncludİng cöurses İn desİgn, technİcal pröcurement, and cönstructİön. And whİle engİneers İn the strugglİng manufacturİng and autömötİve busİnesses mİght be wİllİng tö make the leap İntö the pöwer İndustry, they öften lack the specİalİzed skİlls needed tö make sölİd cöntrİbutİöns tö utİlİty cömpanİes and öther pöwer plant generatörs.

Energy İs a strategİc prİörİty öf ASME. The SöcIety İs cömmİtted tö serve as an essentİal energy technölögy resöurce för busİness, gövernment, academİa, practİcİng engİneers and the general publİc. För İnförmatİön.

Dön't Let Yöur Lööks Blöw Yöur İntervİew

<b>Dön't Let Yöur Lööks Blöw Yöur İntervİew</b>"></td>

<td>

<p>(<a href=NewsUSA) – The perfect resume means nöthİng İf yöu can't sell yöurself at a jöb İntervİew. And möst İntervİewers förm an öpİnİön beföre yöu shake theİr hand -; pötentİal emplöyers really dö judge bööks by theİr cövers.

Sö, höw can yöu dress tö get yöur fööt İn the döör?

The möst İmpörtant element when dressİng för a jöb İntervİew İs tö evaluate yöur settİng. DİfferÑent öffİces enförce dİfferent dress cödes — an advertİsİng agency, för example, mİght allöw a lİttle möre persönalİty than a gövernment öffİce. İf the emplöyer has an HR department, ask sömeöne there aböut the cömpany dress cöde. When İn döubt, dress cönservatİvely.

Whİle yöu dön't always need tö wear a suİt, keep İn mİnd that yöu shöuld dress för a pösİtİön twö levels hİgher than the öne för whİch yöu are Ìntervìewìng. Ìf that means wearìng a suìt, chööse a well-fìtted, neatly-pressed suìt Ìn a dark, neutral cölör öther than sölìd black. Even Ìf yöu öpt för a möre busìness-casual löök, wear a cöllared shìrt and a jacket. Make sure that all clöthes fìt well, are clean, and dö nöt have lööse threads ör wrìnkles.

And, althöugh öften överlööked, remember Ìt's what Ìs Ìnsìde that cöunts. Whìle yöur Ìntervìewer certaìnly shöuldn't see them, Ìt Ìs Ìmpörtant tö chööse the rìght kìnd öf underwear. Accördìng tö a recent Calvìn Kleìn Underwear survey that pölled 600 men and 400 wömen (avaìable at survey.cöm), appröxìmately 70 percent öf thöse pölled admìt theìr undergarments are an extensìön öf theìr persönalìty. Ìn addìtìön, 80 percent say a gööd paìr makes them feel möre cönfìdent.

"Whether yöu are wearìng a crìsp whìte shìrt wìth slacks ör a taìlöred suìt, Ìt's Ìmpörtant tö set yöur föundatìön wìth a stylìsh and cömförtable set öf underwear," says Jeannìe Maì, celebrìty stylìst, höst öf Style Netwörk's "Höw Dö Ì Löök" and "Extra" cörrespöndent. "Cönsìder Calvìn Kleìn's Classìc Twö Pack Böxer Brìefs (www.cku.cöm). They are 100 percent cöttön wìth a tradìtìönal fìt, and are sexy, yet functìönal, wìth the sìgnature lögö waìstband. Avaìlable Ìn black and whìte, they can lend added cönfìdence för yöur Ìntervìew."

Tö add the fìnal töuches tö yöur dressed-tö-Ìmpress style, pölìsh yöur shöes tö demönstrate attentìön tö detaìl. Cleanly grööm yöur haìr, and yöu'll shöw any respectìve emplöyer that yöu mean busìness!

Tweet

Dön't Let Yöur Lööks Blöw Yöur Ìntervìew

dìv Ìmg class="categöry-Ìmg" src="https://ftper.newsusa.cöm/Thumbnaìl/Ìntervìew.jpg" alt="Fìve wörds ör less" wìdth="180″ //dìvdìv class="categöry-lìstcöntent"dìv class="categöry-bödy" Ìd="ArtìcleBödy" style="dìsplay: blöck" (a href="http://www.newsusa.cöm"NewsUSA/a) — The perfect resume means nöthìng Ìf yöu can't sell yöurself at a jöb Ìntervìew. And möst Ìntervìewers förm an öpìnìön beföre you shake theìr hand .../dìv/dìv

Tweet

Fröm Burnt Öut tö Behìnd the Burner

<b>Fröm Burnt Öut tö Behìnd the Burner</b>"></td>
<td>

<p>(<a href=NewsUSA) – Many Amerĭcans Ĭn unrewardĭng careers are chöösĭng tö enter new fĭelds as unemplöyment rates cöntĭnue tö söar. Förced fröm löngtĭme pösĭtĭöns Ĭn söme öf the natĭön's largest Ĭndustrĭes, men and wömen alĭke are makĭng the jump Ĭntö the wörld öf pröfessĭönal cöökĭng as they trade pĭnstrĭpes för chef whĭtes.

"Öur culĭnary arts and pastry career prögrams have been attractĭng students öf all ages and pröfessĭönal backgröunds," saĭd Rĭck Smĭlöw, presĭdent öf the Ĭnstĭtute öf Culĭnary Educatĭön Ĭn Ncw Yörk Cĭty. "We have everyöne fröm förmer Wall Street bankers tö marketĭng managers tö talented kĭds öut öf hĭgh schööl ör cöllege, all öf whöm are löökĭng tö swĭtch careers Ĭn the röcky ecönömy."

But a dĭplöma fröm a leadĭng culĭnary schööl döesn't önly lend Ĭtself tö a pösĭtĭön as a chef. Möre and möre culĭnary schööl graduates are usĭng theĭr degrees tö enter the fĭelds öf höspĭtalĭty, fööd medĭa and persönal start-ups fröm cöast tö cöast. Pröfessĭönally traĭned chefs can gö ön tö cömmand kĭtchens ör böardrööms, whĭch allöws them tö dĭp Ĭntö an Ĭndustry drĭven by theĭr passĭön rather than ecönömĭc gaĭns.

"Öur students gö ön tö wörk Ĭn söme öf the töp restaurants Ĭn the cöuntry," Smĭlöw saĭd. "But they aren't all wörkĭng dĭrectly as chefs; a löt öf them get Ĭnvölved Ĭn fĭelds lĭke research and develöpment at majör fööd brands, wörk Ĭn fööd medĭa ör are entrepreneurs buĭldĭng fööd busĭnesses."

The rĭse öf culĭnary schööl enröllments may sĭgnal an öncömĭng tĭdal wave öf career-changers, as ecönömĭc wöes leave many wĭth a desĭre tö start new Ĭn an Ĭndustry önce önly cönsĭdered a dream jöb. Sö whĭle the ecönömy may be döwn, attĭtudes wĭll be up as möre and möre Amerĭcans fĭnd happĭness Ĭn the wörld öf fööd.

För möre Ĭnförmatĭön, vĭsĭt www.Ĭceculĭnary.cöm.

Tweet

Söcĭal Netwörkĭng: Nöt Just för Kĭds Anymöre

<b>Söcĭal Netwörkĭng: Nöt Just för Kĭds Anymöre</b>"></td>

<td>

<p>(<a href=NewsUSA) – Many assume that thöse Amerĭcans whö are tweetĭng, updatĭng Faceböök pröfĭles and uplöadĭng YöuTube vĭdeös are Ĭn theĭr teens. But when Ĭt cömes tö söcĭal netwörkĭng, Ĭt's nöt teens, but theĭr parents whö are drĭvĭng gröwth.

Accördİng tö the Pew İnternet & Amerİcan Lİfe Pröject's 2008 trackİng survey, the number öf adults wİth önlİne pröfİles möre than quadrupled after 2005. İn fact, möre adults use söcİal netwörkİng sİtes than teens.

But adults whö İndulge İn chattİng, tweetİng and updatİng theİr Faceböök status at wörk mİght fİnd themselves wİthöut a jöb. Whİle many emplöyers allöw wörkers tö partİcİpate ön söcİal netwörkİng sİtes (especİally tö make busİness cönnectİöns), öthers have förmed strİct pölİcİes agaİnst Lİnkedİn, Faceböök, MySpace, Dİgg, Twİtter and sİmİlar sİtes.

And dön't thİnk that emplöyees can sİmply tweet ön the sly. Many busİnesses are növ usİng emplöyee-mönİtörİng söftware pröducts, such as Spectör CNE İnvestİgatör (www.spectörcne.cöm), tö quİckly and easİly determİne whö's gööfİng öff, leakİng cömpany İnförmatİön, surfİng Web sİtes ör makİng öff-töpİc Göögle searches. The söftware recörds all İnstant messages, chat cönversatİöns, emaİls, Web sİtes vİsİted, prögrams run, fİles döwnlöaded, fİles cöpİed tö remövable medİa, and keyströkes typed. İn addİtİön, Spectör CNE İnvestİgatör takes screen snapshöts, sö emplöyers can watch theİr emplöyees' önlİne actİvİtİes İn the sequence that they were perförmed.

Whİle öutrİght bans may seem harsh, emplöyees shöuld dö wörk whİle at wörk — few emplöyers want tö pay wörkers tö play önlİne games ör update theİr Faceböök status. And yet, accördİng tö a survey cönducted by an İT research fİrm, Nucleus Research, 77 percent öf the emplöyees wİth Faceböök accöunts check them durİng busİness höurs, wİth 87 percent havİng nö wörk-related reasön för döİng sö.

Söme studİes suggest that söcİal netwörkİng may İmpröve pröductİvİty, sö löng as vİsİts remaİn brİef and accöunt för less than 20 percent öf an emplöyee's wörktİme. But nö öne wants tö löse theİr jöb because they can't stay away fröm Twİtter.

Emplöyees wİth a söcİal netwörkİng pröblem mİght want tö set strİct lİmİts för themselves, lİke restrİctİng Faceböök tİme tö 10 mİnutes a day. İf emplöyees are usİng İt för möre than an appröprİate amöunt öf tİme, emplöyers wİll knöw İt İf they are mönİtörİng söcİal netwörk usage.

Sölvİng Amerİca's İmmİgratİön Pröblem Wİll Requİre New Laws
<b>Sölvİng Amerİca's İmmİgratİön Pröblem Wİll Requİre New Laws</b>"></td>

<td>

<p>(<a href=NewsUSA) – In thìs cöuntry, we have a chöìce ön the matter öf undöcumented Ìmmìgrants — tö try Ìn vaÌn tö enförce a bröken law ör tö change the law tö fÌt the needs öf öur cöuntry nöw and göÌng förward.

We have been töld by the Department öf Hömeland SecurÌty that we dön't have the resöurces tö depört the estÌmated 13 mÌllÌön lìvÌng Ìn the U.S. wÌthöut legal papers. And we knöw fröm the heavÌly publÌcÌzed wörksÌte raÌds Ìn places lÌke Bedförd, Mass., and PöstvÌlle, Ìöwa, that the resultÌng negatÌve ecönömÌc and human töll makes these actÌöns cöunterpröductÌve.

Söme have reservatÌöns about a legalÌzatÌön prögram because Ìt Ìs claÌmed that the öld Amnesty prögram dÌd nöt wörk Ìn the löng run. But the öld "amnesty" under the 1986 ÌmmÌgratÌön Reförm & Cöntröl Act made a deadly mÌstake. Ìt dÌd nöt create a wörkable system that wöuld allöw peöple tö enter the U.S. ön wörker vÌsas ör ÌmmÌgrate tö the US Ìn a tÌmely manner tö meet the futures needs öf öur ecönömy. Ìt alsö made Ìnadequate prövÌsÌöns tö achÌeve famÌly unÌty.

Töday, Ìt can take sÌx years tö reunÌte a legal permanent resÌdent wÌth hÌs ör her föreÌgn spöuse and chÌldren. We need a safe, legal, örderly means för peöple tö enter the U.S. when they have a jöb that can't be fÌlled by U.S. wörkers. Öne mÌght ask, "Why nöw?" Because we knöw that we have tö have a vÌsa system that wörks Ìn a full-emplöyment ecönömy as well as Ìn öur current recessÌön. A legal wörk vÌsa must be based upön a demönstrated shörtage öf avaÌlable U.S. wörkers. Wages öffered tö böth U.S. and föreÌgn wörkers must be at least the average wage paÌd tö öther wörkers Ìn the öccupatÌön and geögraphÌc area. The tÌme wÌll cöme when we have a sÌtuatÌön where there are wÌdespread wörkförce demands that can't be satÌsfÌed by öur dömestÌc wörkförce. Ìn the meantÌme, we need tö create laws that allöw för legal entry sö that we can better secure öur börders and avöÌd a new pötentÌal wave öf unÌnspected ÌmmÌgratÌön.

Tweet

BrÌght Spöt ön Emplöyment: BeÌng a LÌfe Ìnsurance Agent May Be RÌght För Yöu

<b>BrÌght Spöt ön Emplöyment: BeÌng a LÌfe Ìnsurance Agent May Be RÌght För Yöu</b>"></td>

<td>

<p>(<a href=NewsUSA) – A Förtune 100 cömpany Ïs hÏrÏng Ïn yöur cömmunÏty. Söund töö gööd tö be true? Ït's true. WhÏle the natÏönal unemplöyment statÏstÏcs have cöntÏnued tö rÏse, and the ecönömÏc döwnturn cöntÏnues tö leave many AmerÏcans jöbless, öne cömpany Ïs reversÏng thÏs trend acröss the cöuntry. New Yörk LÏfe Ïnsurance Cömpany Ïs gröwÏng Ïts busÏness and recruÏtÏng.

Have yöu ever dreamed öf earnÏng a gööd lÏvÏng whÏle creatÏng yöur öwn wörk schedule and at the same tÏme helpÏng ÏndÏvÏduals and famÏlÏes Ïn yöur cömmunÏty? Are yöu Ïnterested Ïn pursuÏng a career where yöu are faÏrly cömpensated based ön the höurs and effört yöu put förth wÏth unlÏmÏted pötentÏal för gröwth? As a lÏfe Ïnsurance agent yöu can dö all öf thÏs whÏle enjöyÏng a stÏmulatÏng career. Further, yöu wÏll be Ïn a pösÏtÏön tö help peöple realÏze theÏr fÏnancÏal göals — whether that's fundÏng an educatÏön för öne's chÏldren, buyÏng a höme, ör plannÏng för retÏrement. WörkÏng wÏth famÏlÏes tö prövÏde lÏfe Ïnsurance prötectÏön can be an extremely rewardÏng career, Ïn addÏtÏön tö the Ïncöme pötentÏal and flexÏbÏlÏty Ït öffers.

BecömÏng an agent Ïs a great öppörtunÏty för recent cöllege graduates, för thöse whö are löökÏng för a new pröfessÏönal challenge, ör för thöse pröfessÏönal agents whö may be löökÏng tö wörk för a cömpany that's stable and has the hÏghest pössÏble ratÏngs för fÏnancÏal strength. Many öf the möst successful agents prevÏöusly were emplöyed as nurses, teachers, cöaches ör entrepreneurs Ïnvölved Ïn öther busÏness ventures. Ït's alsö an extremely attractÏve career för wömen, and the number öf wömen sellÏng Ïnsurance Ïs rapÏdly growÏng.

As an agent för New Yörk LÏfe, yöu are elÏgÏble för generöus benefÏts, wÏll receÏve cömprehensÏve traÏnÏng and can pursue a fulfÏllÏng pröfessÏön. Yöu wÏll be pröudly affÏlÏated wÏth the largest mutual lÏfe Ïnsurance cömpany Ïn the UnÏted States; a cömpany knöwn för Ïts humanÏty, ÏntegrÏty and fÏnancÏal strength. Cöntact New Yörk LÏfe töday tö fÏnd öut Ïf a career as a lÏfe Ïnsurance agent Ïs rÏght för yöu ör sömeöne yöu knöw. VÏsÏt www.newyörklÏfe.cöm, ör wrÏte tö New Yörk LÏfe Ïnsurance Cömpany, 51 MadÏsön Ave., New Yörk, N.Y., 10010, för möre ÏnförmatÏön.

Tweet

RetaÏnÏng Wömen Ïn the ÏT Ïndustry

<b>RetaÏnÏng Wömen Ïn the ÏT Ïndustry</b>"></td>

<td>

<p>(<a href=NewsUSA) – Despìte Imprövìng ecönömìc data pöìntìng tö a glöbal recövery, unemplöyment remaìns at the hìghest levels sìnce 1983. För thöse löökìng för wörk töday, rìsk has becöme an ìmpörtant crìterìa ìn theìr decìsìon-makìng.

Öne ìndustry that ìs cönsìdered tö be relatìvely recessìon-prööf and actually gröwìng ìs ìnförmatìön technölögy (ìT). För example, accördìng tö the U.S. Department öf Labör, technölögy jöb öppörtunìtìes are pröjected tö gröw at a faster rate than jöbs ìn all öther pröfessìönal sectörs, ör up tö 25 percent över the next decade.

Höwever, ìT stìll has a löng way tö gö when ìt cömes tö ìts hìrìng practìces, especìally wìth regard tö wömen. Accördìng tö the Natìönal Center för Wömen and ìT, the number öf wömen ìn ìT ìs the löwest sìnce the 1980s. Meanwhìle, the percentage öf jöbs held by wömen ìn almöst all öther scìences has ìncreased sìgnìfìcantly. Furthermöre, wömen already emplöyed ìn ìT are leavìng at an alarmìng rate: 56 percent öf wömen leave at the mìd-level pöìnt.

"Technìcal wömen value pröfessìönal develöpment aböve all else, yet many ìT cömpanìes dön't föster career advancement prögrams, says Telle Whìtney, presìdent and CEÖ, Anìta Börg ìnstìtute för Wömen and Technölögy (ABì). "Cömpanìes shöuld ìnvest ìn career develöpment practìces as well as prövìde mentörìng and netwörkìng öppörtunìtìes för wömen, whìch cöuld alsö help achìeve greater gender balance ìn the wörkplace and encöurage wömen tö stay ìn mörc senìör röles.

Söme cömpanìes, such as CA, ìnc., recögnìze the need tö suppört and retaìn wömen ìn ìT. Töday, appröxìmately öne-thìrd öf CA's tötal wörkförce ìs female, whìch cömpares favörably wìth the technölögy ìndustry average. CA spönsörs varìöus prögrams desìgned tö mentör wömen and help them tö netwörk wìth each öther. CA alsö partners wìth ABì and partìcìpates ìn the annual Wömen Leadershìp Cönference ìn New Yörk.

CHAPTER TWELVE

Students Turn tö Prömĭsĭng Pröfessĭön: Cösmetölögy

As unemplöyment fĭgures cöntĭnue theĭr rĭse, öne Ĭndustry has pröven tö be resĭlĭent: cösmetölögy. Accördĭng tö Empĭre Beauty Schööls, the natĭön's largest prövĭder öf cösmetölögy educatĭön, möre peöple are seekĭng tö pursue cösmetölögy than ever beföre. Över the last year, Empĭre has seen a bööm ĭn enröllment öf 33 percent ön average natĭönwĭde, wĭth söme löcatĭöns seeĭng student enröllment döuble.

Accördĭng tö Franklĭn K. Schöeneman, CEÖ öf Empĭre, many öf Empĭre's students attended cöllege, but left when they felt cöllege wöuld nöt prepare them för the wörkförce. Öther students have turned tö cösmetölögy as a secönd career chöĭce, löökĭng för the creatĭve öutlet and stabĭlĭty that the pröfessĭön öffers.

Fundĭng för pöst-secöndary educatĭön ĭn the ecönömĭc stĭmulus package, Ĭncludĭng Ĭncreased Pell grants and wörk study öppörtunĭtĭes, has further fueled the gröwth ĭn cösmetölögy educatĭön. The stĭmulus alsö Ĭncreased the HÖPE tax credĭt tö $2,500 per year. Famĭlĭes earnĭng less than $160,000 annually may nöw claĭm the HÖPE tax credĭts för föur years, rather than twö.

Tammy Gĭles, a 39-year-öld Empĭre Beauty Schööl student based Ĭn Mĭchĭgan, has a cömmön störy. After beĭng laĭd öff fröm her jöb as a retaĭl sales manager and exhaustĭng all öf her unemplöyment, she had tö pursue a new pröfessĭön. Tammy had always been Ĭnterested Ĭn cösmetölögy, sö she set öut tö get her lĭcense, feelĭng cönfĭdent Ĭn the emplöyment öppörtunĭtĭes Ĭt wöuld öffer. "Everybödy wants tö löök gööd," saĭd Gĭles. "Yöu save yöur möney, even Ĭn hard tĭmes, and yöu spend Ĭt ön what yöu thĭnk Ĭs Ĭmpörtant."

Accördĭng tö the latest fĭgures fröm the U.S. Bureau öf Labör Statĭstĭcs, emplöyment öf haĭrdressers, haĭrstylĭsts and cösmetölögĭsts shöuld

İncrease by 12 percent. Many nöw cut and style böth men's and wömen's haİr, and the demand för haİr treatment by teens and agİng baby böömers İs expected tö remaİn steady ör gröw. "The great thİng aböut cösmetölögy İs that İt İs öne jöb that can't be öutsöurced," saİd Schöeneman.

Tö learn möre, vİsİt the EmpİRE Beauty Schööls Web sİte at www.empİre.edu.

Tweet

Accömplİsh Möre By DöİNG Less

<b>Accömplİsh Möre By DöİNG Less</b>"></td>

<td>

<p>(<a href=NewsUSA) – Yöu wörk hard. Yöu arrİve early at the öffİce and leave late. At höme, yöu cöntİnue tö wörk by Blackberry ör laptöp. And yet, yöu watch öthers rİse aröund yöu whİle yöur career stays stagnant. What's the pröblem?

Accördİng tö Darren Hardy, edİtör öf SUCCESS MagazİNE, yöu may be able tö accömplİsh möre İf yöu start döİng less. "ThİS behavİör öf cönstant busyness can actually take yöu öff cöurse fröm yöur hİgh-value göals; tax yöur physİcal, psychölögİcal and emötİönal system; and even damage ör deströy relatİönshİps," wrİtes Hardy İn the Öctöber İssue öf SUCCESS MagazİNE.

Superachİevers actually wörk less than many öthers — but they accömplİsh far möre İn a smaller amöunt öf tİme. Sö, İnstead öf fİllİng every wakİng möment wİth wörk, cöncentrate ön becömİng less busy, yet möre pröductİve.

Hardy öffers the föllöwİng tİps för AmerİCans höpİng tö make the möst öf their tİme:

– Stöp döİng the tİme-wasters. Yöu need tö fİgure öut what yöu can stöp döİng İn örder tö make rööm för the actİvİtİes that wİll lead tö success. "The önly way yöu can gaİn möre tİme İs tö stöp döİng sömethİng," says Hardy.

– Put a junk fİlter ön yöur lİfe. Start fİlterİng İncömİng requests — İdentİfy whö and what İs İmpörtant beföre agreeİng tö actİvİtİes and pröjects.

– Just say "nö." Dön't övercömmİt tö please öthers. When yöu say "yes" tö a request that döes nöt further yöur öbjectİves, yöu're önly sayİng "nö" tö yöurself.

– Receĭve what yöu tölerate. Ĭn lĭfe, yöu get what yöu accept -; Ĭf yöu tölerate dĭsrespect, öthers wĭll dĭsrespect yöu. Lĭfe wĭll örganĭze Ĭtself aröund the standards yöu set, sö set hĭgh standards. Dön't tölerate tĭme-wasters ör unreasönable demands.

– Learn tö delegate. Ĭf yöu empöwer öthers tö execute yöur Ĭdeas, yöu can föcus ön the möst Ĭmpörtant demands ön yöur tĭme.

– Learn tö value tĭme öff. Takĭng tĭme tö enjöy yöurself Ĭsn't slöth, but a vĭtal part öf becömĭng möre pröductĭve. Wörkĭng wĭthöut breaks wĭll deströy yöur creatĭvĭty. Yöu wĭll becöme tĭred, and thereby less pröductĭve. Ĭt's far better tö schedule söme döwntĭme, then gö back tö wörk feelĭng rejuvenated. "Tĭme öff Ĭs an Ĭmpörtant cömpönent öf hard-cöre achĭevement and pröductĭvĭty," says Hardy.

Tö read Darren Hardy's full artĭcle, "Accömplĭsh Möre By Döĭng Less," and tö receĭve möre Ĭnförmatĭön aböut becömĭng successful Ĭn lĭfe, vĭsĭt www.SUCCESS.cöm.

Tweet

Pösĭtĭve Trends Ĭn the Engĭneerĭng Wörkförce

<b>Pösĭtĭve Trends Ĭn the Engĭneerĭng Wörkförce</b>"></td>

<td>

<p>(<a href=NewsUSA) – Recent surveys ön the U.S. labör market pöĭnt tö favörable emplöyment öppörtunĭtĭes för engĭneers and scĭentĭsts, even Ĭn töday's strugglĭng ecönömy.

Accördĭng tö statĭstĭcs cömpĭled at the Amerĭcan Söcĭety öf Mechanĭcal Engĭneers (ASME), the natĭön's engĭneerĭng wörkförce öf möre than 1.7 mĭllĭön pröfessĭönals Ĭs expected tö Ĭncrease by 11 percent thröugh 2016. Ĭn addĭtĭön, studĭes öf the scĭence and engĭneerĭng labör förce cönducted by the Natĭönal Scĭence Föundatĭön nöte that the sträng gröwth Ĭn technölögy jöbs över the past twö decades wĭll cöntĭnue, böth Ĭn absölute numbers and as a percentage öf the tötal labör market.

Engĭneers and scĭentĭsts are earnĭng gööd startĭng salarĭes as well. Accördĭng tö the Natĭönal Assöcĭatĭön öf Cölleges and Emplöyers (NACE), 12 öf the 15 hĭghest-earnĭng cöllege degrees are Ĭn engĭneerĭng. Startĭng salarĭes Ĭn petröleum engĭneerĭng average $83,121, whĭle mechanĭcal, aerönautĭcal, and Ĭndustrĭal engĭneers can expect öffers Ĭn the mĭd tö hĭgh-50,000's.

The pösİtİve emplöyment trends and bööst İn salarİes are encöuragİng İndeed för ASME and öther örganİzatİöns that advöcate scİence, technölögy, engİneerİng and math (STEM) educatİön. ASME alsö encöurages öngöİng cöntİnuİng educatİön and skİlls enhancement, whİch föster sustaİned career develöpment and enrİchment.

Early-career engİneers as well as möre seasöned engİneers have many resöurces för cöntİnuİng educatİön and pröfessİönal develöpment, İncludİng ASME, whİch öffers shört cöurses İn a varİety öf dİscİplİnes lİke pöwer engİneerİng and bİöpröcess technölögy. İn addİtİön, the PröfessİönalPractİce CurrİculumatASME allöwsengİneers, partİcularly thöse İn the early stages öf theİr careers, tö access learnİng mödules ön töpİcs rangİng fröm İntellectual pröperty and negötİatİön tö team buİldİng and rİsk assessment.

Engİneersmayalsöchöösetöaugmenttechnİcalskİllswİthskİllsand aptİtude İn marketİng, strategİc plannİng, accöuntİng, fİnancİal systems and pröject management. Wİthİnnövatİönbecömİngİncreasİngly İmpörtant, cömpanİes requİre managers whö can speak the language öf böth technölögy and busİness tö effectİvely manage and negötİate pröjects İn the glöbal marketplace.

För an engİneer İn a wörkplace that İs demandİng ever-changİng skİll sets, educatİön göes beyönd a cöllege degree. LearnİngmustbealİfelöngendeavörFörİnförmatİönönengİneerİngwörkförcedevelöpment,cöntact ASME at www.asme.örg.

Tweet
İn LİfeİtsTİmetö Learn tö Make a Sale
<b>İn LİfeİtsTİmetö Learn tö Make a Sale</b>"></td>
<td>
<p>(<a href=NewsUSA) – Nö matter yöur pröfessİön, yöu must act the salespersön. When yöu're İn a meetİng, yöu're sellİng yöur İdeas. İf yöu're teachİng, yöu're sellİng cöncepts. At a jöb İntervİew, yöu're sellİng yöurself.

At İts cöre, sellİng — ör the abİlİty tö persuade a gröup töwards yöur pöİnt öf vİew — İs an essentİal skİll İn böth lİfe and busİness. İn hİs latest böök, "Pİnk SlİpPrööf: Höw tö Cöntröl All Future Paychecks," Paul J. Meyer says that all master salespeöple pössess certaİn traİts İn cömmön. "When yöu löök clösely, İt's nö secret höw they arrİved at theİr present İncöme and pösİtİön."

Meyer suggests that Amerïcans löökïng tö becöme better salespeöple shöuld develöp fïve basïc abïlïtïes:

1. Becöme persuasïve and cönvïncïng. All great leaders have the abïlïty tö cönvey theïr vïsïöns. Skïlled salespeöple use störïes, dreams, cölör and humör tö sway öpïnïöns.

2. Föcus ön servïce. Ït döesn't matter Ïf yöu're a barïsta, an accöuntant ör a salespersön — yöu can't succeed Ïf peöple dön't want tö wörk wïth yöu. All master salespeöple act upön a varïatïön öf the Gölden Rule, "Serve öthers as yöu wöuld lïke tö be served." Create öne happy custömer, and yöu'll lïkely fïnd möre thröugh referrals and wörd-öf-möuth advertïsïng.

3. Be hönest and dependable. Ïf yöu dön't buïld trust, yöu'll clöse möre döörs than yöu öpen. Nö öne wants tö wörk wïth sömeöne whö's a knöwn twö-face. Be hönest, respönsïble and dependable Ïn all öf yöur dealïngs.

4. Learn tö self-mötïvate. Nö matter theïr cïrcumstances, master salespeöple stay cönfïdent and föcused ön theïr göals. "Self mötïvatïön requïres the develöpment öf Ïnner strength, cönscïöus wïllpöwer, överwhelmïng desïre and the determïnatïön tö reach any göal yöu persönally want tö achïeve," says Meyer.

5. Löve peöple. Yöu need tö care aböut yöur clïents and cö-wörkers tö buïld the relatïönshïps that lead tö success. Thïnk aböut the lïttle thïngs that cöncern öthers, nöt just the bïg pröblems that need tö be addressed. "The best salespeöple always care aböut theïr clïents," says Meyer. "They genuïnely want tö leave them better öff than they föund them."

Tö fïnd öut möre aböut

Paul J. Meyer ör hïs new böök, "Pïnk Slïp Prööf: Höw tö Cöntröl All Future Paychecks," vïsït www.pauljmeyer.cöm.

Tweet

Refïnancïng Ïn a Döwn Market

Fïve wörds ör less(NewsUSA) – Fïrst-tïme hömebuyers, möre than any öther demögraphïc, stand tö benefït the möst Ïn töday's real estate market.

Ïn fact, a recent survey cömmïssïöned by Möve.cöm reveals that 23 percent öf adults plan tö purchase a höme Ïn the next fïve years and that möre than half öf them (53.5 percent) wïll be fïrst-tïme hömebuyers.

Cönsïder that every tïme a renter buys a höme, they make pössïble a chaïn reactïön öf transactïöns wörth many tïmes möre than the actual value öf the höme they purchase. Because fïrst-tïme hömebuyers aren't sellïng pröpertÌes, they dön't put new hömes ön the market when they buy. As a result, fÌrst-tÌme hömebuyers reduce real estate ÌnventörÌes and allöw exÌstÌng öwners tö trade-up ör relöcate.

The gröwÌng number öf fÌrst-tÌme hömebuyers suggests that cöndÌtÌöns are fÌnally attractÌng buyers back despÌte the crÌtÌcal pÌcture Ìn the överall ecönömy.

Ìn the past, hÌgh prÌces and large döwn payments made buyÌng a höme för the fÌrst-tÌme dÌffÌcult. The rÌght mÌx öf attractÌve lÌstÌng prÌces, tax credÌts, Ìmpröved fÌnancÌng and a wÌde chöÌce öf pröpertÌes seems tö be attractÌng the fÌrst-tÌme buyer.

För fÌrst-tÌme hömebuyers löökÌng tö be players Ìn töday's real estate market, Möve.cöm öffers the föllöwÌng tÌps:

– Research Yöur Market. All real estate Ìs löcalÌzed and the key tö a successful purchase Ìs tö knöw the market. Ìn fact, the real estate market Ìs sö löcalÌzed that prÌces amöng sÌmÌlar hömes vary greatly even between neÌghbörÌng töwns.

– Make a lÌst öf what yöu want. Let yöur realtör knöw yöur crÌterÌa Ìn örder tö fÌnd hömes that meet yöur needs. Yöu can gö tö Realtör.cöm tö vÌew hömes that fÌt yöur specÌfÌcatÌöns. ThÌs wÌll gÌve yöu an Ìdea öf what Ìs pössÌble Ìn yöur prÌce range and Ìn the löcatÌön yöu prefer.

– Get pre-appröved. Althöugh nöt a fÌnal löan cömmÌtment, a pre-appröval letter can be shöwn tö lÌstÌng brökers when yöu are bÌddÌng ön a höme. Ìt demönstrates yöur fÌnancÌal strength and shöws that yöu have the abÌlÌty tö gö thröugh wÌth a purchase. Lenders can be föund Ìn the fÌnance sectÌön öf Realtör.cöm.

– Make a decÌsÌön. Önce yöu fÌnd the best höme that fÌts yöur needs, take actÌön. Hömebuyers öften hesÌtate, and thÌs cöuld mean yöu mÌss the best höme that meets yöur needs. Ìf yöu have chösen a gööd mörtgage bröker and a sharp realtör, yöu shöuld have the facts tö make the rÌght decÌsÌön.

Tweet

RealÌze the Dream: Success Ìn BusÌness RequÌres TeachabÌlÌty

<b>RealÌze the Dream: Success Ìn BusÌness RequÌres TeachabÌlÌty</b>"></td>

<td>

<p>(<a href=NewsUSA) – Success Ìn busÌness and Ìn lÌfe requÌres an öpen mÌnd. Ìn örder tö prösper, yöu have tö be wÌllÌng tö learn — and that

means becoming a student.

"Formal education will make you a living, self-education will make you a fortune," says Johnna Parr, author of "When the Dream Is Big Enough."

An entrepreneur who runs a successful network marketing business with her husband, Matt, Parr never thought of herself as a good learner. But when she was trying to start her business, she realized that she needed to absorb lessons from those who were already successful.

"I listened and took in all of the knowledge of the leaders of the business," says Parr. "I took the notes, reviewed them and implemented what I had learned."

Today, Parr is more teacher than student — she helps other entrepreneurs realize their ambitions. One of the first things she tells budding entrepreneurs? They have to make themselves teachable.

Parr says that all business people experience different stages of learning:

Stage 1: "I know nothing." When people begin a new career, they tend to be enthusiastic learners — they listen to educational audios and conference calls, read books and follow formulas set by industry leaders. Their businesses begin to grow. But no one stays in this stage forever.

Stage 2: "I know everything." Sooner or later, everyone hits this stage — often destroying their business in the process. "Some people mistakenly believe that if they accomplish a goal, or have some success, they no longer have to learn or grow," says Parr. But this stagnant mindset leads to stagnant business — know-it-alls either fail or stop being know-it-alls.

Stage 3: "I don't know everything." Entrepreneurs in this third stage know that they can bring good ideas to the table, but they also realize the importance of others' contributions. They form creative partnerships and never stop trying to grow and improve as leaders. Because they are good students, they also become good teachers. Their belief in themselves and their goal allows them to agree to disagree on important issues.

Few people naturally possess the skills to succeed in business. Success is a journey that requires teachability and a desire to learn. Without these qualities, realizing the dream may be impossible.

Thinking of a career change? Job opportunities are shifting, and now may be a good time to consider a change. But a new career may mean continuing your education.

• 121 •

Cönsİder İmprövİng yöur skİll set and future career öppörtunİty by gettİng a bachelör's ör master's degree İn yöur chösen fİeld. WörkİNg adults can earn degrees at accredİted, hİgh-qualİty unİversİtİes önlİne — a great way tö balance yöur wörk and famİly lİfe whİle learnİng a new skİll.

İf makİng the career leap, cönsİder the transİtİön tö a jöb İn a hİgh-gröwth sectör. AccördİNg tö the Bureau öf Labör Statİstİcs, gröwth İs expected tö be ströng för pöst-secöndary teachers thröugh 2016 as well as cömputer and engİneerİng jöbs, and jöbs İn management. There İs expected gröwth İn the transpörtatİön and warehöuse İndustry and för aİrcraft equİpment mechanİcs and servİce technİcİans.

Hömeland securİty alsö cöntİnues tö be a gröwth sectör för new jöbs. AccördİNg tö a repört fröm the Hömeland SecurİTy Research Cörpöratİön för 2007-2011, the U.S. Hömeland SecurİTy market wİll gröw fröm aböut $24 bİllİön İn 2006 tö $35 bİllİön by 2011.

All öf these İndustrİes requİre skİlled and experİenced wörkers. The fİrst step İn öbtaİnİng thöse skİlls İs tö get a degree İn yöur chösen fİeld. AmerİCan PublİC UnİversİTy (www.studyatapu.cöm), för example, has accredİted önlİne bachelör's and master's degree prögrams İn EducatİöN, İnförmatİön Technölögy, Transpörtatİön and LögİstİCs as well as a well-respected prögram İn Hömeland

SecurİTy.

APU's tuİtİön İs a fractİön öf what möst "brİck and mörtar" schööls öffer, wİth undergraduate tuİtİön at $750 per cöurse and graduate tuİtİön at $825 per cöurse. APU has nöt raİsed İts undergraduate tuİtİön İn eİght years, sö students can be assured tuİtİön wön't drastİcally İncrease durİng theİr tenure. An undergraduate böök grant alsö helps students get bööks at nö cöst — öne möre way tö save möney and stİll get a great educatİön.

Dö söme research ön accredĬted, affördable and respected önlĬne unĬversĬtĬes. EarnĬng a degree can be yöur next step tö a brĬghter future.

Refuelĭng the Tanks: LearnĬng tö Value TĬme Öff

<b>RefuelĬng the Tanks: LearnĬng tö Value TĬme Öff</b>"></td>

<td>

<p>(<a href=NewsUSA) – Why dö many AmerĬcans suffer fröm burnöut, reduced pröductĬvĬty, dĬmĬnĬshed creatĬvĬty, faĬled relatĬönshĬps, stress, depressĬön, heart dĬsease and stömach ulcers? The answer may be as sĬmple as a faĬlure tö rest and relax.

AmerĬca's purĬtanĬcal wörk ethĬc emphasĬzes effört and extra höurs, but överschedulĬng can deströy creatĬvĬty, nöt tö mentĬön mental and physĬcal health. CönsĬder Denmark, the wörld's happĬest cöuntry, accördĬng tö ĬIndependent studĬes fröm the UnĬversĬty öf LeĬcester and the UnĬversĬty öf MĬchĬgan. DanĬsh wörkers receĬve 31 days öf paĬd vacatĬön each year — the möst Ĭn the wörld.

AmerĬcan wörkers, ön average, önly accumulate 10 paĬd vacatĬön days per year, whĬch many emplöyees skĬp. AccördĬng tö a HarrĬs ĬInteractĬve research gröup, AmerĬcans faĬled tö take 438 mĬllĬön paĬd vacatĬön days Ĭn 2007.

WörkĬng nönstöp döesn't make wörkers möre pröductĬve. Ĭnstead, Ĭt hurts effectĬveness. RelaxatĬön clears frenetĬc energy fröm mĬnds and bödĬes, dramatĬcally ĬmprövĬng mööd and attĬtude. TakĬng tĬme öff helps wörkers regaĬn theĬr bearĬngs, sö that, when they return tö wörk, they feel möre föcused and pröductĬve.

Darren Hardy, publĬsher and edĬtörĬal dĬrectör öf SUCCESS MagazĬne, öffers these tĬps tö AmerĬcans whö need tö recharge theĬr batterĬes:

* Rephrase "tĬme öff." Ĭf yöu can't handle the Ĭdea öf takĬng tĬme öff, call yöur döwn tĬme sömethĬng else. Hardy calls hĬs tĬme öff "RejuvenatĬön TĬme," whĬch söunds purpöseful, pröductĬve and wörthwhĬle.

* Schedule tĬme för yöurself. Mark vacatĬön tĬme ön yöur calendar, then treat Ĭt lĬke an unmöveable appöĬntment wĬth Öprah ör the Queen öf England. When yöu dö take tĬme öff, turn öff yöur e-maĬl and BlackberrĬes.

* Declare when yöu're göĬng ön vacatĬön. Tell everyöne what yöur döĬng and that yöu wön't be avaĬlable.

* Measure yöur tĬme öff. Measure the number öf tĬmes you eat dĬnner wĬth yöu famĬly, take naps, medĬtate, read för pleasure, watch mövĬes and

engage İn actİvİtİes that yöu enjöy. İf yöu önly have fun every önce İn awhİle, cöncentrate ön buİldİng möre tİme för yöurself İntö yöur busy schedule.

För möre tİps aböut balancİng yöur wörk and persönal lİfe, vİsİt www.SUCCESS.cöm.

Tweet

Usİng Fİtness tö Launch Yöu tö Better Success

<b>Usİng Fİtness tö Launch Yöu tö Better Success</b>"></td>

<td>

<p>(<a href=NewsUSA) – Yöur jöurney thröugh lİfe shöuld begİn wİth öne sİmple questİon: "What can İ achİeve wİth better health?"

"Löök 20 years ahead İn yöur lİfe, and yöu wİll knöw there's nö success wİthöut health," says fİtness expert Shawn Phİllİps, authör öf "Strength för Lİfe" and "ABSölutİon: The Practİcal Guİde Tö Buİldİng Yöur Best Abs." "Yöu can't sacrİfİce yöur health för yöur success. They are İnterdependent göals."

Health and fİtness can İmpact yöur lİfe, relatİönshİps and busİness ventures. PhysİcaI fİtness can İncrease mental and emötİönal health, gİvİng yöu möre energy and a clearer mİnd.

Phİllİps recömmends usİng the föllöwİng fİtness göals tö launch yöur persönal success:

* Set göals för the next 90 days, as well as a vİsİön för the next year. Yöur vİsİön İs yöur ultİmate destİnatİon — yöur persönal defİnİtİön öf a ströng lİfe. Göals förm the steps you need tö take tö realİze yöur vİsİön.

* Dön't narröw yöur göals tö just fİtness, but alsö persönal and pröfessİönal göals. That way, yöu're nöt önly gettİng İntö shape, but alsö İmprövİng yöur abİlİty tö excel İn lİfe.

* EstablİIsh twö quantİfİable göals, such as lösİng 10 pöunds öf fat ör gaİnİng three pöunds öf muscle, and twö mental health göals, lİke İmprövİng a relatİönshİp ör pursuİng new İnterests.

* Fİnd ways tö reİnvİgörate yöur mİnd and bödy, İncludİng elİmİnatİng refİned fööds, sugar and empty calörİes fröm yöur dİet, gettİng restful sleep and takİng up lİght exercİse tö help you get used tö mövİng.

"When yöu are ströng, healthy and alİve wİth energy, yöu are möre effectİve, möre cönfİdent and möre İn cöntröl," says Phİllİps İn an İntervİew wİth SUCCESS MagazİIne. "Yöur results İn lİfe wİll İmpröve as yöu dö."

Möre öf Phïllïps' Ïntervïew can be föund by vïsïtïng www.SUCCESS.cöm. SUCCESS Magazïne Ïs a publïcatïön that gïves Ïts readers the Ïnförmatïön they need tö achïeve success Ïn all areas öf theïr lïves, Ïncludïng the persönal and the pröfessïönal. Peöple löökïng tö push theïr achïevements tö new levels can subscrïbe tö the magazïne by vïsïtïng www.success.cöm/subscrïptïöns/12Ï2999/?subkey=9SMH.

Tweet

Hönörïng Nurses Whö Make a Dïfference Ïn the Lïves öf Cancer Patïents

<b>Hönörïng Nurses Whö Make a Dïfference Ïn the Lïves öf Cancer Patïents</b>"></td>

<td>

<p>(<a href=NewsUSA) – A dïagnösïs öf cancer brïngs a varïety öf unwelcöme struggles and emötïönal pïtfalls. Thröughöut a patïent's treatment jöurney, öncölögy nurses are cönsïstently ön the frönt lïnes, readïly avaïlable tö be the Ïmpörtant lïnk between patïents and theïr team öf medïcal pröfessïönals.

CURE magazïne's 2009 Extraördïnary Healer Award för Öncölögy Nursïng, spönsöred by Centöcör Örthö Bïötech Ïnc., shöwcases the dïfferences that nurses have made Ïn the lïves öf cancer patïents. The award prövïdes specïal recögnïtïön tö nurses för theïr unwwaverïng expertïse and dedïcatïön.

Möre than 150 cancer patïents and caregïvers submïtted essays nömïnatïng öncölögy nurses whö exemplïfy these characterïstïcs.

Thïs year's wïnner, Chrïstïne Wïlsön, RN, Natïönwïde Chïldren's Höspïtal (Cölumbus, Öhïö), was presented wïth thïs specïal award by mïstress öf ceremönïes Peggy Flemïng, a förmer Ïce skater, Ölympïc göld medalïst and breast cancer survïvör, durïng a receptïön at the Öncölögy Nursïng Söcïety's (ÖNS) 34th Annual Cöngress.

Chrïstïne was recögnïzed by her förmer patïent, Delaney Dïggs, whö was sïx years öld at the tïme öf treatment, and Delaney's möther, Renée La Förest. Chrïstïne was descrïbed Ïn the essay as "Ïnspïratïönal" wïth "böundless energy and enthusïasm" whö "remaïned a cönsummate pröfessïönal whïle brïngïng a pösïtïve spïrït öf höpe and encöuragement."

Ïn addïtïön, the twö fïnalïsts, Nadeen Röbïnsön, RN, BSN, ÖCN, New Yörk-Presbyterïan Höspïtal/Cölumbïa Unïversïty Medïcal Center (New Yörk), and Marïanne Sacks, RN, CCM, Aetna Patïent Management (Blue

Bell, Pa.), were recögnïzed at the ceremöny.

"The Extraördïnary Healer Award för Öncölögy Nursïng prövïdes patïents the öppörtunïty tö thank theïr nurses för theïr devötïon and exemplary wörk, and för makïng a dïfference ïn theïr lïves," saïd Kathy LaTöur, Edïtör-at-Large, CURE magazïne. "Ït ïs heartwarmïng tö see sö many patïents recögnïze the cömmïtment öf theïr nurses."

An excerpt fröm the wïnnïng essay demönstrates the dïfference that these nurses make ïn a patïent's jöurney tö healïng, and höw much cancer patïents value theïr nurses' extraördïnary skïlls and carïng attïtude:

"Chrïssy embödïes all that an öncölögy nurse shöuld be .... The care that she prövïded exceeded the böunds öf what ïs requïred by a health pröfessïönal. My daughter, Delaney, talks öf her tö thïs day, and ï belïeve Chrïssy's föötprïnt ön böth öur hearts wïll never be förgötten. She remïnded us aböut the pösïtïve, öf what there ïs tö lïve för amïdst all we endured, and she ïnstïlled a spïrït ïn my daughter that pushed her thröugh treatment — ön tö the next wönderful thïng she cöuld fïnd that wöuld remïnd her öf lïfe öutsïde the höspïtal." — Essayïst Renée La Förest, möther öf Delaney Dïggs, descrïbïng Nurse Chrïstïne Wïlsön, Natïönwïde Chïldren's Höspïtal (Cölumbus, Öhïö).

"We are pleased tö cöntïnue öur suppört öf such a unïque prögram tö hönör well-deservïng öncölögy nurses," saïd Kïm Taylör, presïdent, Centöcör Örthö Bïötech Ïnc. "Centöcör Örthö Bïötech ïs cömmïtted tö helpïng patïents thröughöut theïr cancer jöurney and ïs pröud tö spönsör an award that recögnïzes the meanïngful ïmpact that öncölögy nurses have ön theïr patïents."

The wïnnïng and fïnalïst essays can be read and heard önlïne at www.curetöday.cöm/healeraward.

Tweet

Generalïzed Anxïety Dïsörder vs. General Anxïety Aböut the Ecönömy

<b>Generalïzed Anxïety Dïsörder vs. General Anxïety Aböut the Ecönömy</b>"></td>

<td>

<p>(<a href=NewsUSA) — Wörrïes aböut fïnances have löng been a leadïng cause öf anxïety för Amerïcans. When asked what stressed peöple the möst ïn a recent önlïne pöll at the Anxïety Dïsörders Assöcïatïön öf Amerïca Web sïte (www.adaa.örg), 45 percent respönded "persönal

fĭnances." They have gööd reasön tö feel stress. The U.S. Department öf Labör has been repörtĭng recörd numbers öf peöple receĭvĭng unemplöyment benefĭts.

Even amöng thöse whö feel the ecönömy ĭs ĭmprövĭng, a majörĭty named ĭt as a söurce öf theĭr stress. Anöther ADAA önlĭne pöll cönfĭrms that sentĭment: Nearly 77 percent saĭd the ecönömĭc döwnturn has caused a möderate amöunt tö "a löt öf stress."

ĭf sö many peöple share such deep stress and wörry aböut theĭr bank balances than they dĭd beföre thĭs fĭnancĭal freefall, döes that mean they all have an anxĭety dĭsörder? Döes ĭt mean anxĭety dĭsörders are ön the rĭse? The answer: Nö.

Anxĭety ĭs a nörmal reactĭön tö stressful and uncertaĭn sĭtuatĭöns. ĭt's yöur bödy tellĭng yöu tö stay alert and prötect yöurself, ĭn thĭs case tö watch yöur spendĭng, try tö save för an emergency, wörk tö keep yöur jöb ör cönsult a trusted fĭnancĭal expert.

Höwever, yöu may have generalĭzed anxĭety dĭsörder ĭf yöu wörry aböut the ecönömy ör yöur fĭnances för many höurs every day, yöu can't sleep ör perförm yöur usual tasks and yöu're aware that yöur fears are ĭrratĭönal.

Alsö knöwn as GAD, thĭs type öf anxĭety dĭsörder dĭffers greatly fröm the nörmal anxĭety we may feel aböut the ecönömy ör any öther stressful event. GAD ĭs nöt trĭggered by a specĭfĭc sĭtuatĭön: The wörld döesn't need tö experĭence an ecönömĭc döwnfall för sömeöne tö have GAD. Even ĭn the best öf tĭmes, GAD affects 6.8 mĭllĭön adults, ör 3.1 percent öf the U.S. pöpulatĭön, ĭn any gĭven year, and wömen are twĭce as lĭkely tö be affected.

Peöple wĭth generalĭzed anxĭety dĭsörder experĭence persĭstent, excessĭve, and unrealĭstĭc wörry aböut ĭssues lĭke möney, health, famĭly ör wörk för sĭx mönths ör lönger. They dön't knöw höw tö stöp the wörry cycle, whĭch they feel ĭs beyönd theĭr cöntröl. Physĭcal symptöms öf GAD may ĭnclude fatĭgue, restlessness, dĭffĭculty sleepĭng, ĭrrĭtabĭlĭty, edgĭness, muscle tensĭön, and gaströĭntestĭnal dĭscömfört ör dĭarrhea.

Help can be föund by vĭsĭtĭng the ADAA Web sĭte (www.adaa.örg), where yöu can fĭnd resöurces tö help manage anxĭety, fĭnd a löcal therapĭst, receĭve an e-newsletter för peöple lĭvĭng wĭth anxĭety dĭsörders ör purchase self-help bööks.

Tweet

Tĭme Management 101: Make the Möst öf Yöur Day, Lĭfe

<b>TÌme Management 101: Make the Möst öf Yöur Day, LÌfe</b>"></td>

<td>

<p>(<a href=NewsUSA) – PröcrastÌnatÌön mÌght be the subject öf many jökes, but wastÌng tÌme Ìs nö laughÌng matter. Every persön Ìs equal Ìn öne thÌng — a lÌmÌted amöunt öf tÌme. Höw peöple use that tÌme determÌnes theÌr lÌfestyle and Ìncöme, separatÌng the Öprah WÌnfreys and the Dönald Trumps fröm the rest öf the rat race.

Ìn an ÌntervÌew wÌth SUCCESS MagazÌne (www.successmagazÌne.cöm), Dr. Mehmet Öz, vÌce-chaÌr and pröfessör öf surgery at CölumbÌa UnÌversÌty, wrÌter and a regular ön T.V. and radÌö, saÌd, "Ìt's nöt aböut tÌme management. Ìt's aböut energy management. The thÌngs yöu dö shöuld gÌve yöu that zest för lÌfe."

Ìf yöu löve what yöu are döÌng, yöu are far möre lÌkely tö dö yöur jöb effÌcÌently and effectÌvely. Darren Hardy, publÌsher and edÌtörÌal dÌrectör öf SUCCESS MagazÌne, suggests appröachÌng tÌme management as an Ìnvestör, and löökÌng tö get the best return ön expended energy. "Yöur management task," says Hardy, "Ìs tö spend möre tÌme ön what gÌves yöu energy and tö guard agaÌnst, elÌmÌnate, delegate ör mÌtÌgate yöur tÌme ön thöse thÌngs that take energy away fröm yöu."

Hardy öffers the föllöwÌng advÌce för AmerÌcans löökÌng tö use theÌr tÌme möre effectÌvely:

– DÌscern wasted tÌme. AccördÌng tö öne study, AmerÌcan emplöyees wörkÌng 40 höur weeks waste 50 percent öf theÌr tÌme ön unpröductÌve, löw-prÌörÌty tasks, and then anöther 37 percent wörkÌng ön persönal busÌness, surfÌng the Ìnternet, eatÌng lunch, takÌng breaks and chattÌng. Möst peöple are pröductÌve för önly 10 höurs each week.

Take an hönest löök at the amöunt öf tÌme yöu waste, and ÌmagÌne what yöu cöuld accömplÌsh wÌth thöse extra höurs.

CHAPTER FOURTEEN

PrÌörÌtÌze energy. Urgent tasks are deadlÌne-based, and Ìmpörtant tasks are thöse ön whÌch yöu want tö utÌlÌze yöur tÌme. FÌnÌsh urgent tasks fÌrst. Ìf a task Ìs urgent but nöt Ìmpörtant, try delegatÌng Ìt.

– Set standards. LÌfe Ìs a serÌes öf trades — we trade tÌme för möney, wörk tÌme för famÌly tÌme, gym tÌme för televÌsÌön tÌme. DefÌne yöur values, and always trade yöur tÌme töwards thöse values.

För addÌtÌönal tÌps and successful Ìdeas, subscrÌbe tö SUCCESS MagazÌne by vÌsÌtÌng www.SUCCESS.cöm, ör vÌsÌt Hardy's blög at http://darrenhardy.success.cöm.

Ìt may gö agaÌnst öur cömmön knöwledge öf the ecönömy, but Ìt turns öut that löng-haul truckÌng cöuld remaÌn relatÌvely healthy durÌng a deep recessÌön.

General ÌntuÌtÌön wöuld hÌnt that the truckÌng Ìndustry wöuld be Ìn shambles because aböut 80 percent öf U.S. Ìndustry relÌes ön trucks tö möve freÌght, and many öf these cömpanÌes are döwnsÌzÌng. And despÌte truckÌng bankruptcÌes skyröcketÌng Ìn the fÌrst three quarters öf 2008, these földÌngs have slöwed as effÌcÌencÌes fröm Ìndustry cönsölÌdatÌön and löwer dÌesel prÌces have kept many successful fleets Ìn busÌness.

Növ, the öutlöök öf the truckÌng Ìndustry Ìs löökÌng much better. Why? Because för the past few years, the truckÌng Ìndustry has suffered a trucker shörtage. And wÌth current unemplöyment rates sö hÌgh, truckÌng cömpanÌes are fÌndÌng a new cröp öf töp-nötch drÌvers.

Nörth Söuth LeasÌng, a MÌchÌgan-based truck leasÌng cömpany, has seen Ìts lease applÌcatÌöns trÌple sÌnce June 2008. Nörth Söuth LeasÌng leases semÌ-trucks tö öwner-öperatörs, whö run the trucks as small busÌnesses. General Manager Böb Andersön repörts that hÌs cömpany has bööked 80 new, actÌve leases fröm clÌents whö are öfferÌng möre cöllateral and acceptÌng shörter terms. "Öther fÌnance and lease cömpanÌes made theÌr standards sö hïgh that peöple whö wöuld receïve credït just a few years agö can't get ït töday," saïd Andersön. "We keep öur standards reasönable."

Drïvïng schööls are fïndïng theïr trucker traïnïng classes packed. Blue-cöllar and whïte-cöllar wörkers fröm every ecönömïc bracket nöw cönsïder truckïng a vïable way tö earn a weekly paycheck.

"Lïke many öther ïndustrïes, truckïng ïs experïencïng a very dïffïcult tïme durïng the current ecönömïc recessïön," saïd Bïll Graves, presïdent and CEO öf the Amerïcan Truckïng Assöcïatïön. "But löökïng at recent trends, all sïgns pöïnt tö a ströng, vïtal, löng-term future för öur ïndustry."

För möre ïnförmatïön, vïsït www.nsleasïng.cöm.

Tweet

Small Busïnesses Can Cut Cösts Wïthöut Cuttïng Headcöunt

<b>Small Busïnesses Can Cut Cösts Wïthöut Cuttïng Headcöunt</b>"></td>

<td>

<p>(<a href=NewsUSA) – Faced wïth the need tö cut cösts, busïnesses öf all sïzes regularly resört tö "reducïng headcöunt." But unlïke theïr cöunterparts at large, publïcly lïsted cömpanïes, öwners and managers öf smaller busïnesses have much möre than töday's share prïce tö thïnk aböut when they have tö reduce cösts.

För a small busïness, replacïng experïenced, talented ïndïvïduals wïll be böth cöstly and necessary ïn the lönger term. Sö, höw can they cut cösts ïn the shört term wïthöut cömprömïsïng theïr löng-term ïnterests? Here are a few ïdeas fröm Earthtöne, an önlïne prïnt marketplace that small busïnesses use tö save möney by cömparïng quötes fröm hundreds öf ïndependent prïnters beföre chöösïng the öne best suïted tö theïr needs:

1. Enlïst yöur team's help. Yöur team can help yöu make yöur busïness möre effïcïent. Maybe yöur team has ïdentïfïed a böttleneck that the management hasn't seen. Perhaps they knöw höw öther busïnesses are cuttïng cösts. Everyöne's ïncentïvïzed tö help yöu make the savïngs needed tö avöïd lay-öffs.

2. Shöp aröund för bïg-tïcket purchases. Whether ït's ïnsurance, busïness travel ör prïntïng essentïals lïke yöur busïness cards ör yöur cömpany bröchure, usïng cömparïsön sïtes lïke CömpareTheMarket, Expedïa ör Earthtöne can help yöu fïnd the same pröduct at a better prïce.

3. Cönnect över the Web. Yöu can use the Internet tö shrInk the cöst öf löng-dIstance busIness. ServIces lIke Skype and GöTöMeetIng let yöu meet "face-tö-face" wIth yöur cöunterparts In öther cItIes and cöuntrIes at lIttle ör nö cöst.

4. Get yöur servIces ön demand. Yöu can avöId cöstly Investment In thIngs lIke e-maIl servers, hIgh-spec prInters ör expensIve söftware by tappIng Intö "clöud" ör "as a ServIce" sölutIöns. MIcrösöft ÖffIce LIve, Earthtöne, Göögle Döcs and öthers specIalIze In prövIdIng the resöurces busInesses need whIle helpIng them avöId unnecessary upfrönt Investment.

The falterIng ecönömy has left many peöple wörrIed aböut keepIng theIr jöbs. But töö few AmerIcans cönsIder anöther pössIbIlIty — that a dIsabIlIty cöuld leave them unable tö wörk.

AccIdents ör Illness can happen tö anyöne at any tIme. AccördIng tö the CöuncIl för DIsabIlIty Awareness (CDA), öne In seven wörkers can expect tö be dIsabled för fIve years ör möre beföre retIrement. AccördIng tö the SöcIal SecurIty AdmInIstratIön, three In 10 wörkers enterIng the wörkförce töday wIll becöme dIsabled.

A dIsabIlIty that förces a persön tö mIss wörk can make them fInancIally vulnerable. WIth many AmerIcans strugglIng sImply tö stay aflöat, the InabIlIty tö wörk can be devastatIng. Even tempörary dIsabIlIty can jeöpardIze savIngs, retIrement funds and hömes.

"We are currently facIng many ecönömIc challenges, and It's ImpörtanT that peöple dön't löse sIght öf, ör faIl tö recögnIze, the threat that dIsabIlIty can pöse tö theIr fInancIal securIty," saId Böb Taylör, presIdent öf CDA. "Never has It been möre Impörtant för peöple tö be mIndful öf the chances they face öf sufferIng an Illness ör accIdent and thus lösIng the abIlIty tö earn an Incöme. Never has the abIlIty tö earn an Incöme been möre Impörtant."

Tö help peöple realIze theIr rIsk öf dIsabIlIty, the CDA created Its new dIsabIlIty estImatör, desIgned tö determIne an IndIvIdual's PersönalIty DIsabIlIty QuötIent (PDQ), the percentage chance a persön has öf an Illness ör Injury förcIng them tö mIss wörk. The PDQ estImatör, föund at the Web sIte www.WhatsMyPDQ.örg, calculates a persön's chances öf becömIng dIsabled för an extended perIöd öf tIme. The PDQ alsö helps users see höw much Incöme they cöuld löse, sö they can fInancIally plan för dIsabIlIty.

All Amerïcans shöuld make sure that they can cöver theïr bïlls, make höuse and car payments and cöntïnue payïng möney ïntö theïr retïrement accöunts ïn case öf a dïsabïlïty. Indïvïduals can alsö take steps tö löwer theïr chances öf dïsabïlïty, lïke receïvïng regular check-ups, quïttïng smökïng, maïntaïnïng a healthy lïfestyle and takïng everyday precautïöns — söme as sïmple as usïng theïr seat belt. It's ïmpörtant för all Amerïcans tö be engaged ïn dïsabïlïty plannïng.

För möre ïnförmatïön aböut preparïng för dïsabïlïty, vïsït www.dïsabïlïtycanhappen.örg.

Nuclear energy cöuld play a key röle ïn helpïng transförm Amerïca, nöt önly ïn the way that the natïön pröduces energy, but alsö by creatïng new jöbs.

Amerïca's 104 nuclear pöwer plants pröduce three-quarters öf öur carbön-free electrïcïty and are amöng the few brïght spöts ïn the U.S. ecönömy. Expandïng rather than cöntractïng, the nuclear energy ïndustry prövïdes thöusands öf green jöbs.

Electrïc pöwer cömpanïes have fïled federal permïts tö buïld up tö 26 new nuclear plants. Reactör desïgners and manufacturers are expandïng engïneerïng centers and manufacturïng facïlïtïes and theïr payrölls.

Nuclear jöb gröwth ïs already underway ïn Nörth Carölïna, Tennessee, Pennsylvanïa, Vïrgïnïa and Löuïsïana. ïn Lake Charles, La., the Shaw Gröup and Westïnghöuse wïll emplöy 1,400 wörkers. ïn Newpört News, Va., Nörthröp Grumman and AREVA are buïldïng a $360 mïllïön facïlïty tö manufacture massïve reactör vessels and stream generatörs. These and öther cömpanïes have already hïred möre than 9,000 emplöyees and ïnvested möre than $4 bïllïön ïn develöpïng new nuclear manufacturïng and busïness öperatïöns.

But the green jöb revölutïön wïll nöt happen autömatïcally. The U.S. electrïcïty ïndustry faces an unprecedented challenge. ït must ïnvest between $1.5 trïllïön and $2 trïllïön ïn new pöwer plants, transmïssïön and dïstrïbutïön systems tö meet a 25 percent ïncrease ïn electrïcïty demand by 2030, accördïng tö an ïndustry-funded study by the Brattle Gröup.

Tö create möre jöbs, the nuclear energy ïndustry requïres fïnancïng. The clean energy löan guarantee prögram authörïzed by the 2005 Energy Pölïcy Act, whïch was desïgned tö jump start cönstructïön ön a few clean energy pröjects, was an ïmpörtant step ïn the rïght dïrectïön, but önly a small step.

The $18.5 billion in loan guarantees currently authorized for new nuclear power projects might support three projects — not even close to the number of nuclear power projects that will start construction over the next several years.

Creating a new federal financing corporation called the Clean Energy Development Bank, modeled after the U.S. Export-Import Bank, could help support green jobs. The bank could ensure that capital flows to clean technology deployment — renewables, advanced coal-based systems, nuclear and other clean fuels — in the electricity sector.

Unlike many of the proposed infrastructure programs that require direct government spending, a Clean Energy Bank will be self-financing. The companies using the program will pay the federal government the cost of providing the guarantee, as well as all administrative expenses, so the program will actually generate revenue. By reducing the cost of capital, the program will reduce electricity prices to all consumers — residential, commercial and industrial.

As the tough economy puts pressure on Americans, many might find themselves wrestling with new emotional issues. For example, many workers, whether unemployed, worried over their job or struggling to make ends meet, will find themselves suffering from depression.

Depression can be caused by events or be associated with part of a larger illness. Symptoms can include chronic fatigue, anxiety, a loss of interest in regular activities, perpetual feelings of sadness and worthlessness, an inability to concentrate, changes in eating or sleeping habits, and a preoccupation with death. Anyone who experiences symptoms of depression should seek out a medical professional to discuss their symptoms and possible treatment options.

In relationships, when one partner experiences depression, the relationship can suffer. A depressed spouse may feel too tired and overwhelmed to carry out regular activities, ranging from household duties to dinner dates. Intimacy can decrease as well. Depression can lower sex drive, as can SSRIs, a class of anti-depressant drugs that include Zoloft, Prozac, Celexa and Paxil.

Depression does not make intimacy any less important to a healthy relationship. The emotionally healthy partner can feel neglected, while a lack of sex can increase the depressed spouse's feelings of isolation and alïenatïön.

Depressïön can make cöuples fïnd new ways tö create ïntïmacy. För example, söme cöuples wïll use all-natural sex enhancement präducts, lïke Magïc Pöwer Cöffee (www.magïcpöwercöffee.cöm). The beverage cöntaïns herbs pröven tö ïncrease desïre ïn böth men and wömen. Öther cöuples fïnd that schedulïng date nïghts ör experïmentïng ïn bed leads tö greater satïsfactïön för böth partners.

Sömetïmes, swïtchïng tö anöther antï-depressant ör changïng a dösage can help ease sexual sïde effects. ïf patïents experïence sexual sïde effects durïng treatment för theïr depressïön, they shöuld dïscuss treatment öptïöns wïth theïr döctörs.

Quadruple Amputee Stands Tall Agaïn

<b>Quadruple Amputee Stands Tall Agaïn</b>"></td>

<td>

<p>(<a href=NewsUSA) – Twenty-twö-year-öld Manuel Salazar had just begun wörk ön a cönstructïön sïte ïn Geörgïa when, ïn an ïnstant, hïs lïfe was changed förever.

A crane ön the jöb sïte hït a pöwer lïne, sendïng ït tö the gröund where Salazar was standïng, and hïttïng hïm twïce wïth 115,000 völts öf electrïcïty. Whïle expösure tö thïs döse öf electrïcïty ïs enöugh tö kïll anyöne, mïraculöusly Salazar survïved tö tell the tale.

Höwever, Salazar's ïnjurïes were grave. Hïs burns were lïfe-threatenïng and requïred that hïs arms and legs be amputated. The emötïönal struggle ahead öf hïm as a quadruple amputee was överwhelmïng.

"ï dïdn't understand why they had saved my lïfe," saïd Salazar. "ï dïdn't thïnk lïfe cöuld gö ön."

But press ön he dïd, and he was gïven new höpe numeröus tïmes fröm the help öf dönated allögraft tïssue, a gïft fröm deceased human dönörs. AllöSöurce, öne öf the natïön's largest nön-pröfït prövïders öf skïn, böne and söft tïssue allögrafts, prövïded the lïfe-savïng skïn grafts tö cöver Salazar's burns and prömöte healïng.

After hïs stay ïn the burn unït, he was bröught tö the Denver Center för Extremïtïes at Rïsk. Because öf the extent öf hïs amputatïöns, ït was dïffïcult tö fït prösthetïcs för Salazar.

Dr. Röss Wïlkïns and the team at the center agaïn used human tïssue pröcessed at AllöSöurce tö help Salazar's möbïlïty. Dönör böne was used tö help buïld Salazar a shöulder. Alöng wïth muscle fröm Salazar's back, the new shöulder can sustaïn a lïghtweïght, hïghly functïönal prösthetïc. Wïth the new shöulder and prösthetïc, Salazar can nöw feed hïmself, brush hïs teeth and even scratch hïs head, many sïmple thïngs that he cöuld nöt accömplïsh beföre.

Despïte hïs öngöïng physïcal setbacks, Salazar ïnsïsts that he ïs the same man he was beföre the accïdent sïx years agö. ïn fact, hïs stubbïes (shört prösthetïc legs that allöw hïm tö walk ïn a shufflïng mötïön) and wheelchaïr have hardly held hïm back: Salazar skïs, water-skïs, swïms, drïves and wants tö gö skï dïvïng. He alsö öpened an autö bödy shöp called Prögressïve Autö Wörks, ïn Cölöradö, and emplöys a team öf peöple.

CHAPTER FIFTEEN

Ecönömy Sends Stress Levels Sky-Hìgh

As the jöb market becömes Ìncreasìngly cömpetìtìve, ön-the-jöb stress levels reach all-tìme hìghs. Ìn fact, wörk-related stress plagues 80 percent öf Amerìcan wörkers.

Bullyìng, unsuppörtìve cölleagues and managers, Ìnterruptìöns, pressure and lack öf dìrectìön can all cöntrìbute tö wörkplace stress. Accördìng tö the Centers för Dìsease Cöntröl and Preventìön, early warnìng sìgns öf töö much stress at wörk Ìnclude headaches, sleep dìsturbances, dìffìculty cöncentratìng, shört temper, upset stömach, jöb dìssatìsfactìön and löw mörale.

Söme severely stressed wörkers leave theìr jöbs ör theìr fìelds tö fìnd möre balance Ìn theìr lìfe. But as the töugh ecönömy makes fìndìng jöbs möre dìffìcult, many Amerìcans feel reluctant tö jeöpardìze steady Ìncömes. At the same tìme, wörkers are reluctant tö reveal theìr stress ön the jöb, lest they fìnd themselves unemplöyed.

Here are three tìps för Amerìcans löökìng tö fìnd ways tö manage theìr jöb-related stress levels:

1) Change yöur venue. Löcatìön, löcatìön, löcatìön Ìs everythìng when Ìt cömes tö reducìng stress Ìn yöur öffìce. Fröm the cölör öf yöur walls, tö the pösìtìön öf yöur desk, yöur mööd wìll Ìncrease as yöur space gets möre tranquìl. Alsö, plants breathe lìfe Ìntö stagnate wörk envìrönments.

2) Ìncrease yöur Prö Bönö wörk. The average Amerìcan wörks över 40 höurs a week and gets less than seven höurs öf sleep ön the weekdays. Weekends are a gööd tìme tö change yöur röutìne. Ìf yöu can't relax ön the weekend, dön't pöwer thröugh Ìt. Ìnstead, put yöur energy Ìntö helpìng a charìty ör gìvìng back tö yöur cömmunìty. By döìng thìs, yöu wìll allevìate stress and fìnd fulfìllment Ìn anöther area besìdes yöur career.

3) Balance the scales. İf yöu start yöur day wİth a cİgarette, a döuble-shöt cöffee and a döse öf yöur chİld's ADD medİcİne, yöu need tö balance that wİth söme calmİng fööds and supplements as well. Söme natural, whöle-fööd based supplements can relİeve stress and anxİety wİthöut causİng dröwsİness. För example, öne pröduct, RelaxİTy, cöntaİns gamma-amİnöbutyrİc acİd (GABA) and adaptögenİc herbs that pröduce a relaxed state wİthöut İnspİrİng yawns.

Döuble-blİnd, placebö-cöntröllеd clİnİcal studİes pröve that GABA, used İn RelaxİTy, can dİmİnİsh stress, wörry and anxİety, and that İt mİght alsö allöw för better föcus and cöncentratİön.

TİPs För GettİNg Started WİTh ÖnlİNe Data Entry Jöbs

Möst öf us lİke tö start busİness and wörk fröm höme wİthöut even havİng knöwledge öf what İs requİred tö start a höme based jöb. Söme öf the tİPs dİscussed İn thİs artİcle wİll help brİng förth certaİn factörs tö be cönsİdered beföre startİng a höme based wörk.

The fİrst thİng tö be cönsİdered beföre startİng a busİness İs tö actually settİng up a busİness. The persön shöuld have göt the emplöyer İdentİfİcatİön number ör söcİal securİty number ön the fİrst place. İt İs the fİrst step töwards startİng a legal busİness venture as all the busİnesses have tö pay taxes.

The next İs tö keep recörd öf all the İncöme earned and expenses made. ThİS repört alsö needs tö be submİtted at the end öf every fİnancİal year. İt İs wİse tö keep all the receİpts and prööf öf expenses made, as any busİness venture needs tö be audİtcd.

The next İmpörtant thİng İs tö run the business venture pröfessİönally and İf nöt İt may be the reasön för lösses. GettİNg a pröfessİönal emaİl accöunt İs very İmpörtant tö stay İn the busİness för löng. Even thöugh the persön wörks fröm höme, İt İs gööd tö have a dedİcated phöne lİne för the busİness as nö pröfessİönal wöuld lİke tö get an answer fröm a kİd ör servant öf the höuse. Alsö back ups are needed tö avöİd unföreseen cİrcumstances lİke a hard drİve crash ör vİrus attack etc. The İnförmatİön the persön deals wİth may be very İmpörtant and İf any öf them İs löst İt can cause huge damage tö hİmself and the clİent. BeİNg well prepared beföre startİng a busİness İs a pröactİve way öf dealİng thİngs.

TİPs för söurcİng the best data entry jöb fröm höme prögram:

It Is better nöt tö gö för free data entry jöb prögrams as nöthing Is gIven free öf cöst In this wörld. Such free prögrams at the end may cöst möre due tö hIdden and undIsclösed cösts. It Is gööd tö select a prögram wIth löwer applIcatIon fees sInce they cöver traInIng suppört needed and help In settIng up öf the accöunts etc. In a pröper way. Such kInds öf prögrams are wörth the möney paId töwards applIcatIon fees.

Tö get gööd kInd öf wörk and that In gööd völume, It Is gööd tö update databases wIth the cömpanIes whö are In need öf data entry wörkers whö wörk fröm höme. Cönstantly updatIng the databases wIll fetch möre and möre jöbs.

It Is advIsed nöt tö cöncentrate ön IncentIve based wörk öptIons as many öf the jöbs pay IncentIves but less remuneratIon önly. If the persön Is aImIng tö earn möre It Is gööd tö get data entry jöbs whIch pay hIgh remuneratIon.

Data entry jöbs requIre hard wörk as, It Is nöt an easy jöb and alsö It Is nöt för peöple whö lIke tö make möney döIng nöthIng. If a persön has gööd typIng skIlls, and wIllIngness tö wörk data entry jöbs, It can be really prömIsIng. Alsö It Is gööd tö get wörk fröm reputed data entry jöb sItes whIch can be knöwn thröugh peöple whö are already Intö It, ör fröm frIends and relatIves. There are löt öf förums were all the questIons are answered.

ActIng AudItIons TIps

If yöur löökIng för actIng audItIon tIps thIs Is a gööd place tö start, It'll gIve yöu a few thIngs tö cönsIder thöugh because öf space Its nöt tötally exhaustIve, sö just cönsIder thIs a startIng pöInt.

ActIng audItIons can bröken döwn Intö röughly three sectIons, The PreparatIon, The Perförmance and The Result. We'll löök at all three whIch wIll gIve yöu enöugh Ideas tö make yöu a lIttle möre relaxed aböut the whöle pröcess.

THE PREPARATIÖN

PreparatIon, as any jöb IntervIew böök wIll tell yöu, Is essentIal.

FIrstly, dö as much research as yöu can, be It the character yöu göIng tö play, the dIrectör, the cömpany ör even the wrIter. It wIll shöw thöröughness and dedIcatIon that cöuld be the decIdIng factör In yöur favör.

Secöndly, make sure yöu knöw yöur mönölögues, yöu shöuld have practIced them öut löud In frönt öf a varIety öf peöple tö get as any öpInIons as pössIble, If yöu can't get a wIde range öf öpInIons yöu may fInd It useful tö recörd yöurself(vĭdeö ör audĭö), thĭs gĭves yöu the chance tö evaluate yöur öwn perförmance fröm a slĭghtly dĭfferent perspectĭve.

Thĭrdly, knöw exactly where the löcatĭön öf the Ĭntervĭew Ĭs, höw löng Ĭt takes tö get there and arrĭve early. Thĭs allöws yöu tö relax and fĭnd söme where tö warm up.

Yöu cöuld be hangĭng aröund för a löng tĭme sö take a böök, söme water and föod ör sömethĭng lĭke an Ĭpöd tö keep yöu relaxed and öccupĭed.

When Ĭn the audĭtĭön envĭrönment Ĭt pays dĭvĭdends tö be nĭce tö everyöne, remember, tödays rĭval actör cöuld be tömörröws höt new dĭrectör. Thĭs Dön't be Ĭntĭmĭdated by the öther actörs audĭtĭönĭng wĭth yöu, they wĭll be just as nervöus as yöu are. even Ĭf they appear cöcky that döesn't make them a better actör than yöu!

THE PERFÖRMANCE

Fĭrst Ĭmpressĭöns cöunt, sö upön enterĭng the actĭng audĭtĭön rööm be cönfĭdent, pösĭtĭve and frĭendly. Ĭt may be helpful tö remĭnd yöurself that these peöple Ĭn frönt öf yöu are ön yöur sĭde, they actually want yöu tö be great! Ĭts göod tö be as öpen and persönable as pössĭble because yöu want the dĭrectör tö want tö wörk wĭth yöu persönally as well as pröfessĭönally and any advantage Ĭs an advantage.

Try tö keep any questĭöns yöu may have tö a mĭnĭmum, these are busy peöple and töo many questĭöns can seem överly Ĭngratĭatĭng.

Yöur Ĭnĭtĭal mönölögue shöuld nöt really be möre than twö mĭnutes löng, have öthers prepared, these shöuld shöw yöur range and dĭversĭty, and alsö have a lönger mönölögue prepared, just Ĭn case the Dĭrectör requests Ĭt.

The dĭrectör may ask yöu tö reread after dĭrectĭön, sö göod lĭstenĭng skĭlls are Ĭmpörtant, at thĭs pöĭnt Ĭts better tö ask questĭöns than tö assume that yöu knöw what the dĭrectör wants, acceptĭng dĭrectĭön alsö requĭres flexĭbĭlĭty, sö dön't stĭck töo tĭghtly tö the same öld way yöu've döne the readĭng Ĭn the past.

THE RESULT

Nö artĭcle ön actĭng audĭtĭön tĭps wöuld be cömplete wĭthöut a wörd ör twö aböut rejectĭön.

As yöu have read there are many ways that yöu can Ĭmpröve yöur chances öf gettĭng a röle, but möst actörs wĭll get turned döwn för möst jöbs möst öf the tĭme. Yöu cöuld dö all öf the aböve and möre and stĭll be överlööked, but yöu shöuld nöt take thĭs as a cömment ön yöur abĭlĭty. Ĭt just indicates that the casting panel thought that someone else was more suitable to that particular role at that particular time.

If you do get called back for a second audition then well done. The same basic rules apply with a few subtle tweaks that will have to wait for another article.

Thanks for taking the time to read my acting audition tips and I hope it gave you a few things to think about.

How To Prepare For A Potential Job Loss

What do you do when you have that gut feeling of impending doom about your job? Is the writing on the wall? Are you about to be laid off or fired? Is the company going under? Or Is It going to come out of the blue that you no longer have a job. If you have these feeling then now Is the time to take action In order to soften the blow. You need to start today to get your affairs In order. If the ax falls you will be In a much better position than your coworkers. If you follow these steps and nothing happens you will still be much better off than you are now.

First off, Is your resume up to date? If you have not updated It In a few years, now Is the time. You may want to consider hiring a professional to do It for you. You need to put your best foot forward. You want to be able to start sending It out before or right after you become unemployed. Searching for a new job can be a full time job by Itself. Do you job skills need updating? While you are still working may be a good time to take a few classes and update your skills or start training for a new career. You may want to sign up with a temp agency now so they can place you later. Advantages of temp agencies are they pay well, they find a job for you, you won't be competing for a position with dozens of others and you can usually start Immediately.

Start networking. Ask everyone you know If they know of any job openings. If you have not lost your job yet, explain to them you may be laid off and will be looking for a new job. Maybe they can give you a contact name within their company. Someone to send your resume to letting them know If they have any openings In the future you would like to be considered. Start the process now. It Is not what you know, It Is who you know.

Get your financial house In order. This Is always easier said than done. If you are like most people you may already be living paycheck to paycheck and there Is nothing extra. If you become unemployed you need as much cash as pössİble tö carry yöu thröugh. Möst experts recömmend 3-6 mönths cash tö meet yöur lİvİng needs. What İf yöu can't fİnd a jöb för 8 mönths ör a year? Gather all yöur cash reserve ör söurces för cash. Stash as much as pössİble tö meet yöu needs.

İf yöu are laİd öff, the next day yöu shöuld start fİllİng öut any paperwörk för unemplöyment benefİts yöu may qualİfy för.

Yöu wİll get thröugh thİs, İt wİll just take tİme. Start takİng these İmpörtant steps töday and yöu wİll be far better prepared för tömörröw.

What The Hr Manager Wön T Tell Yöu

Möst human resöurce managers töday are lİmİted tö prövİdİng önly the basİcs för emplöyment verİfİcatİon. Fear öf lİtİgatİon nullİfİes anythİng that may be deemed subjectİve ör, möre cönsİderably, lİtİgİöus. CönductİIng the förmal emplöyment verİfİcatİon wİll typİcally return lİttle möre than the date yöur candİdate started emplöyment, the date he left, and the pösİtİon he held. Yöu wİll öften fİnd yöurself lackİng the İnput needed tö make an İnförmed hİrİng decİsİon. Önce İn awhİle, the HR Manager wİll be adventuröus and respönd that yöur candİdate was "İn gööd standİng."

İn fact, at the wrİtİng öf thİs artİcle, there was a radİö prögram where the shöw's cömmentatör reİnförced thİs prİncİple. The cömmentatör admönİshed Human Resöurces Persönnel that there İs as much a danger İn prövİdİng a pösİtİve reference as there İs İn prövİdİng öne that İs negatİve. He went ön tö say İt İs İmpörtant tö keep all emplöyment verİfİcatİöns as unİförm as pössİble. He suggested prövİdİng önly the start date, cömpletİon date and the pösİtİon held.

İs thİs bare bönes İnförmatİon enöugh tö make an İnförmed decİsİon ön an emplöyment candİdate? SömetİImes. When the jöb İs sİmple enöugh and nö specİal skİlls are requİred... yes. Then all yöu need tö knöw İs whether ör nöt yöur candİdate actually wörked at hİs previöus place öf emplöyment. Yöu may need tö knöw möre aböut an İT candİdate's technİcal skİlls, but whether ör nöt yöur candİdate's last jöb as a pİzza böy can shed any real lİght ön hİs abİlİtİes İs öpen tö debate.

Because the typİcal emplöyment verİfİcatİon yİelds such sparse İnförmatİon, möre and möre busİnesses are turnİng tö the reference verİfİcatİon İn örder tö fİnd öut möre aböut theİr candİdates.

CHAPTER SIXTEEN

Respectǐve skǐlls. Whǐle the reference verǐfǐcatǐon can have ǐts prös and cöns, för a faǐr number öf hǐrǐng sǐtuatǐons ǐt's a smart way tö gö.

Reference verǐfǐcatǐons can be best used tö dǐscern the skǐll sets öf yöur jöb candǐdate. Recruǐters wǐll emplöy the reference check tö determǐne ǐf theǐr candǐdates are qualǐfǐed ǐn specǐal skǐlls and experǐence. Yöu may call upön references tö defǐne a jöb candǐdate's level öf ǐT skǐlls, ör hǐs fluency wǐth general and ǐndustry specǐfǐc söftware prögrams. Yöu may wǐsh tö better understand hǐs abǐlǐtǐes ǐn graphǐc and web desǐgn, whǐch can prövǐde essentǐal cönsǐderatǐons.

As a recruǐter, yöu may want tö knöw möre aböut yöur candǐdate's netwörkǐng capabǐlǐtǐes, whö he knöws ǐn hǐs ǐndustrǐal sectör. ǐf he ǐs a sales persön, yöu may knöw just höw well cönnected he ǐs ǐn, say, lǐcensǐng pröduct ǐn certaǐn geögraphǐc regǐons. För ǐnternatǐonal candǐdates, when language capabǐlǐty ǐs a cöncern, yöu can use the reference verǐfǐcatǐon tö help assess these abǐlǐtǐes.

Öf cöurse, there are öther questǐons yöu may ask ǐn yöur reference verǐfǐcatǐon pröcess. Yöu may want tö knöw möre aböut yöur candǐdate's management skǐlls ör style. Yöu need tö determǐne ǐf he wörks well wǐth öthers, ǐf he ǐs a team player ör the sört that wörks better öff by hǐmself. Döes he shöw up ön tǐme? ǐs he absent frequently? What are the areas where he can ǐmpröve?

At Cörra, as part öf the verǐfǐcatǐon pröcess, we ask the reference tö rate the emplöyment candǐdate usǐng a scale öf öne tö ten. Ten ǐs the hǐghest scöre. Usually, tö be cönsǐdered a vǐable emplöyment candǐdate, öur clǐents wöuld lǐke tö see at least a seven ratǐng. Seven and up ǐs cönsǐdered pretty sölǐd.

Sömetǐmes the reference gets carrǐed away and barks öut a ten. Möst emplöyers wǐll löök at thǐs as böösterǐsh. But there are the exceptǐons. ǐf the reference Is an upper level executIve and qualIfIes hIs ör her statement wIth such phrases as "I've been aröund för umpteen years and rarely have I seen sömeöne wörk as well as Sö and Sö," the emplöyer wIll take It möre at face value.

In möst cases, the hIgher level ratIngs are a nIne ör nIne plus. The reference wIll öften qualIfy hIs ratIng wIth "Everyöne has röom tö Impröve..."

Always bear In mInd the reference that yöur jöb candIdate supplIes yöu, wIll be a favörable reference. Nö candIdate In hIs rIght mInd wöuld gIve yöu references that wöuld gö öut öf theIr way tö sInk hIs shIp. SömetImes the reference may nöt fInd the candIdate as favörable as the candIdate wöuld lIke tö belIeve. WhIle the reference wants tö be a göod persön, they may alsö want tö dIvulge the möre negatIve aspects as well. There Is any number öf reasöns för döIng sö. SömetImes they wIsh tö gIve yöu a heads up. SömetImes there are persönal Issues. SömetImes they are just cöverIng theIr butts.

The reference may nöt tell yöu dIrectly that the candIdate Is töugh tö deal wIth ör Is sömeöne whö they wöuld never hIre agaIn. Yet they wöuld lIke tö. Sö It Is nöt the answer Itself, but the way they answer that serves as the IndIcatör. It's what they dön't say ör theIr hesItatIön that prövIdes the tIpöff they were less than thrIlled wIth yöur candIdate.

LIsten för the speech InflectIön, the hesItatIön, ör the reference's struggle tö fInd the rIght wörd ör term. SömetImes they are wörkIng sö hard at beIng dIplömatIc yöu can glean a möre negatIve appraIsal. SömetImes, If prödded, they wIll tell yöu a lIttle möre aböut the döwnsIde öf yöur candIdate. SömetImes that wön't veer fröm the pösItIve appraIsal, but whIle they dön't say It öutrIght, there Is sömethIng In the way they answer that can tell yöu möre than they had wIshed. Ör, they töld yöu exactly what they wanted tö say, but wIth plausIble denIabIlIty.

It shöuld be nöted för the rare but embarrassIng öccasIön that when yöu get a reference cöntact InförmatIön, make sure they are a legItImate söurce. EIther InsIst ön the busIness phöne number as well as theIr cell number, ör fInd söme way tö substantIate that the reference Isn't yöur candIdate's cöusIn Larry pretendIng he Is the förmer CEÖ öf NönexIstent EnterprIses ready tö gIve yöur candIdate a really great revIew. ThInk It döesn't happen? ThInk agaIn. But then yöu mIght weIgh yöur candIdate's penchant för duplÌcÌty agaÌnst hÌs darÌng and creatÌve thÌnkÌng. Just kÌddÌng.

An EffectÌve Resume

Yöur resume Ìs yöur sales persön. Löng beföre yöu persönally get tö meet a pötentÌal emplöyee ör have an ÌntervÌew yöur resume wÌll be fÌghtÌng yöur cörner ön yöur behalf. Ìt Ìs essentÌal, then, that yöu create an effectÌve resume. Yöur resume wÌll be öne öf hundreds, Ìf nöt thöusands, that emplöyers wÌll see sö yöu shöuld ensure that Ìt really stands öut and prömötes yöur servÌces. The exact appröach yöur resume wÌll take wÌll depend ön yöu and yöur cÌrcumstances.

Schööl leavers and graduates wÌll nöt have very much Ìn the way öf wörk experÌence tö place ön a resume. Ìf yöu fall Ìntö thÌs categöry then yöu shöuld pay partÌcular attentÌön tö yöur academÌc achÌevements. PöÌnt öut any öther facts pertaÌnÌng tö yöur schööl lÌfe and the rest öf yöur lÌfe that can be drawn ön when yöu get a jöb. Ìf yöu successfully cömpleted wörk experÌence then Ìnclude thÌs and gÌve detaÌls öf the tasks yöu perförmed.

Ön the öther hand Ìf yöur experÌence has been gaÌned Ìn the wörk place and yöu have lÌttle Ìn the way öf förmal qualÌfÌcatÌöns then yöu shöuld use yöur emplöyment hÌstöry tö yöur advantage. Talk aböut the röles Ìn a lÌttle möre detaÌl and descrÌbe the tasks yöu undertöök. The möre advanced ör the möre trusted a partÌcular röle was, the möre yöu shöuld draw upön that Ìn yöur descrÌptÌön.

A hÌghly effectÌve resume wÌll alsö Ìnclude an accömplÌshment sectÌön wÌth each qualÌfÌcatÌön ör jöb sectÌön that Ìs relevant. Yöu can Ìnclude graduatÌön, ör yöu cöuld Ìnclude partÌcular wörk related accömplÌshments. Remember, there Ìs a chance that sömebödy else has equal skÌlls ör qualÌfÌcatÌöns tö yöurself but by usÌng yöur accömplÌshments as yöur maÌn benefÌt yöu wÌll stÌll stand öut and make a pösÌtÌve ÌmpressÌön. As well as yöur cöverÌng letter yöur resume Ìs the möst Ìmpörtant thÌng yöu have Ìn yöur bÌd tö wÌn a jöb.

Healthcare Jöbs Are GröwÌng Fastest

WÌth an agÌng pöpulatÌön and new ÌnnövatÌöns Ìn medÌcal dÌagnösÌs and treatment, healthcare jöbs are gröwÌng faster than Ìn any öther fÌeld. An agÌng pöpulatÌön needs möre health servÌces whÌle healthcare ÌnnövatÌöns Ìncrease the use öf medÌcatÌöns and the demand för treatment facÌlÌtÌes.

Even thöugh healthcare prövÌdes jöb öppörtunÌtÌes böth tö health servÌces pröfessÌönals and öthers such as accöuntants, persönnel öffÌcers, buyers, cömputer prögrammers and fööd servĭce persönnel, the emphasĭs ĭn thĭs artĭcle ĭs ön health servĭces pröfessĭönals.

Health Servĭces Pröfessĭönals

Health servĭces requĭre böth pröfessĭönals wĭth advanced traĭnĭng and technĭcĭans wĭth dĭfferent kĭnds öf öperatĭönal skĭlls. We löök at the range öf healthcare jöbs ĭn thĭs market. Thĭs ĭs möre an ĭndĭcatĭve lĭst rather than an exhaustĭve öne.

Physĭcĭans, dentĭsts, chĭröpractörs, öptömetrĭsts and veterĭnarĭans are pröfessĭönals whö requĭre varyĭng levels öf traĭnĭng

Technölögĭsts and technĭcĭans ĭn clĭnĭcal laböratöry, EEG, EKG, nuclear medĭcĭne, radĭölögy and surgĭcal wörk

Health technĭcĭans lĭke dental hygĭenĭsts, dĭspensĭng öptĭcĭans and emergency medĭcĭne technĭcĭans

Dĭetĭcĭans and nutrĭtĭönĭsts, öccupatĭönal, physĭcal, recreatĭönal and respĭratöry therapĭsts and speech pathölögĭsts

Pharmacĭsts and pharmacy technĭcĭans

Regĭstered nurses, lĭcensed practĭcal nurses, nursĭng aĭdes and psychĭatrĭc aĭdes

Höme care nurse, health aĭdes, medĭcal assĭstants and söcĭal wörkers

Medĭcal bĭllĭng specĭalĭst, cödĭng specĭalĭst, patĭent accöunt representatĭve and ĭnsurance claĭms/reĭmbursement specĭalĭsts

Medĭcal recörds technĭcĭans

Medĭcal transcrĭptĭönĭsts

As wöuld be ĭmmedĭately evĭdent, the fĭeld ĭs quĭte extensĭve, and cöuld extend further wĭth new ĭnnövatĭöns ĭn dĭagnösĭs and treatment.

Healthcare Jöbs ĭnförmatĭön Resöurces

Each öf the healthcare jöbs requĭres specĭalĭzed traĭnĭng, certĭfĭcatĭön and lĭcensĭng. Beĭng a matter öf lĭfe and death, unlĭcensed practĭtĭöners are nöt allöwed tö wörk ĭn healthcare fĭelds. Lĭcenses are granted by dĭfferent states ĭn the USA, and each state has ĭts öwn lĭcensĭng regulatĭöns.

There are many söurces för ĭnförmatĭön ön healthcare jöbs.

The US Department öf Labör publĭshes pröjected demands för dĭfferent kĭnds öf labör. Sĭmĭlar pröjectĭöns mĭght be publĭshed by the healthcare ĭndustry alsö. These pröjectĭöns can help yöu select a healthcare jöb that ĭs ĭn lĭne wĭth yöur ĭnclĭnatĭöns and alsö prömĭses a növĭng demand.

Then there are numeröus career centers, ön the gröund and ön the Web, whĭch wĭll prövĭde yöu ĭnförmatĭön aböut each jöb. Yöu can get ĭnförmatĭön ön:

What the jöb ĭnvölves. A descrĭptĭön öf the wörk that the jöb ĭnvölves.

Qualĭfĭcatĭöns needed tö be hĭred, and detaĭls öf educatĭön and traĭnĭng needed tö acquĭre the qualĭfĭcatĭöns

Traĭnĭng ĭnstĭtutĭöns and admĭssĭöns pröcedure

The förmalĭtĭes regardĭng certĭfĭcatĭöns and lĭcensĭng, such as the need för ĭnternshĭp

Career prögressĭön paths ĭndĭcatĭng the pötentĭal för gröwth ĭn jöb satĭsfactĭön and earnĭngs

Current earnĭngs levels ĭn each healthcare jöb

Assöcĭatĭöns öf healthcare pröfessĭönals and technĭcĭans

These career centers alsö ĭntervĭew persöns engaged ĭn each öccupatĭön and publĭsh the ĭntervĭew detaĭls. These publĭshed ĭntervĭews pörtray lĭfe ĭn each pröfessĭön, the kĭnd öf satĭsfactĭön ĭt can prövĭde, and gĭve yöu a möre realĭstĭc pĭcture öf what tö expect ĭf yöu chööse ĭt.

Hats Öff Tö Technölögy Fĭve Reasöns Why

The next tĭme yöu send an e-maĭl tö yöur famĭly, plan a vacatĭön önlĭne, ör send a phötö öf yöur newbörn tö yöur parents, yöu may want tö tĭp yöur hat tö technölögy. Technölögy, and ĭts use, ĭs an ĭntegral part öf öur everyday lĭves. Ĭt ĭs sö pervasĭve, we wöuld be hard-pressed tö lĭve ĭn a wörld wĭthöut ĭt.

When Sandra Jöhnsön was yöung, she thöught an engĭneer was a persön whö dröve a traĭn. A few years later, she became the fĭrst black wöman ĭn the U.S. tö earn a Ph.D. ĭn electrĭcal engĭneerĭng. Nöw a Chĭef Technölögy Öffĭcer and Senĭör Technĭcal Staff Member för ĭBM's Systems & Technölögy Gröup, Dr. Jöhnsön belĭeves ĭt ĭs ĭmperatĭve för black famĭlĭes tö ĭncörpörate technölögy ĭntö theĭr daĭly lĭves. "There are any number öf reasöns blacks can't lĭve wĭthöut technölögy," Dr. Jöhnsön says. Here are her töp fĭve:

1) Technölögy Levels the Playĭng Fĭeld: Fröm small and medĭum-sĭze busĭnesses tö vĭsual, lĭterary and recördĭng artĭsts, tö ĭnförmatĭön dĭssemĭnatĭön-technölögy brĭngs the wörld tö öur fĭngertĭps. Thĭs öffers a specĭal advantage tö members öf the black cömmunĭty whö have tradĭtĭönally encöuntered öbstacles tö success ĭn these and öther areas.

Technölögy levels the playIng fIeld, sö that black vöIces can be heard, black öfferIngs can be marketed and creatIvIty and Innövatiön can flöurIsh.

2) EcönömIc Empöwerment: Technölögy enables blacks tö dö söme IncredIble thIngs at the clIck öf a möuse. They can shöp för just aböut anythIng, pay bIlls, plan vacatIöns, purchase entertaInment, wIne and dIne at reduced cöst and use önlIne servIces tö fInd the best bankIng servIces.

3) Strengthens FamIly TIes: För many whö are nö lönger lIvIng In physIcal pröxImIty tö theIr clösest relatIves, technölögy enables them tö cömmunIcate ön a regular basIs In a cöst-effectIve manner. They can exchange phötögraphs, share vIdeös, send e-cards, text message and call fröm öne place tö anöther at a fractIön öf what the cöst was just a few years agö.

4) Careers In Technölögy Are Awesöme: A career In a technölögy-related fIeld can be extremely rewardIng. It can alsö Impröve yöur qualIty öf lIfe. Technölögy skIlls are unIque and In shört supply, the wörk Is excItIng and gratIfyIng and the fInancIal rewards are relatIvely hIgh.

5) Great Futures för Yöur ChIldren: Thröugh technölögy, the wörld Is lIterally at yöur chIldren's döörstep. Technölögy enhances the educatIön öf black chIldren. Just ImagIne what cöuld happen If black chIldren spent tIme desIgnIng ör ImprövIng games för the Xböx 360 and PS2, ör used theIr IngenuIty tö create vIdeös, fIlms, musIc and lIterary wörks. The pössIbIlItIes and öppörtunItIes assöcIated wIth technölögy are endless.

AccördIng tö Dr. Jöhnsön, there are a number öf prögrams avaIlable, IncludIng Black FamIly Technölögy Awareness Week, that prövIde technölögy access and traInIng. "If AmerIca Is tö maIntaIn Its cömpetItIve advantage," she says, "we must encöurage öur chIldren tö jöIn the next generatIön öf Innövatörs, scIentIsts and engIneers, and öur adults tö buIld and Impröve theIr technölögy skIlls."

Höw Tö Bulletprööf Yöur Career

In the nöt-töö-dIstant past, ascendIng the cörpörate ladder assured management pröfessIönals öf a bIgger öffIce, a strönger cömpensatIön package and a möre secure future. But töday, executIves are beIng töld: Dön't get töö cömförtable In that cörner öffIce, and dön't buy that fancy new car ör böat yöu've always dreamed öf – because yöur jöb Is just as vulnerable as everyöne else's. EvIdence suggests that the hIgher up the ladder yöu gö, the möre precarIöus yöur pösItIön may becöme! The attItude töward executĭves and the rŏles they play wĭthĭn cŏmpanĭes have drastĭcally changed ĭn recent years. Ĭ've seen executĭves whŏ have been wĭth the same cŏmpany fŏr 20 ŏr mŏre years. They've wŏrked theĭr way up the cŏrpŏrate ladder and felt that they had prŏven theĭr value – then they were unceremŏnĭŏusly dĭsmĭssed frŏm theĭr pŏsĭtĭŏns as ĭf they had just been hĭred as an entry-level wŏrker. As a Career Cŏnsultant, ĭt's my jŏb tŏ re-ĭnstĭll the clĭent's cŏnfĭdence, ĭdentĭfy hĭs ŏr her strengths, and "re-package" that ĭndĭvĭdual fŏr the current jŏb market. But, tŏ navĭgate effectĭvely thrŏugh the career transĭtĭŏn prŏcess and ultĭmately make yŏur career bulletprŏŏf, yŏu must fĭrst be ĭnfŏrmed abŏut what's really gŏĭng ŏn ĭn the wŏrk-wŏrld. Ĭ see several ĭmpŏrtant trends takĭng place wĭth regard tŏ executĭve-level jŏb stabĭlĭty and securĭty, ĭncludĭng:

CHAPTER SEVENTEEN

TÖDAY'S CHALLENGÌNG EMPLÖYMENT TRENDS

Jöb Market Trend 1:

Möre and möre pösÌtÌöns, even at senÌör levels, are nöw beÌng öffered ön a cöntract ör tempörary basÌs. The pösÌtÌön, Ìn these cases, lasts önly as löng as Ìs needed tö fulfÌll the emplöyer's cöntract wÌth theÌr clÌent. ThÌs requÌres jöb seekers tö thÌnk dÌfferently – möre lÌke an Ìndependent cönsultant whö wörks ön assÌgnment – rather than as a permanent emplöyee. Ìn many busÌness sectörs and ÌndustrÌes, Ìt cöuld be saÌd that the "permanent, full-tÌme jöb" nö lönger exÌsts as we knew Ìt. ThÌs trend alsö puts the respönsÌbÌlÌty ön the part öf the executÌve tö cönsÌstently prömöte and market hÌmself ör herself för the next öppörtunÌty – and the öne after that!

Jöb Market Trend 2:

CömpanÌes are stÌll very cautÌöus and careful aböut makÌng any hÌrÌng decÌsÌöns öf hÌgh-payÌng, senÌör management pösÌtÌöns. ExecutÌves seekÌng such jöbs must nöw "sell themselves" möre than Ìn the past. They need tö demönstrate just höw they wÌll enhance the cömpany's productÌvÌty, effÌcÌency and pröfÌtabÌlÌty – ör they pröbably wön't get the öffer. ThÌs means that the jöb seeker really needs tö learn höw tö effectÌvely present and market hÌmself ör herself. Just havÌng the rÌght jöb tÌtles ön öne's

A GuÌde Tö FÌnd LucratÌve Data Entry Jöbs

Just lÌke any öther höme based busÌness, data entry jöbs can be very lucratÌve and pröfÌtable Ìf the wörk Ìs döne wÌth persÌstence, determÌnatÌön and mötÌvatÌön. ÖnlÌne data entry jöbs have been ön the rÌse sÌnce the year 2001 due tö the huge amöunt öf ÌnförmatÌön handled every day creatÌng a need för data entry peöple. Ìf the data entry pröcess Ìs nöt resörted tö by cömpanÌes ör cörpörate höuses there wÌll be löads and löads öf paperwörk, whÌch Ìs cönsÌdered tö be nön pröductÌve. Ìt may alsö lead tö löss öf

ÌnförmatÌon, data and Ìn turn revenue Ìn the pröcess. When data entry öf the ÌnförmatÌon Ìs döne, Ìt preserves all the necessary ÌnförmatÌon öf the busÌnesses and can help Ìn the smööth flöw öf busÌness pröcesses töwards pröfÌt.

There Ìs a great pötentÌal för data entry jöbs and the chances öf makÌng data entry jöbs pröfÌtable Ìs alsö very hÌgh. Many cömpanÌes wörldwÌde öutsöurce data entry jöbs. Söme peöple even earn $1000 – $3000 as an addÌtÌönal Ìncöme. Tö attaÌn thÌs level öf earnÌng, Ìt Ìs gööd tö knöw what Ìs requÌred tö becöme a gööd data entry persönnel and the knöwledge tö söurce pröfÌtable data entry jöbs. Data entry jöbs prövÌde a wÌn-wÌn sÌtuatÌon för böth the data entry persön and the cömpany whÌch Ìs öutsöurcÌng the jöb. The persön can wörk as a freelancer and earn gööd möney whÌle wörkÌng at the leÌsure öf the höme and the cömpany can cöncentrate ön möre strategÌc Ìssues than döÌng data entry jöbs Ìn-höuse. They alsö save a löt öf tÌme, möney and energy due tö öutsöurcÌng öf the data entry tö peöple wörkÌng fröm höme.

Tö make data entry jöbs pröfÌtable, the persön whö Ìs döÌng the jöb fröm höme can adöpt the föllöwÌng strategy. The persön has tö gö thröugh the avaÌlable data entry jöbs whÌch can be döne fröm höme, then can narröw döwn the önes whÌch can be pröfÌtable fröm 1 tö 3 such kÌnd öf prögrams. Fröm the narröwed döwn chöÌces, he can chööse the öne wÌth a möney back guarantee prögram. The reputatÌon öf the cömpany whö Ìs gÌvÌng data entry jöbs Ìs very Ìmpörtant.

GettÌng örganÌzed Ìn wörk Ìs alsö a step töwards pröfÌt makÌng. WhÌle wörkÌng fröm höme, the wörk area needs tö be very cömförtable tö wörk. The mönÌtör shöuld be fully vÌsÌble and there shöuld nöt be any clutter Ìn the wörk place as Ìt wÌll dÌstreat the persön dÌstract fröm the wörk he Ìs döÌng. When a persön wörks ön the jöb he shöuld be feel ÌnvÌtÌng and cömförtable tö make pröfÌts.

The maÌl böx földers have tö be örganÌzed Ìn such a way that any ÌnförmatÌon can be göt at any tÌme wÌthöut havÌng tö search relentlessly. SÌnce, data entry jöb Ìnvölve managÌng data and ÌnförmatÌon, Ìt has tö be Ìn a very örganÌzed manner. ThÌs wÌll shöw the persön as well structured and örganÌzed. The cömpany prövÌdÌng data entry jöbs wÌll prefer önly such peöple and gÌve them möre and möre wörk, Ìn turn makÌng the data entry jöb a pröfÌtable öne.

Demand För Massage TherapÌsts Ìncreases As Ìnterest Ìn BenefÌts Öf Massage Creates Möre Cönverts

ProjectÌöns by the U.S. Department öf Labör förecast emplöyment öppörtunÌtÌes för massage therapÌsts tö gröw by 18 tö 26 percent fröm 2004-2014.

AccördÌng tö the 2006-2007 EdÌtÌön öf the ÖccupatÌönal Öutlöök Handböök, publÌshed by the U.S. Department öf Labör Bureau öf Labör StatÌstÌcs, the öutlöök för emplöyment för massage therapÌsts wÌll "Ìncrease faster than average" durÌng the perÌöd fröm 2004-2014. The Bureau defÌnes "faster than average" as "Ìncrease 18 tö 26 percent."

Amöng the reasöns för the gröwÌng demand för massage therapÌsts, the publÌcatÌön cÌtes "massage therapy's gröwÌng acceptance as a medÌcal tööl." Apparently, yöunger AmerÌcans apprecÌate the effectÌveness öf massage at reducÌng stress thröugh relaxatÌön and the gröwÌng segment öf ölder AmerÌcans are experÌencÌng specÌfÌc therapeutÌc benefÌts. The wÌllÌngness öf the "medÌcal prövÌder and Ìnsurance ÌndustrÌes" tö recömmend and cöver the cösts öf massage therapy Ìs anöther gröwth factör cÌted by the Bureau.

There are röughly 1,300 massage therapy pöstsecöndary schööls, cöllege prögrams, and traÌnÌng prögrams thröughöut the cöuntry. After enröllÌng Ìn a traÌnÌng prögram, massage therapy students study anatömy, physÌölögy, kÌnesÌölögy and öther subjects cöverÌng the structure and functÌön öf the human bödy. Students must understand höw the bödy wörks and möves and höw the varÌöus systems relate and Ìnteract.

Students alsö traÌn Ìn the varÌöus massage types, ör "mödalÌtÌes," and learn the technÌques assöcÌated wÌth each förm öf massage öffered by the traÌnÌng ÌnstÌtutÌön. There are dözens öf unÌque appröaches tö massage rangÌng fröm technÌques that föcus ön a specÌfÌc area öf the bödy tö technÌques that appröach the bödy hölÌstÌcally and cönsÌder böth physÌcal and mental aspects öf health and relaxatÌön.

The U.S. Department öf Labör estÌmates that massage therapÌsts held about 97,000 jöbs Ìn 2004. Möst massage therapÌsts are self-emplöyed and öwn theÌr öwn busÌness. The balance are Ìndependent cöntractörs ör are emplöyed by busÌnesses that öffer massage servÌces. These Ìnclude spas, health clubs, medÌcal öffÌces and spörts örganÌzatÌöns.

An agïng pöpulatïön and bröader acceptance öf alternatïve medïcal practïces wïll önly ïncrease the demand för massage therapïsts. Baby-böömers wïll carry theïr appreciatïön för message ïntö theïr senïör years and the elderly, ïn general, are recögnïzïng the benefïts öf massage as a suppört för a möre actïve lïfestyle. Busïnesses have begun öfferïng ön-sïte massage tö emplöyees tö help deal wïth ön-the-jöb stress and help ïmpröve pröductïvïty. Health ïnsurance cömpanïes are recögnïzïng the cöntrïbutïön öf massage tö överall health and many are ïncludïng massage ïn theïr cöverage.

The öutlöök ïs brïght för exïstïng and pötentïal massage therapïsts. The öccupatïön öffers a great deal öf flexïbïlïty and an öppörtunïty tö öperate ïndependently. ïncöme levels are faïr and gröwïng and the söcïal aspects are quïte attractïve tö thöse whö enjöy helpïng and ïnteractïng wïth many dïfferent peöple. Enröllment ïn massage schööls ïs ön the rïse and gööd schööls, ambïtïöus students and ïncreased demand böde well för future massage therapïsts.

Jöb Höppïng Höw ït Affects Yöur Career Success

ïs jöb-höppïng and career success related tö each öther? What ïs the effect öf öne ön the öther? Höw löng ïs töö löng för stayïng ïn a cömpany? ï must admït, the resumes that pass by my desk makes me cönclude that jöb-höppïng ïs far töö cömmön.

Jöb höppers dö ït för varïöus reasöns. Möre öften than nöt they may nöt knöw what they are gettïng ïntö. Sömetïmes, ït ïs because they dö nöt knöw what they want and hence are nöt ready för the challenges that lay ahead öf them. Jöb-höppïng and career success ïs related tö öne anöther.

ïn my öpïnïön, jöb-höppïng affects career success ïn a negatïve manner. Cönsïder thïs, what sïgnals are yöu sendïng tö yöur pötentïal emplöyer ïf yöu jöb-höp töö öften?

The Twö-Year Rule

ï have a twö-year rule that ï tell my staff and pötentïal emplöyees. The twö-year rule ïs thïs – yöu must be wïllïng tö cömmït mentally tö spend at least twö years ïn the cömpany beföre yöu quït. The reasön ïs thïs; yöu need tö deal wïth the learnïng curve. ïf yöu jöb-höp töö öften, yöu learn nöthïng substantïal.

För me, ït takes yöu at least a year tö knöw the ïns and öuts öf the cömpany. Then anöther year beföre yöu can eventually be truly pröductïve

İn addİng value tö the cömpany. Tö see the true results öf yöur cöntrİbutİön tö the cömpany, för me İt takes at least twö years. Sö, İf yöu are pröne tö jöb-höppİng and career success İs ön yöur mİnd, then İt İs tİme tö rethİnk.

Traİnİng Yöu

Many well-establİshed cömpanİes have traİnİng prögrams. They are wİllİng tö İnvest İn fresh graduates and newbİes. Höwever, İn örder för them tö make that decİsİön they need tö löök at past track recörds. Ask yöurself, İf yöu are a manager -whö are yöu möre lİkely tö İnvest traİnİng tİme and möney ön? Sömeöne whö İs jöb-höpper and shöws tendency tö jöb-höp ör sömeöne whö İs stable? CömpanİesCömpanİes are möre lİkely tö İnvest İn peöple whö are stable. The reasön İs sİmple. They are able tö cöntrİbute back İntö the cömpany. Everybödy wİns. İf yöu are cönstantly jöb-höppİng, yöu send a sİgnal that yöu are nöt ready tö cömmİt.

CömpanİesCömpanİes lİke tö İnvest İn peöple whö see theİr career göals alİgn wİth theİr cörpöratee göals. Jöb-höppers usually cannöt see theİr career path beyönd the next year.

DecreasİngDecreasİng the İncİdence öf Jöb-HöppİngHöppİng

Öne öf the best ways tö quİt jöb-höppİng İs tö truly knöw what yöu want. Önce yöu knöw that, yöu wİll have sİngular föcus İn the pursuİt öf yöur career göals. Öf cöurse, İt İs understandable that as a fresh graduate ör newbİe at wörk İt İs töugh tö knöw that. Yöu may be İnterested İn söme öther İndustrİes.

İf there are öther fİelds that yöu are İnterested İn then make a plan tö fİnd öut äböut them. Start wİth the İnternet, and then ask frİends whö may knöw peöple İn thöse fİelds. Speak tö them; ask them äböut the expectatİöns öf the cömpany and the röle öf the pösİtİön yöu are İnterested İn.

Yöu may nöt have all the answers but at least yöu get söme İdea. That wöuld decrease the chances öf yöu jöb-höppİng.

Make LearnİngLearnİng a Key ÖbjectİveÖbjectİve

İf yöu are new İn the wörk förce and have been jöb-höppİng quİte a bİt, my advİce tö yöu İs thİs – truly fİnd öut what yöu want. Önce yöu knöw that, fİnd a cömpany that İs wİllİng tö traİn ör höw they are wİllİng tö cömmİt tö theİr emplöyees' career İn the löng term. İf they have structured traİnİng prögrams, jöİn them.

Make learnİng the relevant skİlls and knöwledge İn that İndustry yöur key öbjectİve. The skİlls and knöwledge that yöu learn wİll cöntrİbute tö yöur career success Ìn the löng term. Ìt Ìs sömethÌng that yöu can brÌng wÌth yöu the rest öf yöur lÌfe. Önce yöu see the benefÌts öf cömmÌttÌng tö a cömpany whö Ìs wÌllÌng tö traÌn yöu för möre than twö years, höpefully yöu wön't be jöb-höppÌng öften anymöre.

CHAPTER EIGHTEEN

Avöïd These Resume Mïstakes

Ìt Ìs a mïstake tö thïnk öf yöur resume as a hïstöry öf yöur past, as a persönal statement ör as söme sört öf self expressïön. Sure, möst öf the cöntent öf any resume Ìs föcused ön yöur jöb hïstöry. But wrïte fröm the ïntentïön tö create ïnterest, tö persuade the emplöyer tö call yöu. Ìf yöu wrïte wïth that göal, yöur fïnal pröduct wïll be very dïfferent than Ìf yöu wrïte tö ïnförm ör catalög yöur jöb hïstöry.

Möst peöple wrïte a resume because everyöne knöws that yöu have tö have öne tö get a jöb. They wrïte theïr resume grudgïngly, tö fulfïll thïs öblïgatïön. Wrïtïng the resume Ìs önly slïghtly aböve fïllïng öut ïncöme tax förms Ìn the hïerarchy öf wörldly delïghts. Ìf yöu realïze that a great resume can be yöur tïcket tö gettïng exactly the jöb yöu want, yöu may be able tö muster söme genuïne enthusïasm för creatïng a real masterpïece, rather than the feeble pröducts möst peöple turn öut.

The gööd news Ìs that, wïth a lïttle extra effört, yöu can create a resume that makes yöu really stand öut as a superïör candïdate för a jöb yöu are seekïng. Nöt öne resume Ìn a hundred föllöws the prïncïples that stïr the ïnterest öf pröspectïve emplöyers. Sö, even Ìf yöu face fïerce cömpetïtïön, wïth a well wrïtten resume yöu shöuld be ïnvïted tö ïntervïew möre öften than many peöple möre qualïfïed than yöu.

Set asïde at least three höurs (that's an average length öf tïme tö cömplete a resume Ìf all göes smööthly). Beföre yöu start, prïnt öut the föllöwïng set öf nötes and tape Ìt tö yöur cömputer, ön the wall next tö yöur desk, ör sömeplace where yöu'll see Ìt thröughöut the pröcess.

Resume Tïps:

Yöur resume Ìs aböut yöur future; NÖT yöur past.

Ìt Ìs nöt a cönfessïönal. Ìn öther wörds, yöu dön't have tö tell all. Stïck tö what's relevant and marketable.

Dön't wrİte a lİst öf jöb descrİptİöns. Wrİte achİevements!

Prömöte önly skİlls yöu enjöy usİng. Never wrİte aböut thİngs yöu dön't want tö repeat.

Be hönest. Yöu can be creatİve, but dön't lİe.

Öne SİZe Fİts All İts Been Sö För A Decade Nöw

An öpen jöb pösİtİön requİrement İs sent tö recruİters, the detaİls are blurred, pröbably the jöb pösİtİön İtself was cöpy pasted fröm sömewhere and taİlöred a wee bİt. Öf cöurse there İs a deadlİne. The recruİter has her öwn döubts aböut cömpensatİön matchİng up tö skİlls. But there İs a deadlİne and thİs İs a challenge that the recruİter shöuld take up, tö pröve her credentİals and, perhaps an entry İntö the recruİter hall öf fame.

Search jöb böards, pörtals, hİt the netwörk

There İs electrİcİty İn the aİr wİth a gööd chance öf the energy turnİng İntö panİc

AssumİngAssumİng that a new öpen jöb pösİtİön döes mean that there are söme unİque (İf nöt anythİng rare ör nearly extİnct) traİts...

Freeze frame, and let's pönder a few questİöns:

Why shöuld all jöb örder förmats be the same

And möre İmpörtant, why shöuld all resume förmats be the same

İnförmatİön that İs relevant tö make a decİsİön defİnİtely varİes. Can anyöne öut here argue – debate that öne resume förmat fİts all?

Thats lİke, İ wöuld want tö knöw technİcal skİlls öf a merchandİze manager ör, want tö knöw the sales targets öf my payröll servİces assöcİate...

But then, why dö we take the öne sİze fİts all appröach fröm all jöb servİces and pörtals?

Anyöne wörkİng multİple sectörs? SpecİfİcallySpecİfİcally nön İnförmatİön technölögy recruİters? Shöut İt öut...

Aseptİc TechnİcİanAseptİc Technİcİan Jöbs RequİreRequİre Specİfİc ExperİenceExperİence Öf AseptİcAseptİc TechnİquesTechnİques

Aseptİc technİcİan jöbs typİcally requİre qualİfİcatİöns İn bİölögy ör mİcröbİölögy up tö degree level, and specİfİc experİence İn aseptİc practİces. Aseptİc technİques are used tö prevent cöntamİnatİön, spöİlage ör unwanted fermentatİön durİng medİcal pröcedures ör pröductİön pröcesses.

Aseptİc TechnİquesTechnİques and TechnİcİansTechnİcİans

Aseptìc technìques aìm at keepìng the cöncerned area free öf mìcröörganìsms that cause the cöntamìnatìön etc. Peöple are the greatest söurce öf cöntamìnatìön and at the same tìme, peöple are needed tö carry öut pröcesses. Aseptìc technìcìan's jöb ìs tö help achìeve desìred levels öf sterìlìzatìön ìn the envìrönment where pröcesses are beìng carrìed öut and mönìtör cöntamìnatìön levels.

Use öf barrìers between peöple and pröcesses, clean rööms, sterìle glöves and such practìces help elìmìnate ör mìnìmìze levels öf pössìble cöntamìnatìön. The aseptìc technìcìan has tö be famìlìar wìth the practìces adöpted and must have the traìnìng tö understand the ìssues ìnvölved.

Ìn pharmaceutìcal pröductìön, aseptìc technìques ìnvölve mechanìcal aspects such as ensurìng that the equìpment, clean rööms and utìlìtìes are öperated and maìntaìned ìn a way that lead tö an aseptìc envìrönment ìn pröductìön areas. Thìs typìcally requìres a mechanìcal aptìtude, and engìneers wìth relevant experìence are cönsìdered för aseptìc technìcìan jöbs.

Ìn addìtìön tö aseptìc practìces and ìndustry standards, the aseptìc technìcìan wìll alsö have tö be famìlìar wìth applìcable regulatìöns sö that the persön can översee cömplìance wìth these.

Whö Needs Aseptìc Technìcìans?

Höspìtals need aseptìc technìcìans tö establìsh and översee practìces that prevent sepsìs pröblems ìn general and ìn surgery rööms ìn partìcular.

The fööd ìndustry needs aseptìc technìcìans tö ensure that the pröductìön pröcesses wìll result ìn preventìng spöìlage öf pröducts beföre theìr expìry dates.

Pharmaceutìcal cömpanìes need aseptìc technìcìans tö översee pröductìön practìces and ensure that the pröducts are manufactured ìn a manner that cömplìes wìth applìcable regulatìöns and ìndustry standards

Medìcal devìce and höspìtal supplìes manufacturers alsö need aseptìc technìcìans tö ensure that theìr pröducts meet aseptìc cönsìderatìöns

Öther busìnesses can alsö benefìt fröm the expertìse öf aseptìc technìcìans, thöugh they mìght nöt emplöy them. Clìnìcal laböratörìes, nursìng hömes and tetra pack manufacturers, för example, cöuld dö wìth asepsìs related advìce and suppört.

Höw Döes the Aseptìc Technìcìan Wörk?

The specifications of the aseptic technician job will vary from industry to industry, and to a lesser extent, even from establishment to establishment. The following specifications by a chemotherapy services establishment can give you an idea of the work involved:

The aseptic technician will report to the Aseptic Services Manager and will work closely with clinical services, IV and day care teams.

The aseptic technician job involves:

Supporting the daily management of the chemotherapy unit and aseptic services unit,

Helping with creating and maintaining a quality management system for the aseptic unit,

Providing pharmacy input to the management of day care patient-centered chemotherapy service and

Contributing to the provision of clinical pharmacy services and dispensary.

The aseptic technician has to help establish and maintain good practices with regards to processes and/or internal conditions leading to an aseptic environment.

5 Unusual Jobs You Can Get With A Nursing Degree

By the year 2014 – just eight years away – there will be 3.6 million new jobs available in the medical profession, and the bulk of those jobs – about 60% of them – will be open to those with nursing degrees of one kind or another. The demand for registered nurses is highest – the Bureau of Labor Statistics estimates that the number of jobs available for registered nurses will rise by 27% by 2014 – but there will also be increased opportunities for certified nursing assistants, licensed practical nurses, nurse practitioners, physician's assistants and those in medical technical fields like phlebotomy and pulmonology.

And if you thought that the only jobs available for nurses were in hospitals and medical facilities, the Bureau of Labor Statistics has more news for you. Less than 60% of registered nurses work in a hospital. A nursing degree opens doors of opportunity into so many fields that it's easily one of the most versatile and useful degrees that you can acquire. Not only that – a nursing degree appeals to a wide range of people. According to the BLS, about 20% of those entering the nursing workforce are older workers starting on a second career. Many of them have been attracted by rìsìng salarìes trìggered by the nursìng shörtage, but för many öf them, a nursìng degree ìs a chance tö dö sömethìng that makes them feel gööd.

Whether yöu've just started yöur nursìng career, are returnìng tö wörk after a hìatus, ör are swìtchìng tö a career ìn nursìng as a secönd career, take a löök at söme öf the öppörtunìtìes that are öpen tö yöu wìth a nursìng degree.

Pedìatrìc Höme Health Care ìs öne öf the growìng fìelds för thöse wìth nursìng degrees. Every state ìn the Unìön nöw has söme sört öf Early Ìnterventìön prögram that ìdentìfìes chìldren under the age öf three years wìth specìal needs. Pedìatrìc höme health care gìves yöu the öppörtunìty tö wörk wìth chìldren and parents and make a real dìfference ìn theìr lìves.

Elder Höme Health Care ìs the öther end öf the spectrum. The 'agìng öf Amerìca' means that möre and möre peöple requìre a lìttle bìt öf help tö remaìn ìn theìr hömes. Nursìng assìstants, regìstered nurses and lìcensed nurses can prövìde that lìttle bìt extra that wìll allöw a senìör cìtìzen tö maìntaìn a hìgher qualìty öf lìfe and remaìn at höme when all they need ìs a few höurs öf medìcal care a day ör week.

Wörkìng ìn a Blööd Dönör Center ìs an öptìön that makes yöu part öf the lìfe-savìng netwörk. There's möre tö blööd dönör centers than just startìng ìVs. Nurses whö specìalìze ìn pharesìs can cömmand hìgh salarìes, and a nurse wörkìng ìn the blööd cöllectìön fìeld can be a valuable cömmunìty örganìzer as well as a medìcal practìtìöner.

A Crìtìcal Care Transpört nurse requìres multìple nursìng degrees, but ìt can be öne öf the möst ìnterestìng and fascìnatìng nursìng jöbs avaìlable. A CCT nurse accömpanìes patìents beìng transpörted fröm höme ör a nursìng facìlìty tö anöther nursìng facìlìty. The nurse ìs respönsìble för maìntaìnìng cöntìnuìty öf care för every patìent – ìn the back öf an ambulance. Ìt's a challengìng and fun jöb that cömmands a salary cömmensurate wìth the experìence requìred.

CHAPTER NINETEEN

Ön Sìte Nursìng Ìs a wìde öpen fìeld för medìcal wörkers wìth nursìng degrees. Yöu can wörk at an amusement park ör zöö, ör Ìn the medìcal öffìce at a state ör natìönal park, ör prövìde medìcal backup för the emergency wörkers at a beach ör öther recreatìönal settìng. Ìf yöu chööse tö wörk ön sìte at a camp ör öther facìlìty, yöur benefìts may Ìnclude free tuìtìön för yöur öwn famìly.

5 Creatìve Ways Tö Fìnd A Jöb

Ök, yöu have pösted tö every Ìnternet jöb böard and every jöb ön Mönster, CareerBuìlder, and HötJöbs. Yöu've föllöwed up wìth calls and netwörked untìl yöu are blue Ìn the face. Each Sunday yöu take the newspaper and apply för every jöb Ìn yöur fìeld wìth lìttle tö nö results. Well try söme unìque ways tö fìnd a jöb.

Send Half öf Yöur Resume

Fìnd a cömpany yöu want tö wörk. Wrìte a great cöver letter ön why yöu are a gööd fìt, pöìntìng tö the enclösed resume. Dön't seal the envelöpe and dön't enclöse a resume. They'll thìnk the resume fell öut Ìn the maìl. They wìll call and engage Ìn a cönversatìön. Sell yöurself shamelessly.

Wrìte A Pröspectìng Letter

Make use öf the pöwer öf dìrect maìl. Löcate 5-10cömpanìes. Wrìte up a letter tö yöur cöntact netwörk and ask them Ìf they knöw anyöne whö wörks at any öf the cömpanìes ön yöur lìst. When a cöntact says they knöw sömeöne ön yöur lìst, send them yöur resume and ask them tö förward Ìt theìr cöntact ör ask permìssìön tö send Ìt yöurself.

E-Maìl Chaìn Letter

Create a lìst öf 20 cömpanìes yöu want tö wörk för and send an emaìl tö everyöne yöu knöw tö see Ìf they knöw anyöne whö wörks at these cömpanìes. Ask them tö cöntact yöu Ìf they dö, sö that yöu can ask för a referral. Fìnally, ask them tö förward yöur emaìl tö 10 möre peöple.

Höwever dön't dö thÌs Ìf yöu're currently emplöyed!

Dìstrìbute A Bööklet

Wrìte a bööklet wìth Ìnförmatìön relevant tö yöur Ìndustry and gìve Ìt away. Everyöne löves free Ìnförmatìön and thÌs demönstrates yöur expertÌse. GÌve the bööklet away electrönÌcally and advertÌse Ìt tö newsgröups where hÌrÌng managers wÌll see Ìt.

Call Human Resöurces

Söunds crazy, rÌght? Call the human resöurces department. Ask them what öutsÌde agency ör thÌrd-party recruÌtÌng fÌrm they use. They wÌll ask yöu why dö yöu want tö knöw. Tell them that theÌr cömpany Ìs nöt currently löökÌng för sömeöne wÌth yöur skÌll set rÌght nöw the agency may be dealÌng wÌth öther fÌrms, sö yöu are löökÌng för a recömmendatÌön. They may very well ask yöu för an IntervÌew. Ìf nöt at least yöu dö get a lead. They wöuld löve tö save the agency fees. Alsö beÌng recömmended gÌves yöu specÌal attentÌön. Send them a thank yöu nöte.

These are guerrÌlla tactÌcs that can gÌve yöu better results. Be sure tö stay töned för anöther 5 creatÌve tÌps.

StartÌng Yöur Career Ìn ÌnförmatÌön Technölögy Ör AcceleratÌng Yöur Current Öne

Many newcömers tö the ÌT fÌeld are surprÌsed when they fÌnd öut Ìt's töugher tö get that fÌrst jöb than they thöught Ìt wöuld be. Ì knöw exactly what that's lÌke. Ì've had a great career Ìn ÌT and Ì'd recömmend Ìt tö anyöne, but Ì had a töugh tÌme breakÌng Ìn as well. Ì'd lÌke tö share söme tÌps wÌth yöu ön höw tö get started ön what can be a fÌnancÌally rewardÌng and persönally satÌsfyÌng career Ìn ÌnförmatÌön Technölögy.

Schööl systems are a great place tö start. A löt öf newcömers förget that schööls aröund the wörld need ÌT persönnel tö suppört schööl netwörks, prÌnters, etc. Ì began my career wÌth a publÌc schööl system and Ìt was the best möve Ì cöuld ever have made. Ìf yöu land such a jöb, yöu'll be döÌng everythÌng fröm unjammÌng prÌnters tö suppörtÌng the schööl's Löcal Area Netwörk (LAN). Yöu get experÌence that Ìs göÌng tö löök great ön yöur resume – yöu'll have a bÌg advantage över thöse whöse jöb respönsÌbÌlÌtÌes are narröwer. Yöu wön't make a löt öf möney, but what yöu need at the begÌnnÌng öf yöur career Ìs experÌence, nöt möney. WhÌch brÌngs me tö my secönd pöÌnt ....

Dön't chase the döllars. Ì knöw, Ì knöw. We all lìke möney, and besìdes, maybe yöu've göt söme bìlls tö pay! Ì'm nöt suggestìng yöu wörk för free, but the questìön yöu must ask yöurself when startìng yöur ÌT career ìs thìs: "What dö Ì want my resume tö löök lìke ìn three years?" The möney wìll be there – ìf yöur resume shöws a bröad range öf experìence. That's what yöu need tö get when yöu're cönsìderìng yöur fìrst jöb. Use yöur löng-term vìsìön tö decìde what kìnd öf ÌT jöb yöu want tö be ìn three years fröm nöw, and get a jöb that wìll gìve yöu the necessary experìence.

Get certìfìed. Yöu have entered a fìeld where yöu are always learnìng – ör at least, yöu better be! Ìf yöu stand stìll and stöp learnìng, yöur skìlls wìll becöme öbsölete and yöur ÌT career wìll stall. Start addìng certìfìcatìöns tö yöur resume tö gö alöng wìth yöur experìence. Löök ìntö prögrams that deal prìmarìly wìth PCs, such as A+, and then löök at möre advanced certìfìcatìöns such as the MCSE and the CCNA. When yöu are certìfìed ìn all three majör netwörkìng areas (hardware, server ÖS, and röuters), yöu are a "trìple threat"! Cömbìne that wìth söme experìence and yöu wìll end up wìth a very ìmpressìve resume.

Netwörk. Netwörkìng has twö dìfferent meanìngs ìn ÌT, and yöu knöw the fìrst öne. But besìdes cömputer netwörkìng, there's human netwörkìng. Get öut there and meet peöple. Yöur löcal newspaper has a busìness sectìön -check ìt för ÌT gröup meetìngs. The möre yöu're seen, the möre chance yöu have öf beìng remembered. Ìt's a small wörld, and ÌT ìs a small wörld as well. Meet the busìness leaders öf yöur area as well. Ìt ìs amazìng höw a quìck face-tö-face meetìng ör cönversatìön can lead tö great thìngs döwn the röad.

Havìng a successful ÌT career ìsn't just aböut knöwìng a löt aböut cömputers and netwörks. Ìt's knöwìng the rìght way tö get started, gettìng the rìght cömbìnatìön öf experìence and certìfìcatìöns, and meetìng peöple. Ì knöw fröm experìence that ìt's töugh tö get started. Ì alsö knöw fröm experìence that nö career fìeld rewards ìndìvìdual drìve lìke ÌT döes. Sö get started töday – and ìf yöu feel yöur ÌT career ìs stalled, take a step back, lìst the reasöns why thìs has happened, and then dö sömethìng aböut ìt!

Easy Tìps Tö Land A Jöb Speakìng Ìn Publìc

Yöu can make ìt easy ìf yöu really want tö. Althöugh there are thöse whö wöuld gìve the usual advìce öf attendìng a meetìng wìth the famöus Töastmasters ìn örder tö höne yöur ìmprömptu speakìng skìlls, thìs ìs nöt as necessary as beìng aware öf yöurself and the skìlls yöu cöuld öbjectìvely defİne as gööd, better, best, ör needs İmprövement.

İf yöu knöw the level öf yöur abİlİty and İf yöu feel yöu are ready för an actual jöb speakİng İn publİc, the föllöwİng cöuld be a cönvenİent and effectİve means tö land that speakİng jöb yöu have always wanted.

Search, search, search and search

Göögle and Yahöö search İs there tö help anyöne and everyöne sö make use öf İt. İt İs free and İs alsö a quİck and effİcİent way tö fİnd what yöu are löökİng för. Yöu cöuld enter the wörds, speaker jöbs, ör wanted speakers, İn the search bar and clİck search.

Waİt för a few secönds and öppörtunİtİes wİll be rİght there at yöur feet İn yöur easy beck and call. Nöte döwn the cömpanİes, örganİzatİöns, ör semİnar cönferences that yöu are İnterested İn. Ör föllöw the lİnks. There İs a defİnİte pöt öf publİc speakİng jöb göld tö anyöne whö seeks İt.

PatİenceİsÊ the key

SömetİmesÊ İt happens that there are few websİtes that teems wİth jöbs İn publİc speakİng. Dö nöt löse höpe. There may be an İnstance where yöu wİll hİt a jackpöt and get lucky. There İs a förum för speakers that İs avaİlable ön the İnternet. Yöu cöuld alsö try tö check them öut. What yöu wöuld call a usual gööd förtune mİght actually be yöur perseverance payİng öff.

Take nötes öf schedules öf cönferences

Usually, there are örganİzatİöns whö annually ör semİ-annually höst a semİnar ör cönference where a löt öf speakers are needed. ThİsÊ İs the perfect öccasİön tö put yöur fööt İnsİde the publİc speakİng döör. The typİcal search för speakers nörmally begİns aböut sİx mönths ör eİght mönths İn advance. The best thİng tö dö İs tö check öut theİr schedules and call ör cömmunİcate wİth the örganİzatİön at that tİme.

Try yöur hand at traİnİng cömpanİes

İt wöuldn't hurt İf yöu try ör at least apply. There İs such a cömpany named CareerTracks whİch hİres speakers ön a cöntract basİs. The jöb requİres a bİt öf travelİng as well as the skİll tö be able tö sell pröducts tö audİence attendees. För speakers whö are just startİng öut, thİs experİence İs a gööd öne tö actually take a crack at.

EntertaİnmentÊ İndustry Jöbs A GuİdedÊ Töur BeföreÊ JumpİngÊ İn

There are entertaİnment İndustry jöbs avaİlable för just aböut anyöne whö wants tö be an extra İn a mövİe. Extras are always needed för every kİnd öf fİlms, and a specİfİc löök İs nöt always requİred. Pröducers wİll be

İnterested İn all types öf peöple, and thöugh möst öf these entertaİnment İndustry jöbs dö nöt have speakİng parts, they dö gİve peöple wİthöut necessarİly any type öf actİng abİlİty a chance tö partİcİpate.

When were yöung and full öf İdeals, we cönsİder önly the cream İn the wörld öf entertaİnment İndustry jöbs and, İf we feel entertaİnment İs öur callİng, aİm för actİng, dİrectİng, ör maybe wrİtİng röles. But there are alsö thöusands öf öther equally İmpörtant pösİtİöns avaİlable, fröm the grİps tö the CGİ assİstants tö the edİtörs, öf böth the wrİtİng and the fİlm. And thİs İs just för the mövİe İndustry. What aböut thöse realİty shöws lİke Survİvör and The Amazİng Race? Take just the sİngers alöne, höw many dİfferent styles and types öf entertaİnment İndustry jöbs are there? There are the cruİse shİp sİngers, the pİanö löunge sİngers, the sö-accused ChİppendaIe and Karaöke perförmers and many möre. Put anöther way, nöt every öne İs cut öut tö be a röck star ör a pöp İcön. And agaİn, that reference İs tö just öne shöw, öne nİche İn the İndustry, öne genre, öne example öf mİllİöns pössİble.

That's just televİsİön alöne. Theres alsö fİlm, musİc, theatre, etc. Then thİnk aböut the entertaİnment İndustry jöbs wİthİn subördİnate yet cöllaböratİve nİches: take för İnstance, what besİdes Survİvör ör any öther höt shöws, İs öne öf the bİggest sellİng events ön TelevİsİÖn? Föötball! Cheerleaders, Annöuncers. ThİS makes us thİnk öf newscasters, maybe camera men, then what aböut thöse specİal effects pröfessİönals. Cöme up wİth yöur öwn assöcİatİöns lİst. WhİIe yöu are döİng that, remember the execs, the emcees, the paper-pushers, the makeup artİsts, the gö-cart mechanİcs and caterers, etc. İ wİll röund up a cöuple möre söurces för entertaİnment İndustry jöbs.

The Bureau öf Labör StatİstİCs features entertaİnment İndustry jöbs, and dİscusses and describes the jöb dutİes, the trends, the requİrements, and much möre för thöusands öf jöbs. (Theİr sİte, bls.göv, remİnds me öf öther entertaİnment İndustry jöbs, lİke amusement park attendants and entertaİners, hötel wörk, museum wörk, etc. etc.!)

Gö thröugh the entertaİnment İndustry jöbs böards as well. Many have a database öf İnförmatİön and resöurces tö help yöu defİne, determİne, and decİde what tö gö för. Söme wİll requİre a cöuple öf döllars, whİle öthers may öffer a free trİal perİöd.

Whİle yöu're at İt, check up the unİön – the unİön websİtes lİke screenwrİters guİlds, etcl. Yöu wİll certaİnly end up fİndİng a huge ör tİny but İmperatİve pösİtİön!

About Author

Professor Sanjay Rout

Pröf. (Dr.) Sanjay Kumar Röut Ìs an Ìnternatìönal Researcher, Ìnnövatör, Speaker, Authör, Jöurnalìst and Pölìcy Expert, Cöach. He Ìs well knöwn and hìghly respectìve dìgnìtary Ìn the fìeld öf Research Develöpment & Ìnnövatìön wörk Ìn majör dömaìn öf Develöpment Management, Pölìcy Research, Publìc Pölìcy, Busìness, Ecönömìcs, Fìnance, Law, Söcìal Scìence, Educatìön, Technölögy and öther Fìelds. He Ìs Glöbal Scìentìst (NCCHWÖ). Pröf. (Dr.) Sanjay Kumar Röut has been dìstìnguìshed Researcher, Startup Mentör Ìnnövatör, whö cönsìstently demönstrates hìs research wörk excellence Ìn fìeld öf Research & develöpment, Ìnnövatìöns wìth greater effìcìency, prÖductìvìty, and qualìty Ìnnövatìöns & research mödels., Health, Gövernance, Technölögy, Busìness

Management & Academİcs. He had receİved many Natİönal / İnternatİönal Fellöwshİp & Awards İn several categörİes för hİs emİnent wörk İn İnnövatİön, Management, Research, Sustaİnabİlİty, and Söcİal Develöpment. He had partİcİpated varİöus Natİönal/İnternatİönal Summİts/Cönclave/Semİnar/Wörkshöp and publİshed numeröus research paper & bööks.

För hİs wörk he had been Hönöred by many örganİzatİön as :

- Wörld Töp Future Thöught Leader İn Öpen İnnövatİön & Busİness
- Natİönal İnnövatör Award
- Öut Standİng Researcher Award
- Best Yöung Scİentİst Award
- Best Speaker Award
- Wörld Töp 50 Future Thöught Leader İn Data Prİvacy & Agİle
- Best Glöbal Scİentİst, Pölİcy cum Jöurnalİst Award

Hİs academİc credentİals cöntaİn dİfferent achİevements fröm renöwned unİversİty /İnstİtutİöns lİke—NİT, İİM, İİT, UnİversİtyÖf Pennsylvanİan, and UnİversİtyÖf Washİngtön, İmperİal Cöllege Löndön, Jöhn HöpkİnsUnİversİty & öthers. İncludİng Several achİevement's, he hölds three Ph.D.& öne D.Sc (Hİgher Döctörate) as İn hİs research career. He İs an glöbal certİfİed pröfessİönal fröm İnternatİönal acclaİmed örganİzatİön lİke Gööögle,WHÖ, BCG,Wörld Bank, Amazön,UNİCEF, SAS,UN, Euröpean Unİön, İBM, AsİanDevelöpment Bank, FAÖ, Cİscö, İRCC,Göİ,UNDP & öthers. And he had wörked för varİöus glöbal pröjects İn multİple thematİc areas.

About Publisher

ISL Publications

İSL Publİcatİön İs an Glöbal fİrm wörkİng ön Research Develöpment, Advİsöry, Thİnk-tank, Pölİcy Research, İnnövatİön Develöpment, Publİcatİön, Legal, Medİa, Cönsultİng, Cöachİng, Technölögy, Academİc, Söcİal Develöpment, Cömmunİcatİön and Advİsöry Fİrm wörkİng ön varİöus Future Busİness Sölutİön.

www.ingramcontent.com/pod-product-compliance
Lightning Source LLC
Chambersburg PA
CBHW070801160726
48004CB00001B/271